ERRORS, MEDICINE AND THE LAW

ALAN MERRY
AND
ALEXANDER McCALL SMITH

CAMBRIDGE
UNIVERSITY PRESS

PUBLISHED BY THE PRESS SYNDICATE OF THE UNIVERSITY OF CAMBRIDGE
The Pitt Building, Trumpington Street, Cambridge, United Kingdom

CAMBRIDGE UNIVERSITY PRESS
The Edinburgh Building, Cambridge CB2 2RU, UK
40 West 20th Street, New York NY 10011–4211, USA
10 Stamford Road, Oakleigh, VIC 3166, Australia
Ruiz de Alarcón 13, 28014 Madrid, Spain
Dock House, The Waterfront, Cape Town 8001, South Africa

http://www.cambridge.org

First published 2001

Printed in the United Kingdom at the University Press, Cambridge

Typeface Minion 10.5/14pt   *System* 3B2   [CE]

A catalogue record for this book is available from the British Library

Library of Congress Cataloguing in Publication data
Merry, Alan.
Errors, medicine, and the law / Alan Merry and Alexander McCall Smith.
p.   cm.
Includes bibliographical references and index.
ISBN 0 521 80631 3 (hb.) – ISBN 0 521 00088 2 (pb.)
1. Medical personnel – Malpractice.
2. Medical jurisprudence.
I. McCall Smith, R. A. II. Title
K4365.M47 2001   344′.0411 – dc21   2001025439

ISBN 0 521 80631 3 hardback
ISBN 0 521 00088 2 paperback

Untoward injuries are unacceptably common in medical treatment, at times with tragic consequences for patients. The phrases 'an epidemic of error' and 'the medical toll' have been coined to describe this problem of 'iatrogenic harm', which it has been suggested may have contributed to 98,000 deaths per year in the USA. Some of these incidents are the result of negligence on the part of doctors, but more usually they are no more than inevitable concomitants of the complexity of modern healthcare. This book is fundamentally about distinguishing the former from the latter. It questions the understandable, but often inappropriate, tendency to blame individuals for these events and points out that the goal of safety is far better served by a sophisticated understanding of the difference between negligence and inevitable error, and by a frank recognition of just why human error occurs and how things go wrong in any complex system.

Although medicine is used as the book's primary example, the points made apply equally to aviation, many industrial activities, and many other fields of human endeavour. The book advocates a more informed alternative to the blaming culture which has increasingly come to dominate our response to accidents, whether in the medical field or elsewhere.

ALAN MERRY is a practising cardiac anaesthetist, whose research focuses on safety, and in particular on reducing error, in anaesthesia. He was the co-founder and co-chair of the New Zealand Medical Law Reform Group, which contributed to the passing of the Crimes Amendment Act 1997 which redefined the threshold for criminal prosecution arising from negligently caused harm in New Zealand. He is the author of a number of papers in medical and legal journals. He has developed a computer-based systems approach to reducing drug administration errors in anaesthesia (the IDAS), which applies many of the principles discussed in this book, and which is in use in several Auckland hospitals.

ALEXANDER McCALL SMITH, Professor of Medical Law at the University of Edinburgh, has been involved in medico-legal issues for more than twenty years and has lectured at universities throughout the world. He is the Vice-Chairman of the Human Genetics Commission of the United Kingdom, a ... ...mmittee of UNESCO, and ... f the *British Medical Journ...* ... the areas of medical law an ... *cs* (with J. K. Mason), which ...

CONTENTS

ACKNOWLEDGEMENTS

We wish to acknowledge the help which we have received in the planning and writing of this book. In particular, we wish to record our gratitude to Bruce Corkill, Dr Denys Court, Margaret Deith, Diana Emmens, Gaeline Phipps, Bill Runciman, Craig Webster and to an anonymous, but immensely helpful, reviewer in the USA. We were enabled to spend several periods working together in Canada thanks to the hospitality of Barbara Parker and Iona and John Copping of Vancouver, and of Douglas and Nadia Parker of Toronto, during which, and other times, Dr Sally Merry and Dr Elizabeth McCall Smith provided unstinting support for the project. Finally, no praise would be too great for the editorial support of Finola O'Sullivan of Cambridge University Press.

INTRODUCTION

Modern medicine is highly effective. It is also available to greater numbers of people than ever before, but preventable injury has been identified as a strikingly common occurrence in all aspects of modern healthcare. The term 'epidemic of error' has been coined. In the United States, the Institute of Medicine, acting under the National Academy of Sciences, has identified errors in healthcare as a leading cause of death and injury, comparable with that of road accidents.[1] The precise extent of this problem is open to question, but it is beyond argument that an unacceptable number of people suffer serious harm or die as a result of 'avoidable adverse events'. Sometimes these events are attributable to negligence. However, it is often simple human error, operating in an intrinsically hazardous system, which results in an unnecessary death or serious injury. For the person concerned, and for the person's family and friends, the consequences of a deceptively simple mistake may be a tragedy of the first order. In addition, there may also be grave implications for a doctor or nurse at whose door the blame for the accident is laid, with consequences for his or her family as well.

This book is a study of how mishaps occur and how people are blamed for them. In many areas of human activity there is a strong tendency to attribute blame for incidents which, on further investigation, may be shown not to involve any culpable conduct. This is a particular issue in medical practice, where the consequences of an error or a violation may be severe. The desire to blame leads to official inquiries and in many cases to legal proceedings. In many parts of the world this has gone hand in hand with a marked increase in medical litigation, reflecting heightened

---

[1] L. T. Kohn, J. M. Corrigan and M. S. Donaldson (eds.), *To Err Is Human: Building a Safer System* (Washington, D.C., National Academy Press, 2000).

1

public concern over the level of iatrogenic harm. The Institute of Medicine has set as a target the reduction of errors in healthcare by 50 per cent over five years, but as one commentator, writing in the *New England Journal of Medicine*, has pointed out, 'Any effort to prevent injury due to medical care is complicated by the dead weight of a litigation system that induces secrecy and silence.'[2]

This book presents an argument that many of these events do not involve moral culpability. This argument is supported by the extensive research which has been carried out into the principles underlying the generation of human errors and into failures in complex systems. We examine the moral and legal basis for the attribution of blame and conclude that in many cases where there is a finding of blameworthy conduct, this in fact may not be justified in respect of the individual, but may often reflect institutional failures or unavoidable human error. Paradoxically, by focusing on an individual, such inquiries or proceedings often fail to identify systemic deficiencies which predispose to error, or fail to protect the patient against the consequences of inevitable error. Blaming the person 'holding the smoking gun' may simply leave the scene set for a recurrence of the same tragedy.

A point which is often misunderstood is that human error, being by definition unintentional, is not easily deterred. Furthermore, to be effective, deterrence must be directed at those who are able to effect change within the system. For example, convicting two junior doctors of manslaughter after the incorrect injection of the drug vincristine into the spinal cord failed completely to prevent the same tragedy from happening again, with two more junior doctors some years later – a mistake which has in fact been made at least ten times in British hospitals. Violations are a different matter from errors. Violations involve choice. Not all violations are reprehensible, and some may be forced upon individuals by the system, but in principle violations can be deterred. The psychological mechanisms which underlie violations are quite different from those which lead to error. It is important to distinguish these different types of human behaviour if we are to make our healthcare systems safer for patients and our legal systems fairer for those whose well-intended care sometimes goes astray. Attempts to modify human behaviour by regula-

---

[2] T. A. Brennan, 'The Institute of Medicine report on medical errors – could it do harm?' (2000) 342 *New England Journal of Medicine* 1123–5.

tion or legal processes are entirely appropriate, but need to be well informed. The current standard by which negligence is assessed in the law is that of reasonableness in respect of knowledge, skill and care. However, a great deal depends on the way in which this is tested. If the line of questioning focuses on the action, many statistically inevitable errors appear unreasonable. An expert can hardly be expected to say that it is reasonable to give the wrong drug, for example. However, if the questioning focuses on the person, who is a human being, and asks, 'Was this the sort of mistake a reasonable practitioner might make?' the answer will be different. As we shall see, there is overwhelming evidence that in fact all doctors make slip/lapse errors at some time, including errors in drug administration. It follows that these are errors which can be made by the reasonable doctor. There are other actions, such as leaving an anaesthetised patient unattended, which no reasonable practitioner would do. In the latter case a punitive response may well be called for. This may be achieved through disciplinary procedures, or the criminal law, or indirectly through civil legal action. In the former situation, such a response may actually be counter-productive. This book is as much about understanding those situations in which blame *is* appropriate as about knowing when it is not. It has at its centre concern for the patients who are injured, but alongside that it makes the point that some doctors, by unwittingly contributing to such injury, become victims themselves – often quite innocently. The impact on the doctor is at times underestimated, and acknowledgement of its true extent should not be seen as diminishing the importance of the primary victim, the patient.

Ultimately, the best response for both patients and doctors is to make healthcare safer. Unfortunately, error will never be completely eliminated, and there will always be some doctors whose behaviour is frankly culpable. Some consideration of how to do better in handling the aftermath of medical accidents is appropriate. Unfortunately, there are no simple answers, but a better understanding of the factors which underlie the different types of human failing associated with iatrogenic harm is the fundamental requirement for improving the way in which we regulate medicine and compensate those who are harmed in the course of receiving treatment.

The problem affects all societies. The issues discussed in this book apply generally, although some of the examples relate to specific countries. The legal principles involved are discussed in the context of common-law systems. While they may differ in detail, these systems share the same basic approach. Reference is therefore made to the decisions of courts in the UK, the USA, New Zealand, Australia and Canada. Because error and negligence raise issues of both civil and criminal liability, and may also fall within the scope of professional discipline, we have taken all these jurisdictions into account.

In chapter 1 we introduce the concept that the pervasive nature of blame in contemporary society is distorting reactions to adverse events in medicine and other activities. To illustrate this we give a number of actual examples of severe consequences that have followed relatively minor errors committed during normal medical practice. The cases are used to exemplify the concepts discussed in subsequent chapters. The language used to describe these events can be important. The term 'accident', for example, is exculpatory, and, may have value in distinguishing between situations of culpability and those not warranting blame.

In chapter 2 we discuss how human beings function, not in isolation, but in the context of today's complex technological organisations. Successful human endeavour in medicine and other fields has been the result of man's ability to communicate, co-operate, develop technology and function within a mechanised and skill-demanding world. The cognitive processes which have produced these successes are the same processes as those which predispose to certain forms of error. These should therefore be viewed as strengths rather than weaknesses, in comparison with the less error-prone but also less flexible attributes of machines.

A proper understanding of the human actions which lead to adverse events in medicine requires a knowledge of the nature of error. In chapter 3 a precise definition of error is followed by a detailed discussion of its underlying cognitive processes and a discussion of its taxonomy. The thesis is that errors should not necessarily be viewed as random acts or manifestations of carelessness, but rather that even inexplicable and bizarre actions or mistakes can often be understood, and even predicted from particular circumstances. Deterrence will not prevent errors – their reduction depends on understanding the processes involved. However, not all unsafe acts are errors. In chapter 4 we discuss violations, beginning with their definition. An understanding of violations facilitates the discussion of the difference between culpable and non-culpable failures in human activity.

The discussion now shifts to culpability. In chapter 5 we explore the concepts of negligence, recklessness and blame, referring to the insights derived from our discussion of errors and violations. Negligence does not necessarily imply blameworthiness, but may carry considerable overtones of moral opprobrium. Drawing on the theory developed in the previous three chapters, we suggest a classification of blame into five levels ranging from pure causal responsibility to intentional harming. The implication of this for our response to adverse events is explored. Negligence in the law is based on the standard of care expected of the reasonable person. In chapter 6 we scrutinise how the standard of care is set by the law. To assist the courts in recognising failures to meet this standard, evidence of professional custom has been relied upon. This chapter explores how this test, while nominally adhered to, has tended to move from what can reasonably be expected to what ought ideally to have been done. This could be corrected if there were to be greater cognisance of the insights of psychology and accident theory discussed in the preceding chapters. The role of the expert witness in setting the standard of care is considered in chapter 7. Evidence provided by experts tends to reflect an ideal rather than a customary standard of care. This has contributed to the development of the unrealistic standard discussed in chapter 6.

In chapter 8, we consider a variety of possible reforms to shift the focus from blame with a view to improving the response of the law to the injured patient, to the need to promote safety in healthcare, and to the reduction of inappropriate findings of culpability in doctors. We address at some length the concept of no-fault compensation and consider various possibilities for improving the tort system.

We conclude, in the final chapter, that a failure to understand the role of blame, along with considerable contemporary enthusiasm for finding scapegoats, has led to what might be termed an inflation of blame. The consequences of this are particularly serious – and costly – in the area of medical mishaps. This chapter draws together the strands developed in the book and argues for coherent, rational and well-informed analysis of blame, in the interests of patients and doctors, and all others for whom safety in medicine is a priority.

1

Accidents

We begin with a chapter of accidents. The accident *par excellence* of the twentieth century was the loss of the *RMS Titanic*, which on the night of 12 April 1912 collided with an iceberg in the North Atlantic. Who, or what, was to blame for this incident, which was to become so enduring and potent a cultural symbol? There are numerous potential explanations: the iceberg might have been sighted in time, but was not. A warning message was sent, but not passed on. The metal used for the construction of the ship's rivets contained impurities, with the result that they gave under strain. The ship's architects had miscalculated the ability of sealed-off compartments to maintain buoyancy. A wireless operator on a nearby ship, which could have arrived on the scene to rescue the passengers, had turned off his set, only twenty minutes earlier, with the result that Mayday messages were not received. If the crew had been equipped with binoculars, the watch might have been alarmed in time. All of these played some role in the final disaster.[1]

The equivalent in our own times of the loss of the *Titanic* – in the sense that it demonstrated the same essential vulnerability of grandiose human ambitions – was the explosion of the space shuttle *Challenger* in 1986, 73 seconds after launch.[2] It is clear that ring seals failed, causing the explosion of escaping fuel, but this failure would not have occurred had

---

[1] The literature on the *Titanic* disaster is extensive. Contemporary official documents include the British and American governmental inquiries, both recently reprinted: Great Britain, Parliament, *Report on the Loss of the SS Titanic* (reprinted 1998) and T. Kuntz (ed.), *The Titanic Disaster: The Official Transcripts of the 1912 Senate Investigation* (reprinted 1998).

[2] United States Government, *Report of the Presidential Commission on the Space Shuttle Challenger Accident* (Washington, D.C., US Government Printing Office, 1986). See also L. C. Bruno, '*Challenger* explosion', in N. Schlager (ed.), *When Technology Fails: Significant Technological Disasters, Accidents and Failures of the 20th Century* (Detroit, Ill., Gale Research, 1994).

the seals not been exposed to low temperatures on the ground. The problem was not a new one: engineers had expressed concern over the issue but this concern had not been translated into action within the labyrinths of the space programme. The launch was approved, but this decision might not have been taken had a number of those responsible not been grossly sleep-deprived at the time of the crucial meeting, and under pressure to meet deadlines. The impact of sleep deprivation on intellectual processes is well understood, and decision makers had been deprived of normal sleep for many days. This, of course, was not necessarily a situation of their own making. They were under immense pressure to ensure that the launch proceeded according to schedule – a pressure which reflected the operational culture of NASA, and which led to managers overruling advice from engineers concerning the risk of ring-seal failure. And this, in due course, stemmed from budgetary pressure applied by politicians.[3] The range of potential causes was therefore wide, and the points of possible responsibility for the accident somewhat scattered. Can any one person, or even group of persons, be said to be to blame for this loss of life and material? What is the liability of organisations involved in this project?

These are well-known, extensively documented incidents, the background of which has been closely scrutinised. Most accidents are considerably more mundane, occurring on the roads, in the home, or, as W. H. Auden observed in his poem on the fall of Icarus, against a backdrop of people simply going about their normal business.[4] Many medical accidents fall into this category. They occur in the context of routine treatment and are frequently not the subject of inquiry or proceedings. The Harvard Medical Practice Study, for example, which investigated the incidence of such accidents in the state of New York, revealed a remarkably high rate of such incidents, but only a small proportion of them resulted in formal legal action.[5] The question of

---

[3] For an account of the human factors involved in the *Challenger* disaster, see R. Boisjoly, E. F. Curtis and E. Mellican, 'The *Challenger* disaster: organizational demands and personal ethics', in M. D. Ermann and R. J. Lundman (eds.), *Corporate and Governmental Deviance* (Oxford University Press, 1996), 207.

[4] W. H. Auden, 'Musée des Beaux Arts', in his *Collected Shorter Poems* (London, Faber and Faber, 1966).

[5] *Patients, Doctors and Lawyers: Medical Injury, Malpractice Litigation and Patient Compensation in New York* (Cambridge, Mass., President and Fellows of Harvard College, 1990); T. A. Brennan, L. L. Leape, N. M Laird, L. Hebert, A. R Localio, A. G. Lawthers, J. P. Newhouse, P. C. Weiler and H. H. Hiatt, 'Incidence of adverse events and negligence in

responsibility for these incidents may be as complicated as the question of responsibility for major, highly publicised accidents, and it is for this reason that medical mishaps can make an extremely useful case study for the general question of responsibility for untoward events.

In all incidents of this nature, whether they are spectacular disasters (*Titanic, Challenger, Chernobyl*), or whether they are small-scale incidents involving the injury or death of a single person, the same questions of causal complexity will be involved. Causal investigations are familiar territory now to the public, which has become accustomed to publicity given to the proceedings of committees of inquiry, coroners and criminal courts, and in general we are rather more sophisticated in our appreciation of the multi-factorial features of many of these incidents. Yet this ability to appreciate that adverse events may be caused by more than one factor has not necessarily been accompanied by a change in blaming behaviour. Locating causal responsibility for an event may precede blaming, but is not in itself sufficient for an attribution of blame. There is a marked tendency to look for a human actor to blame for an untoward event – a tendency which is closely linked with the desire to punish. *Things have gone wrong, and therefore somebody must be found to answer for it.* The crudity of this statement is apparent on the face of it, and yet, to an extraordinary extent, it represents a widely held view. It is this attitude which fuels media and political campaigns for the identification and punishment of those responsible for whatever tragedy or social problem has seized the attention of the public. It is the psychology of the moral panic and it threatens certain fundamental values of a liberal, humane society: namely, that censure and punishment should be reserved – as far as is possible – for those whose actions reveal morally relevant

hospitalized patients: results of the Harvard Medical Practice Study I' (1991) 324 *New England Journal of Medicine* 370–6; L. L. Leape, T. A. Brennan, N. M Laird, A. G. Lawthers, A. R Localio, B. A. Barnes, L. Hebert, J. P. Newhouse, P. C. Weiler and H. Hiatt, 'The nature of adverse events in hospitalized patients: results of the Harvard Medical Practice Study II' (1991) 324 *New England Journal of Medicine* 377–84; and A. R Localio, A. G. Lawthers, T. A. Brennan, N. M. Laird, L. E. Hebert, L. M. Peterson, J. P. Newhouse, P. C. Weiler and H. H. Hiatt, 'Relation between malpractice claims and adverse events due to negligence: results of the Harvard Medical Practice Study III' (1991) 325 *New England Journal of Medicine* 245–51. The Harvard study is discussed in greater detail on p. 43 below. See also P. M. Danzon, *Medical Malpractice: Theory, Evidence, and Public Policy* (Cambridge, Mass., Harvard University Press, 1985) and P. C. Weiler, *Medical Malpractice on Trial* (Cambridge, Mass., Harvard University Press, 1991), 1–16.

wrongdoing.[6] Such analysis is often conspicuously lacking from both moral and legal judgements – a situation prompting the moral philosopher Jean Hampton to remark: 'Accusing, condemning, and avenging are part of our daily life. However, a review of many years of literature attempting to analyze our blaming practices suggests that we do not understand very well what we are doing when we judge people culpable for wrong they have committed.'[7] Morally relevant wrongdoing can only properly be identified if the actions of those whose responsibility is in question are subjected to analysis designed to identify states of mind that are truly culpable. A refined system of criminal justice, with its elaborate notions of *mens rea* (guilty mind doctrine) and its carefully defined defences, is capable of achieving this degree of discrimination between the blameworthy and the blameless. However, many processes of calling to account – including many legal proceedings of both a civil and a criminal nature – fall far short of this goal.[8]

The central argument put forward in what follows is that the process of blaming, as it is practised in contemporary society, is in danger of losing sight of these moral values. It is a matter for remark that this should happen at a time when our understanding of human action, and therefore our ability to appreciate the full complexity of faulty human behaviour, has made substantial progress. The insights of psychology and accident theory are available to the law and to other institutions of blame; yet they are widely ignored. There are a variety of reasons why this should be so. To an extent, it is because of an understandable – and necessary – belief in

---

[6] There will be some circumstances in which strict liability will be acceptable. In these cases punishment may be justified by the community's interest in the protection of a value or interest which cannot otherwise be protected; road traffic offences provide an example of this. Offences which involve real moral opprobrium require correspondingly real moral guilt, a distinction formally recognised in some jurisdictions. For general discussion, see K. W. Simons, 'When is strict liability just?' (1997) 87 *Journal of Criminal Law and Criminology* 1075–1137.

[7] J. Hampton, 'Mens rea', in E. F. Paul, F. D. Miller and J. Paul (eds.), *Crime, Culpability and Remedy* (Oxford, Basil Blackwell, 1990), 1.

[8] In one view, this goal is practically unattainable and, in any event, is not defensible. In criminal-law theory there is a continuing tension between subjectivism and objectivism in the attribution of liability. In practice, most criminal justice systems place objectively determined limits on the extent to which certain conditions are capable of excusing those who cause actual harm to others. For recent discussion of the issue see A. Ripstein, *Equality, Responsibility, and the Law* (New York, Cambridge University Press, 1999), 172–217; and R. H. S. Tur, 'Subjectivism and objectivism: towards synthesis', in S. Shute, J. Gardner and J. Horder (eds.), *Action and Value in Criminal Law* (Oxford, Clarendon Press, 1993), 213–37.

individual accountability. But there are less acceptable reasons behind the phenomenon as well. These are the reasons which find their root in an atavistic human response of scapegoating. It is easier to blame others for mishaps than to accept the inevitability of human loss, and it is for this reason that crude solutions to the problem of human accidents strike a strongly responsive chord.[9]

Our investigation of the phenomenon of blame and negligence focuses predominantly on medical accidents. This is not only because of the frequency of such mishaps, but because such incidents occupy a central role in the contemporary drama of blame. Doctors and others in professions allied to medicine are frequently blamed for bad outcomes of medical treatment. In some of these cases, blame is justified; in others it is clearly not. Our aim is to examine the whole issue of blame in this context, in an attempt to show that the background to a mishap is frequently far more complex than may generally be assumed, and also to demonstrate that actual blame for the outcome must be attributed with great caution. It is our belief that society has become too ready to attribute blame without the discriminating, in-depth analysis which this process requires. This represents not only a moral affront but also threatens the very safety goals which we profess to embrace.

Medical accidents

When a patient unexpectedly dies or is harmed in the course of a medical procedure, a common reaction is to attribute responsibility for the death to the medical practitioner involved. Not only may this be done by the family, but often the hospital itself will tend to lay the blame on the individual doctor. There may be occasions when this will be entirely appropriate, and where the problem clearly does lie with the doctor. Very often, however, the situation is much more complicated. The inadequacies of the system, the specific circumstances of the case, the nature of human psychology itself, and sheer chance may have combined to produce a result in which the doctor's contribution is either relatively or completely blameless.

---

[9] For discussion of blaming behaviour, see H. Tennen and G. Affleck, 'Blaming others for threatening events' (1990) 108 *Psychological Bulletin* 209–32. Also, J. Green, *Risk and Misfortune: A Social Construction of Accidents* (London, UCL Press, 1997). Scapegoating is discussed by T. Douglas, *Scapegoats: Transferring Blame* (London, Routledge, 1995).

Blame is rarely a simple matter. It is our view that the complexity of medical treatment and the human and technological systems involved are such that many of the allegations of medical fault are misplaced. Conversely, current processes may fail to identify the important lessons to be learned from a tragedy simply because they focus on blame. Thus the doctor's behaviour may not constitute a legally actionable wrong or sustain a criminal or disciplinary charge, but may nevertheless warrant constructive intervention.

What is required is an enhanced understanding of the underlying causes of iatrogenic harm. This necessitates a more sophisticated appreciation of how things go wrong. It is also important to distinguish between notions of best practice and the reality of how medical practice is actually carried out in the face of pressing need and limited resources. Finally, the ways in which the standard of care is assessed are themselves subject to a number of limitations: for example, expert evidence may be a very poor indicator of what should reasonably be expected in a particular case.

The case for reassessing our current approaches to harm of this nature is prompted not merely by concern that legal and disciplinary procedures should be properly founded on firm moral and scientific grounds; it is also motivated by the conviction that patients will be better served if the real causes of harm are properly identified and appropriately acted upon. A number of cases, drawn from practice, have been chosen to illustrate some of the issues at stake. They provide a starting point for an analysis of the nature of negligence and the difficulties of determining culpability when injury or death occurs as a consequence of medical intervention.

Illustrative cases

One theme of this book is that quite minor errors may have consequences completely out of proportion to their moral culpability. It is appropriate therefore that most of the cases dealt with involve the death of a patient. Many have been the subject of criminal prosecution, but could equally have resulted in a civil action (and indeed, the former does not rule out the latter). A disproportionate number of the cases are from New Zealand, where the issue of medical negligence has been the subject of particular scrutiny in recent years and where there has been an extended political debate about medical accidents and culpability. They occurred at a time when the New Zealand law provided (under certain circumstances, including but not restricted to medical practice) that there could be criminal liability where death resulted from a relatively low level of negligence – a level no higher than that required for civil purposes. This law has subsequently been amended to allow for such prosecution only where there has been a 'major departure' from the required standard of care. This in effect means that gross negligence is now required and brings New Zealand law into line with the vast majority of common-law jurisdictions (including those of the USA and the UK).[10] We shall return later to the place of criminal prosecution for negligent injury; what concerns us at this stage is the variety and complexity of the influences which contribute to the causation of unintended harm, particularly in medical practice, but also in other potentially hazardous activities. Many of these influences have not been adequately recognised by the law, with the result that there is frequently a gap between legal discussions of negligence and reality.

An anaesthetic drug error[11,12]

Dr Yogasakaran was an anaesthetist who had recently immigrated to New Zealand and had been given provisional registration with the expectation that he would work in a hospital post under some degree of supervision for a year. He obtained a position in the small provincial town of Te Kuiti, where it seems he was probably the best trained anaesthetist in the hospital. While there, he undertook the anaesthetic of a 'high-risk' patient for gall bladder surgery. At the end of the operation an emergency developed. During emergence from general anaesthesia the patient began to bite on her endotracheal tube (by which oxygen is administered to the lungs), became unable to breathe and developed cyanosis. It seems that the help immediately available to Dr Yogasakaran might not have been optimal at this moment, the surgeon and scrub nurse having already left theatre, and the nurse who regularly assisted the anaesthetist having been relieved by someone less experienced in this role. Dr Yogasakaran decided to inject the drug *dopram*, an analeptic agent with the property of stimulating arousal of the central nervous system. Unfortunately,

---

[10] P. D. G. Skegg, 'Criminal prosecutions of negligent health professionals: the New Zealand experience' (1998) 6 *Medical Law Review* 220–46.

[11] *R. v. Yogasakaran* [1990] 1 NZLR 399.

[12] D. B. Collins, *Medical Law in New Zealand* (Wellington, Brooker and Friend, 1992), 195–6.

someone (who was never identified) had placed an ampoule of *dopamine* in the section of the drug drawer labelled dopram. This is an inotrope (a drug used to stimulate the heart), and quite different from dopram. As presented, it would normally require dilution and administration as an infusion over time, not as a bolus injection. There was a similarity in presentation of the two agents, however, and in his haste to treat the developing crisis Dr Yogasakaran injected the entire contents of the dopamine ampoule in error. It has always been accepted that this dose of dopamine produced cardiac arrest and was responsible for the subsequent demise of the patient. Dr Yogasakaran succeeded in resuscitating her, and transferred her to the regional centre of Waikato, in Hamilton, where she was admitted to the intensive care unit for ventilation and further management. Unfortunately, it became clear over the next day or two that she had suffered irreversible brain damage, and she eventually died.

Dr Yogasakaran returned to Te Kuiti, went back to the operating room, and only then discovered (himself) the empty ampoule of dopamine. He realised what had happened and immediately informed the doctors at Waikato Hospital, and reported the matter to the authorities in his own hospital. It was his honesty in bringing to light the drug error which led to the laying of charges by the police and to his ultimate conviction for manslaughter.

At his trial the expert witness for the defence was asked whether he would ever administer a drug without checking it. He said that he would not, and that one should always check every drug before administration. He then sought to qualify this position by a description of certain well-known features of human psychology, including the concept of 'mindset' and the fact that people often see what they expect to see in any given situation, not what is actually there – especially when there is a similarity between the two. This further evidence was objected to on the grounds that the witness was an anaesthetist, not a psychologist, and was ruled inadmissible (personal communication, Dr H. Spencer). Dr Yogasakaran was convicted, and then discharged without sentence. It was acknowledged that the conviction alone was a serious punishment for a doctor in these circumstances. His conviction was upheld at the Court of Appeal; the Privy Council in London (the ultimate court of appeal from New Zealand) declined to interfere with what was seen as a policy decision of the New Zealand courts.

On the face of it, this was a straightforward example of negligence. Dr

Yogasakaran failed to check the drug, a requirement acknowledged even by the expert called by the defence. On closer inspection, a number of other factors emerge as important contributors to this incident. In the first place, a small provincial hospital was hardly a suitable place for a doctor deemed to require supervision, even if the level of supervision needed was fairly minimal. A system which sets such a requirement should also ensure that the arrangements actually made are appropriate. This therefore was a systems failure at a fairly general or high level. Similarly, it is questionable whether a high-risk case of this sort should have been dealt with at all in a hospital with limited expertise and resources. It is very likely that this death would have been averted had this patient been transferred to a major centre for her operation.

Many incidents involve a contribution from more than one person, and this case is an example. It illustrates the tendency to blame the last identifiable element in the chain of causation – the person holding the 'smoking gun'. A more comprehensive approach would identify the relative contributions of the other failures in the system, including failures in the conduct of other individuals – in this case the unidentified person who placed the wrong ampoule in the relevant compartment of the drug drawer, for example.

On closer analysis, it seems compelling that Dr Yogasakaran's error was a slip or lapse of the type well recognised as an inevitable part of human behaviour. As we shall discuss in chapters 2 and 3, there are ample data to show that all human beings make mistakes of this general type and that anaesthetists giving drugs are no exception. Stated simply, people frequently see what they expect to see rather than what is there. While the resolution of this problem is in fact very difficult, it seems reasonable to expect that the legal process would take greater account of current knowledge of normal human behaviour. The conclusion that Dr Yogasakaran's act was culpable must therefore be open to question, particularly since his handling of the crisis, once it developed, appeared to have been both responsible and competent.

When attributing blame, we often concentrate on a single, discrete act without paying adequate attention to the overall performance of the individual in the context of the entire event. This is the way in which the law frequently operates. It does not necessarily concern itself with what happened before and after an isolated act of alleged negligence: it focuses upon a single act and draws conclusions as to culpability purely on the basis of this act. It would therefore be quite misleading to describe Dr Yogasakaran as a 'negligent doctor' on the basis of one incident, just as it would be misleading to describe a driver as a negligent driver on the basis of one momentary lapse in attention. Indeed, in his summing up in the Yogasakaran case the judge alluded to this difficulty by saying: 'It is certainly not suggested by the Crown that Dr Yogasakaran is a poor doctor. The Crown says he is a highly trained, experienced, responsible man, whom the Crown says made a mistake, through carelessness, on this one occasion.'[13]

There are obviously times when it is appropriate to judge people on the basis of single acts. In the context of medical practice, though, it is particularly important that the cause of a problem is identified as soon as possible and the way in which the problem is then handled becomes highly relevant. It is often said in medical training that mistakes are inevitable, but that the important thing is to know that one has made them and to deal with them appropriately. Viewed from this perspective, Dr Yogasakaran appears to have met all the requirements that could reasonably be expected of an anaesthetist in the circumstances. His only failing appears to have been a normal human error of the type that all anaesthetists will inevitably make from time to time, particularly in an emergency.

The value of punishment in a case like that of Yogasakaran is far from clear. The need for compensation, of course, is a different matter, and there may well be justification for this. Punishing the last person in the chain, however, usually fails to address the underlying problems. It is doubtful whether deterrence is effective in preventing slips and lapses of this type. Even removing the individual without correcting the system simply creates a situation where his or her replacement will be vulnerable to a recurrence of the same problem.

A matter of 'momentary carelessness'[14]

Dr Morrison, a radiologist, was handed the wrong contrast medium by his assistant, an experienced radiographer, and injected it into a patient's spinal canal without first checking it. Death resulted two days later. Dr

---

[13] Summing up of Justice Anderson, Case no. 56/88 (Hamilton Registry), p. 19.
[14] *R. v. Morrison*, 23 April 1991, s. 7/91, High Court, Dunedin.

Morrison accepted that he had been negligent in injecting fluid without an adequate check, and pleaded guilty to manslaughter. He was convicted and discharged, the judge noting that the omission had been 'contributed to, indeed initiated, by the act of another person also qualified and experienced and with whom the accused was accustomed to work'. He also accepted that the omission 'was a matter of momentary carelessness in circumstances where he had no reason to be on guard'.

At a subsequent hearing the Medical Council placed certain requirements for supervision on Dr Morrison for a defined period, and also asked that guidelines be developed for such injections. These were published in the Medical Council newsletter,[15] and, although headed as coming from the College of Radiology, the implication was that they were applicable to all injections of drugs. The key feature was a requirement for two people to check every injection by means of a 'chant' in which the key information was read out by one to the other. This approach has long been used by nurses, but has not always prevented errors.[16] There is real doubt that it would be practical in other situations such as anaesthesia, where the frequency of injections and potential to disturb other activities is high, or general practice where doctors may give injections in the home without the availability of a suitable second person. Furthermore, a subsequent survey (involving anaesthetists) revealed that only a minority of practising clinicians were aware that the guideline existed.[17]

The negligence in this case is clearer than that in the Yogasakaran case. Unlike the latter, there was no urgency here. However, there was once again an important contribution by a second person, and once again at least part of the problem, not just on the part of Dr Morrison and his assistant, but also on the part of the wider radiological community, lay in the system and its lack of formal procedures for checking during the administration of drugs into the spinal canal. This was acknowledged by the Medical Council, and at least some attempt was made to address this safety issue through the development of guidelines. While this may have gone some distance towards improving the situation in radiology, it does seem that a greater effort to deal with wider problems of injectable drugs

---

[15] Medical Council of New Zealand, 'Safe administration of drugs' (1992) 5 *Medical Council News* 4.

[16] A. F. Merry and D. J. Peck, 'Anaesthetists, errors in drug administration and the law' (1995) 108 *New Zealand Medical Journal* 185–7.

[17] A. F. Merry and D. J. Peck, Unpublished survey data.

across all specialities might have been warranted. In particular, guidelines are of little use if not adequately promulgated.

An important difference between this case and the previous one is the particular vulnerability of the spinal cord. Injections into the spinal canal require meticulous care. The central point of the whole procedure was the administration of a single drug into a hazardous site. Although the error in this case is entirely understandable – in the sense that it is easy to see how it came about – there does, nevertheless, seem to have been a degree of associated carelessness, albeit slight when taken in the context of contemporary practice. This example demonstrates that culpability has to be judged in the light of all aspects of the particular case, including the level of risk and the degree of urgency. Whether an incident of this sort, subsequently handled appropriately and with complete honesty, should merit the severity of a criminal prosecution is a more questionable matter, however, and we shall return to this point in the concluding chapter.

Both these cases also bring to the fore the crucial importance of result in the criminal law. Criminal justice focuses on the effects which wrongful conduct produces. These effects may sometimes be out of all proportion to the seriousness of the wrongdoing, and indeed may be a matter of chance or what in philosophical discussion is referred to as 'moral luck'. A momentary lapse of attention while driving would often go unnoticed and unpunished, or if it were to be detected and punished, the punishment would be very slight. However, if moral luck dictates that a pedestrian is killed, the punishment is likely to be considerably more serious, *even though the wrongdoing is identical in each case.*

Similarly, we know that many, if not most, doctors have administered the wrong drug to a patient at some time.[18] In most cases this is without serious consequence and attracts little comment. However, if a patient dies or is otherwise seriously harmed as a result, two factors may come into play. One is that the likelihood of legal or disciplinary proceedings becomes very high; the other is that the phenomenon known as 'outcome bias' will tend to induce a much harsher appraisal of the degree of negligence involved. This point is further explored in chapter 7.

---

[18] Merry and Peck, 'Anaesthetists'.

Perverting the course of justice[19]

A contrast can be drawn between the manner in which Drs Yogasakaran and Morrison responded to and dealt with the results of their errors, and that followed by a British general practitioner who inadvertently prescribed a beta-adrenergic blocking agent (beta-blocker) to a patient with asthma. Asthma is a known contra-indication to the use of beta-blockers, and predictably produced bronchospasm, which proved fatal. In the resulting criminal trial for manslaughter, the court took a lenient view of the doctor's medical error, but sentenced him to six months' imprisonment for falsifying the relevant records with the intent of perverting the course of justice.

This illustrates neatly the distinction in terms of culpability between an understandable mistake (prescribing the beta-blocker) and a deliberate and unacceptable violation (altering the evidence). The attribution of blame seems entirely appropriate in respect of the doctor's deliberate choice to commit the offence of falsifying evidence.

Unsupervised junior doctors[20]

Malcolm Savage, a sixteen-year old boy, who had had leukaemia since the age of four (and was found at post-mortem examination to be in remission), was admitted to Peterborough District Hospital in 1990 for his monthly treatment with cytotoxic drugs. Under the supervision of Dr Barry Sullman (a house officer), Dr Michael Prentice (a pre-registration house officer) injected vincristine (which should have been given intravenously) into the patient's cerebrospinal fluid instead of methotrexate. It appears that Dr Sullman misunderstood his role, and believed himself to be supervising only the lumbar puncture while Dr Prentice believed his colleague to be supervising the overall procedure of administering the cytotoxic medication. The boy died two weeks later. In summing up, the judge said, 'It seems to me you could have been helped more than you were helped.' He also said, 'You are far from being bad men; you are good

---

[19] D. Brahams, 'Medical manslaughter' (1994) 344 *The Lancet* 256.

[20] G. Korgaonkar and D. Tribe, 'Doctors' liability for manslaughter' (1992) 47 *British Journal of Hospital Medicine* 147; *R. v. Prentice* [1993] 3 WLR 927; C. Dyer, 'Doctors cleared of manslaughter' (1999) 318 *British Medical Journal* 148; *R. v. Prentice and another, R. v. Adomako, R. v. Holloway* [1993] 4 All ER 935; D. Brahams, 'Manslaughter and reckless medical treatment' (1991) 338 *The Lancet* 1198–9.

men who contrary to your normal behaviour on this one occasion were guilty of momentary recklessness.' Both doctors were convicted of manslaughter, and given nine-month suspended prison sentences, but this conviction was overturned by the Court of Appeal.

In a very similar case, also involving junior doctors, vincristine was given intrathecally instead of intravenously once again, this time into a twelve-year-old child, Richie William. Charges against Dr John Lee, a specialist registrar in paediatric anaesthetics, and Dr Dermot Murphy, a registrar in haematology, were withdrawn on the grounds that failures in the system operated by Great Ormond Street Hospital for Children had played a significant part in the events. For example, the patient was admitted to a general ward instead of the ward which specialised in the treatment of malignancies. The injection was then deferred because he had eaten a biscuit. The result of this was that the senior registrar who should have administered the chemotherapy was off duty by the time the injection could be given. Vincristine was incorrectly sent to the operating theatre by a nurse against a rule which prohibited this. It was injected by Dr Lee, who had never previously administered chemotherapy into the spine, after Dr Murphy advised him, over the telephone, to administer the drugs which had been sent to theatre.

The case of Prentice and Sullman was of importance in the development of the English position on the criminal prosecution of negligence, and the decision of the Court of Appeal confirmed the requirement of gross negligence for this purpose. The striking feature of both cases, however, is the lack of any senior doctor or hospital authority amongst the defendants. A second feature is the fact that the very high-profile prosecution of Drs Prentice and Sullman appears to have had little if any benefit in avoiding recurrences of the same mistake. Finally, in both, it can be seen how factors in the system may contribute to the generation of an error.

A highly complicated emergency[21]

Dr Hugel, a specialist anaesthetist, was charged with manslaughter after a thirteen-year-old boy, Benjamin Thorne, died following a minor pro-

---

[21] The details of this case are known to one of the authors (Merry), who acted as an expert witness. See also Skegg, 'Criminal prosecutions of negligent health professionals'.

cedure on an infected knee. The child was fit and active, and the tragedy of this case was particularly poignant. His mother had expressed anxiety about the risks of anaesthesia, but had been told that the operation could not be done under local anaesthetic and that under the circumstances there was little to fear.

After some pre-trial proceedings, the charge was confined to an allegation that Dr Hugel had been negligent in failing to identify and remove a blocked filter. Expert evidence called by both prosecution and defence concurred that the preliminary problems in this case were nothing to do with the filter, but rather the result of aspiration of stomach contents into the larynx. This, it was thought, produced laryngospasm, which led on to the well-recognised syndrome of negative pressure pulmonary oedema and probably bronchospasm as well. Dr Hugel immediately called for the help of an anaesthetic colleague, but this was nearly thirty minutes coming and the contribution of various junior doctors who did arrive was relatively ineffectual. It was accepted by both sides that a filter used to protect the anaesthetic circuit from possible contamination by patient secretions was indeed blocked by the time the second anaesthetist arrived, and that its removal at that point did result in a rapid improvement of the boy's oxygenation and general condition. Unfortunately, he had suffered irreversible brain damage by this stage, and life support was discontinued the following day. The defence led evidence to the effect that it was unlikely that this blockage occurred until relatively late in the proceedings. None of the experts was able to say how the time that irreversible brain damage occurred related to the time at which the filter blocked. All four experts said that the general conduct of the resuscitation was adequate, and none was prepared to criticise without reservation Dr Hugel's failure to identify the problem with the filter. It was agreed that she had not followed a protocol known as 'COVER ABCD'[22] in that she had not expressly eliminated the patient circuit and replaced it with a rebreathing bag. However, in the circumstances of the case none of the experts was able to say confidently that this would have made any difference. Furthermore, one of the witnesses, the author of the protocol, pointed out that the protocol had failed to anticipate this particular problem and, if followed to the letter, would probably have

---

[22] W. B. Runciman, R. K. Webb, I. D. Klepper, R. Lee, J. A. Williamson and L. Barker, 'Crisis management – validation of an algorithm by analysis of 2000 incident reports' (1993) 21 *Anaesthesia and Intensive Care* 579–92.

been interpreted as requiring the filter to be retained because it was the means by which the carbon dioxide sampling line gained access to the circuit gases and the protocol expressly advised the retention of this line. He said the protocol had now been modified to make the need to eliminate a filter explicit. In the result, the jury returned a verdict of not-guilty.

One of the most important features of this case is its 'smoking gun' aspect. A very obvious problem – the blocked filter – suggested itself as the cause of the death. A superficial inquiry might have gone no further, but on more mature reflection and more detailed examination of the facts it became obvious that this was but one of several difficult and dangerous problems which faced the anaesthetist. It was, furthermore, one which seems to have developed late in the proceedings. A second feature underlined by this case is the fact that certain medical procedures (notably the administration of anaesthetics) may be inherently hazardous, and may allow very limited time for response to problems when they do develop. Dr Hugel had no more than a few minutes to evaluate and resolve a complex and rapidly evolving emergency. We are once again confronted with the human being as the limiting factor in the complex system.[23] No matter how competent a person may be, there will always be challenges that exceed his or her ability to react adequately and in time.

The strikingly emotive nature of this case, involving, as it did, the totally unexpected death of a healthy thirteen-year-old undergoing a minor procedure, makes some form of blame attribution almost irresistible. Yet it is important that the desire to blame does not prevent a proper and objective evaluation of what went wrong.

Another feature illustrated by this case is the uncertain nature of medical knowledge. The algorithm COVER ABCD was developed on the basis of an analysis of the first 2,000 incidents reported to the Australian Incident Monitoring Study (AIMS).[24] It was (and is) an excellent approach to facilitating the management of a crisis in anaesthesia. It was understandable for the prosecution to assume that this protocol represented a statement of the standard of care for managing just the sort of situation faced by Dr Hugel. On closer analysis, however, it emerged that the protocol was flawed in the very respect applicable to the case in

---

[23] G. H Sigurdsson and E. McAteer, 'Morbidity and mortality associated with anaesthesia' (1996) 40 *Acta Anaesthesiologica Scandinavica* 1057–63.
[24] Runciman, 'Crisis management'.

question. This was a reflection of the fact that no similar incident had been reported to the AIMS database. A further point is that the protocol was not in fact universally accepted. Not all practising anaesthetists in New Zealand were aware of its existence, and it is uncertain how many anaesthetists outside Australasia would have been familiar with it.

A sleeping anesthesiologist[25]

Joseph Verbrugge, a Denver anesthesiologist, was convicted of negligence after an eight-year-old patient, Richard Leonard, died following ear surgery in 1993. Dr Verbrugge was accused of having fallen asleep during the anaesthetic; he denied this, but admitted colleagues had confronted him about allegedly falling asleep during previous anaesthetics. There were a number of other features of this case which may have influenced the jury, who concluded that Dr Verbrugge's conduct amounted to 'an extreme deviation from generally accepted standards of medical practice', but were unable to agree unanimously that this constituted criminally negligent homicide or reckless manslaughter.

The most important point in this case is the fact that Dr Verbrugge's falling asleep during previous anaesthetics had been raised with him. Whether or not he was in fact asleep on the occasion of Richard Leonard's death, it does seem that something more should have been done to reduce the risk created by this problem. It might be thought that an anaesthetist has a responsibility to respond to manifestations of an inability to stay awake at work. It could also be argued that those who identified this problem had a responsibility to take action. The public is rightly concerned about the repeated failure of the available mechanisms to identify medical practitioners who are a risk to their patients, or to take adequate measures to safeguard patients when such doctors are identified.

A 'systems double-bind'[26]

At about 6 p.m. one evening a mature woman was admitted to a district hospital in New Zealand following a road traffic accident. She had

---

[25] 'Anesthesiologist is convicted in death of patient', *The New York Times* (24 October 1996), A22. The conviction was appealed: *People* v. *Verbrugge* 998 P 2d 43 (1999).

[26] Coroner's Verdict, Coroner's Court, Rotorua, 15–17 October 1997. D. Diaz, 'Doctor's slip led to death, inquest told', *New Zealand Herald* (16 October 1997), A4.

multiple orthopaedic injuries, but none of them was life-threatening. Both the orthopaedic surgeon and the anaesthetist who were on call had completed a long day's work. The anaesthetist assessed the patient soon after admission and then attended to two other urgent cases. At about 10 p.m. he was free to take the patient who had had the accident to the operating theatre. The proceedings became quite protracted and blood loss significant. To manage this better, the anaesthetist elected to insert a central venous catheter (CVC). This procedure was made more difficult by the fact that it was undertaken during the operation rather than before it, and unfortunately, unbeknown to the anaesthetist, in the process of insertion of the CVC, damage was done to the carotid artery. Blood loss became an increasingly difficult problem. What in fact was happening was that blood from the carotid artery was tracking into the thorax. The anaesthetist did consider this possibility, and made some attempts to investigate it. By this time, however, it was after 3 a.m. and these attempts may have been less determined than normal.

The surgery was completed at about 7 a.m. By this time, the doctors concerned had been working for almost 24 hours without rest. The patient was handed over to intensive care staff and the doctors departed. Shortly afterwards, cardiac arrest occurred and the patient died. The post-mortem examination confirmed that the cause of death was bleeding into the thorax from the damaged carotid artery.

At the coroner's hearing (presided over by a district court judge), the expert witness gave evidence that the actual insertion of the CVC had been entirely competent, and that the problem which had occurred was a recognised complication of CVC insertion. She did express criticism, though, of the failure to diagnose and treat the problem adequately. The judge commented on the possible contribution made by fatigue to this failure. He took note of evidence testifying to the adverse effect of fatigue on performance. On the basis of other evidence presented, he eventually acknowledged that the hours worked by the doctors in this case were accepted as inevitable in both anaesthesia and orthopaedic surgery. It was pointed out that it would be difficult to staff hospitals of this type without exposing doctors to the occasional requirement to work all night after a full day. On these grounds the judge declined to criticise the individual doctors, but recommended that the relevant colleges re-evaluate their guidelines with regard to hours of work.

There is now increasingly convincing evidence of the negative impact of fatigue on performance in many fields, including medicine.[27] It is now widely accepted that working continuously for a period such as that involved in this case should be seen as a violation of safe practice.[28] The hours worked, the nature of the work, and the time of day may all have contributed to a decrease in performance. This incident is a prime example of a violation made unavoidable by the system. This has been referred to as a 'system double-bind' – the doctors may understand and wish to avoid the unsafe behaviour, but they are unable to do so because of the constraints of their working arrangements.

Once again, this example reinforces the need to evaluate events in their wider context. Concentrating on human error alone may produce a misleading picture of the true cause of the problem. As we have observed previously, simply to punish, or even to remove the individual without addressing the deficiencies in the system, is to invite a repetition of the event, albeit with different players. It is significant that the judge was prepared to identify fatigue as a possible contributory factor in this patient's death. Such an awareness has been markedly absent in the law and it is only recently that the courts are beginning to be aware of the full impact of fatigue on human activity. The challenge is to translate this awareness into effective measures to promote more sensible practices. We shall return in later chapters to the question of holding organisations accountable for the performance of their employees.

A culpable violation[29]

Dr Channagiri Manjanatha, a Saskatchewan anaesthetist, was the first Canadian doctor to be gaoled as the result of criminal negligence causing bodily harm. He had left the operating room to make a personal telephone call during the anaesthetic of his seventeen-year-old patient, Ryan Braumberger, who was undergoing surgery to repair a broken leg, without arranging for a suitable person to monitor the situation. The patient became disconnected from the ventilator, and was left in a vegetative state. Two of the ventilator's alarms had been switched off. Dr Manjanatha was also found by the judge to have falsified, to some degree, his report of the incident.

---

[27] T. H. Monk (ed.), *Sleep, Sleepiness, and Performance* (New York, John Wiley, 1991).
[28] Violations and errors are distinct: see chapters 3 and 4.
[29] (1995) 131 *Saskatchewan Reports* 316.

For an anaesthetist to leave a patient unattended is quite different from any of the medical errors outlined above. This is a matter of deliberate choice – a clear violation of the rules of safe anaesthesia. A central theme of this book is that genuine human error is inevitable; equally central, however, is the point that violations are a different matter. Thus it is unreasonable to require that, in an entire career, an anaesthetist should never make a slip/lapse error of the type made by Dr Yogasakaran, but it is quite reasonable to require, in the absence of compelling cause, that no patient should be left unattended in the manner of this case.

The Bristol cardiac surgeons[30]

This well-known case involved the performance over an extended period of time of two cardiac surgeons at Bristol Royal Infirmary, in relation to difficult operations on paediatric patients with congenital heart abnormalities. Of fifty-three operations involving arterial switches and atrioventricular septal defects, twenty-nine resulted in the death of the patient. In addition, four of the surviving patients suffered brain damage. These results were considerably worse than those obtained in other centres. The central issue related to the persistence of these surgeons in continuing these procedures in the face of poor results. Attempts to raise the matter by others were discounted by the surgeons and by a hospital administrator. Indeed, it seems that the anaesthetist who expressed concern over the high mortality rate had little choice but to leave Bristol and to find employment outside Britain. The parents of the patients were quoted standard risks rather than being told the actual results of the unit in question.

This complicated story raises a number of issues. It illustrates the

---

[30] Editorial, 'First lessons from the "Bristol case"' (1998) 351 *The Lancet* 1669; R. Horton, 'How should doctors respond to the GMC's judgments on Bristol?' (1998) 351 *The Lancet* 1900–1; I. Murray and A. Lee, 'Baby death surgeons ignored warnings', *The Times* (30 May 1998), 1; C. Dyer, 'Bristol doctors found guilty of serious professional misconduct' (1998) 316 *British Medical Journal* 1924; T. Delamothe, 'Who killed Cock Robin?' (1998) 316 *British Medical Journal* 1757; R. Smith, 'All changed, changed utterly' (1998) 316 *British Medical Journal* 1917–18; J. Warden, 'High powered inquiry into Bristol deaths' (1998) 316 *British Medical Journal* 1925; P. M. Dunn, 'The Wisheart affair: paediatric cardiological services in Bristol, 1990–5', (1998) 317 *British Medical Journal* 1144–5; various correspondents (1998) 317 *British Medical Journal* 1579–82, 1592–3, 1659–60; various correspondents (1999) 318 *British Medical Journal* 1009–11; C. Dyer, 'Whistleblower in Bristol case says funding was put before patients' (1999) 319 *British Medical Journal* 1387.

problem of individual technical competence of doctors, who undertake difficult procedures when they simply are not sufficiently skilled or perhaps sufficiently well supported by their unit, to achieve an acceptable success rate. It also raises issues of audit, of how such doctors are to be identified, and of the difficulties faced by whistleblowers. The culpability in this case is rather different from that in the preceding examples, because of the drawn-out nature of the course of conduct, and also because of the complexity of the issues at stake. For example, the point has been made that the results of a unit such as this depend not only on the surgeons but also on a number of other members of the team. Furthermore, it is no simple matter to demonstrate that results in a relatively small series of high-risk cases are indeed beyond the limits of acceptable variation. Nevertheless, the decision to take a risk and persist with the operations in the face of mounting evidence of unacceptable outcomes was unfortunate. Furthermore, being deliberate, in this case once again the actions of the doctors have the appearance of a violation rather than an error. Disciplinary proceedings by the General Medical Council resulted in the deregistration of both surgeons, and of the medically qualified hospital administrator whose response to expressions of disquiet was considered adequate.

Naming and blaming

Our examples illustrate how failures – at times quite minor failures – in medical care can at times have tragic consequences for the patient. How we react to events of this sort is, in one sense at least, dependent on how the event is described. Event descriptions carry a great deal of moral weight, and our choice of description may well be decisive in determining the outcome of any legal or moral inquiry into the event. For example, to describe an event as an accident is often taken to mean that it was a 'matter of chance' and carries strong implications of blamelessness. At the other end of the spectrum, to describe it as deliberate or intentional implies a high level of culpability.[31] Yet between these two extremes of complete chance and intentional harm, there may be varying degrees by which behaviour knowingly contributes to the risk of harm. For example,

---

[31] R. A. Duff, *Intention, Agency and Criminal Liability: Philosophy of Action and the Criminal Law* (Oxford, Basil Blackwell, 1990).

the drunk driver may not intend harm, but must be held responsible for the consequences of deliberate risk-taking. Such a driver may protest that the knocking down of a pedestrian was unintentional and was therefore an accident. This would not be accepted, and it could be pointed out that the event was not accidental in that it could have been avoided by modifying a decision within his or her control – the decision to drive while under the influence of alcohol.[32] By contrast, if an apparently well-maintained tyre blows out, perhaps because it has run over a jagged stone in the road, that would seem to be beyond the control of the driver and would be truly accidental. It might be viewed as reflecting inadequate maintenance of the road, and in that context be seen as a systems problem. However, systems designs are themselves subject to limits, including those on resources, and in this example there is a sense that, given the current state of tyre design and the impossibility of keeping roads free of all debris, it would have been beyond the ability of anybody to prevent this. This event was simply not preventable – an accident in the purest sense.

If it is the case that the term 'accident' carries with it an exculpatory, or even mitigating, meaning, it is important to identify exactly what this word means. One definition describes an accident as something which is 'largely, if not completely, unintentional, unforeseeable – and harmful'.[33]

Does this definition serve our purposes adequately? Probably not. To begin with, the inclusion of the concept of harm must be taken as a matter of arbitrary definition and is unnecessary; it is possible to imagine an event which all would agree is accidental but which causes no harm. Indeed, there is even the concept of the happy accident, which describes an occurrence which may be fortuitous but which is regarded as positive. Missing a flight which subsequently crashes comes to mind as an example.

Intentionality is certainly relevant. It is obvious that no harm was intended in any of the cases dealt with above. Were these, then, all accidents? If they were, does this imply that there should be no blame attached to any of them?

A particular feature of medical practice, well illustrated in the cases presented, is that, so far from any intention to harm, there is actually an intention to help. This is in contrast to the situation where a driver

---

[32] J. Rumgay, *Crime, Punishment and the Drinking Offender* (London, Macmillan, 1998).

[33] J. Dowie, 'Would decision analysis eliminate medical accidents?', in C. Vincent, M. Ennis and R. J. Audley (eds.), *Medical Accidents* (New York, Oxford University Press, 1993), 116.

knocks over a pedestrian. In the latter case there may be no intention to harm the pedestrian, but in fact, apart from the technical duty of care on the part of the driver not to cause harm to the pedestrian, there is no intent either way in relation to the particular individual. When a doctor accepts responsibility for a patient, there is an explicit intent to help that patient or at the very least not to harm him or her. Sadly, however, unintentionality alone does not provide a sufficiently narrow filter to preclude all cases in which blame may reasonably be attributed. There are many examples of unintended consequences which may be neither intended nor desired by the actor, but which nevertheless may be the subject of blame and may therefore need to be excluded from the category of accidents. In the example of an armed robber who points a weapon at a shopkeeper with the intention only of frightening him, the law nevertheless quite rightly holds the robber responsible for the consequences if the gun goes off and the shopkeeper is killed or injured. It would certainly be unacceptable to describe this as an accident even if the robber genuinely had no intention of shooting. What makes the situation non-accidental is the element of foreseeability. Even if the robber did not foresee the possibility of the weapon going off, any reasonable person would have seen the risk of this happening. The term 'accident' has a strongly normative element to it; it is not merely descriptive and cannot be understood outside the framework of the normative evaluation of the behaviour in question. Clearly, then, in evaluating the sort of case described above, intentionality, although an important component of our definition of an accident, must be taken as given and is of little use on its own.

A more significant element would seem to be foreseeability. As with intentionality, this concept is one of the important elements in determining whether an occurrence is accidental but, of itself, it too is insufficient. By convention, foreseeability in this context means reasonable foreseeability. If an event is foreseeable, then there is a duty to take precautions to prevent its occurrence. A failure to do so is culpable and justifies the conclusion that what happened was not an accident. There is, though, a further requirement. It is only reasonable to hold a person responsible for a foreseeable event if it was realistically within his or her power to prevent it. Thus it is foreseeable that an anaesthetist's failing to stay awake is, in the end, likely to result in a tragedy – and something can be done about this by the practitioner concerned. As with the drunken driver, if a patient died because of a practitioner's known tendency to fall asleep while working we would not call this an accident. Similarly, it is foreseeable that failing to supervise junior doctors will over time increase the number of harmful errors in a hospital. Again, it should be possible to deal with problems of this type, given adequate resources, but in this case the onus would seem to lie primarily with others, and only partly with the junior doctors. The limitations of human behaviour must also be taken into account. In the following chapters we shall argue that it is foreseeable that every practitioner will eventually make certain types of error, and some of these will harm patients. As with the junior doctors, we shall emphasise the importance of designing the system to reduce the likelihood of such harm occurring. However, if it is accepted that certain types of error are an inevitable accompaniment of the human condition, then it follows that it is not realistically within the power of human practitioners to eliminate them. Given a reasonably well-designed and resourced system, a genuine error (as defined in chapter 3) must be accepted as unintended and unavoidable – and therefore as an accident.

We would suggest, then, that an event can be defined as an accident only if the following conditions are met: (i) that it was unintended; and *either* (ii) it was reasonably unforeseeable *or* (iii) it was foreseeable (in a general sense at least) but could not realistically have been prevented.

This might be tested further against others of the cases mentioned above. We have already noted that the first condition is met in all the cases: none of the doctors in question intended to harm the patient. As far as the second and third requirements are concerned, judgements on foreseeability and preventability in these cases depend to some degree on the weight given to the contemporary understanding of the nature of human error. Thus in Dr Yogasakaran's case one might say that failing to read an ampoule's label is preventable, and that one could foresee the risks entailed in such a failure. A view more compatible with our knowledge of human psychology is that this was an example of a lapse. We shall expand on the nature and classification of human error in chapter 3, but all the evidence suggests that lapses are inevitable concomitants of the human ability to deal with complex situations. They cannot be prevented by exhortation, punishment, or any other direct attempt to modify human behaviour. They are particularly understandable in the context of an unplanned and unexpected emergency. By contrast, for the planned injection of a single drug into a hazardous location by Dr Morrison, it does seem that more could have been done to ensure that a proper check was carried out. While no amount of care can guarantee that all such errors will be prevented, the omission of precautions along the lines subsequently recommended by the College of Radiologists does represent a failure which was preventable. In effect, more could reasonably have been done. Furthermore, it could reasonably have been predicted that the failure to follow such precautions might eventually result in a disaster. There are grounds for suggesting, therefore, that the case of Dr Yogasakaran was an accident, while that of Dr Morrison was not.

In spite of this, it seems harsh to place the entire responsibility for the event on Dr Morrison, partly because of the contribution of a second person (the radiologist), but more importantly because the evidence points to the lack of a properly defined procedure for radiologists administering such an injection at the time. Had a proper protocol been in general use when the injection was undertaken, there would be little doubt about Dr Morrison's culpability in choosing not to follow it. In fact, it was only after the event, and at the instigation of the Medical Council, that the College of Radiologists produced a suitable protocol. Dr Morrison chose to plead guilty to the charge against him; it might have been possible for him to defend himself on the grounds that his overall approach was consistent with the norms applicable at the time. If one accepts this proposition, his only error was, like Dr Yogasakaran's, a momentary lapse – something very difficult to prevent. In that context, it was an accident.

Similarly, there was a clearly preventable component in the case involving fatigue, one which might foreseeably compromise performance. It is far from ideal for doctors to work for excessive periods without a break, and it ought to be possible to avoid this. For this reason, in one view, this case should not be called an accident. Yet in an alternative view, even if it was not an accident and was therefore attributable to a deliberate violation of a general principle in relation to fatigue, responsibility for the incident did not rest primarily with the doctors. In chapter 4 we shall consider the contribution of system double-binds to the generation of violations. It may be neither possible nor desirable to single out individuals responsible for the system failure in a situation of this type, although sometimes this can and should be done. For the doctors concerned, in the circumstances, working while fatigued was not preventable. Once again, under this construction, the patient's death might be thought accidental.

In the case of Dr Hugel, it is understandable that the completely unexpected death of an essentially healthy child, taken together with the discovery of a blocked filter, might be construed as a simple matter constituting negligence – and therefore not an accident. On closer enquiry, the case (as we have described) involved multiple factors in a complex and rapidly evolving emergency. It is hard to see how a sequence of events such as this could have been predicted, and at her trial for manslaughter no measures were identified which, without the benefit of hindsight, could reasonably have been expected from a competent practitioner and which would clearly have prevented the loss of the patient. Once again, therefore, we can conclude that this incident was an accident.

An important feature in understanding this case is its progressive nature. The overall incident may be viewed as having been made up of a series of developments which were dependent upon one another. The management of the case cannot be evaluated by looking at a single decision or act within the series. One must take into account the overall picture and how the reaction to each stage may have been affected by what had preceded it. How the boundaries of an event are defined may be crucial to its evaluation. In this case the prosecution laid great store by the doctor's failure to identify a blocked filter. The defence view, though, was that the filter was a late and largely irrelevant development. Furthermore, while one might have expected an anaesthetist to identify a blocked filter as an isolated problem at the beginning of a case, diagnosing a late blockage in the context of numerous other problems is a different matter. The subjective reaction of the anaesthetist to a relentlessly developing crisis in which a child is dying is likely to be severe and, indeed, to become overwhelming as bad event succeeds bad event. The point to be made here is that human behaviour has a chronological dimension and performance must be judged in temporal context. What might be considered preventable at the beginning of a sequence may be made inevitable by the limitations of human beings confronted with the informational and emotional overload which develops as a crisis unfolds.

It is possible to analyse the remaining cases in somewhat similar terms. The point of this exercise is not to endorse or reject the decisions of the courts but rather to emphasise the need for some sophistication in analysis of this type. It is essential to look beyond the 'smoking gun' (the filter in Dr Hugel's case, for example) and identify the full sequence of events, the nature of any antecedent factors, the cognitive processes involved in the incident, and the contribution of other players and of the system in general.

There is no doubt that many people use the term 'accident' rather loosely, and would include within it at least some untoward incidents in which there is an element of fault or blame. Indeed, it is in this sense that we used the word in the opening sentence of this chapter. This usage, though, deprives the term of a useful evaluative role. In a technical context we talk, for example, of *non-accidental injury* in children, and this is a convenient term which signals the presence of some element of culpability. The concept of accident and the accidental, as we have defined it, is a useful aid to differentiate blameworthy from blameless behaviour, and is in accordance with one form of everyday use. It is obvious from the above discussion that the dividing line between acci-dental and non-accidental events may be hazy and subject to differences of interpretation. In chapter 5 we shall extend this distinction, and identify five levels of blameworthiness. Clarifying the boundaries between them depends on a proper understanding of the insights which the science of psychology has brought in relation to the ways in which the limitations of human behaviour contribute to adverse events.

Accidents, errors and violations

A useful starting point in deciding whether an event should be judged as accidental or non-accidental is a proper classification of the cognitive processes underlying the human behaviour which has contributed to its occurrence. Errors need to be distinguished from violations. Errors are characteristically never deliberate. Violations, on the other hand, must be defined in the context of accepted rules, norms or principles, and constitute a deliberate deviation from them. They are not inevitably reprehensible, and indeed may be motivated by the best of intentions. Yet they do involve choice – there is in a violation a clear volitional component. Violations are therefore always avoidable, although factors within the system or organisation may at times make it very difficult in practice to avoid them. Errors, by contrast, are unintentional and cannot be avoided simply through the exercise of choice.

Errors may involve an action or a plan. Skill-based errors are either slips or lapses, and can also be thought of as unintended actions. Errors involving unintended actions can be differentiated from *mistakes*, in which the action is intended but there is some flaw in the plan. Mistakes may be further subdivided according to the type of cognitive processing involved in the generation of the event. Much is known about each type of error and about different forms of violation. Indeed, it is often possible to predict what type of error is most likely to occur in a particular set of circumstances. This systematic approach should greatly facilitate assigning accidental or non-accidental status, or, in a more general sense, blame-worthiness. In chapters 3 and 4, we shall enlarge upon each of these error types and on violations, and relate each to medical practice. A further theme of this book is that the proper understanding of errors and violations goes beyond the knowledge and experience of the lay person, and is not a matter which the court should determine for itself without the help of an expert. On the contrary, analysis of these events requires familiarity with a substantial body of knowledge based on empirical research. Indeed, certain attributes of error are counter-intuitive. For example, we shall see that, surprisingly, although experts are less likely than novices to make errors overall, they are more prone than novices to slips and lapses – a factor of obvious importance in the evaluation of an event.

Explaining and blaming

The quest for truth

Misfortune invites explanation. When things go wrong in human affairs, the almost inevitable response is to seek an explanation for what happened. This can be explained in various ways. At the most general level, human curiosity about the world compels us to try to understand the events which touch upon our lives. It is this curiosity which prompts us to try to understand the past, in order to make sense of our relationship with it. Every human institution, every human life has a history, and the urge to see coherence in the events of our lives and to resolve the unresolved is very powerful. Even if the knowledge that we acquire as to what has happened were to have no practical value – in the sense that it would not alter how we conduct our affairs or even how we deal with them legally – it may still be important to us for its own sake. The truth is always important to people, whatever other motivations may also contribute to the search for the facts.

The pursuit of safety

Curiosity apart, there are good pragmatic reasons for seeking an accurate account of events that have caused harm. Foremost amongst these is the desire to prevent the recurrence of such harm. What distinguishes this motivation from others is the fact that it is forward-looking and is therefore arguably of greatest use. In the scientific and technological realms in general, and in medicine in particular, the need for comprehensive and scientifically based evaluation of incidents is well understood, and significant resources are committed to this sort of inquiry.

The emphasis is on identifying the truth rather than on attributing blame. This is shown by the way in which inquiries of this sort will seek to encourage maximum disclosure by focusing on the information itself rather than by seeking to establish authorship and responsibility. This also recognises that the individual operator is only one component of the complex system, and often the least important one. The use of confidential reporting, notably in aviation and medicine, is widely accepted as being of great value. Typically, in a hospital using this system, a report will be submitted by the doctor concerned with the incident. This may be anonymous, although in practice it may be difficult to conceal the identity of the reporting doctor. The vital requirement is for the doctor not only to explain the facts but also to offer his or her opinion about what went wrong. In this situation, the right to silence is being set aside. There is also a significant chance that the opinion may take too little account of all the circumstances and may even be unnecessarily self-critical. With this in mind, arrangements have been made in many countries for such opinion to be privileged to a greater or lesser degree. This privilege results in no loss for police or other investigative agencies; all the normal sources of information remain open to them, including patient notes and the testimony of witnesses, for example. The process to which privilege applies is additional to the existing avenues of enquiry. It is regrettable that, in a number of countries, legislators struggle to accept the value of such provisions. In aviation, it is useful for this process to be conducted through the submission of confidential reports, compiled by any member of aircrew or ground staff. These reports are analysed centrally by bodies concerned with air safety. One medical example of a similar, centralised process of anonymous incident reporting is that which has been set up under the auspices of the Australian Patient Safety Foundation.[34]

The overriding goal of all these activities is the pursuit of greater safety. The aim is to circumvent the barriers created by the legal process – whether civil or criminal – to the comprehensive and open elucidation of adverse events. It should, of course, be possible to obtain an understanding of an event through the use of legal or disciplinary proceedings, but in practice such proceedings may be unreasonably protracted, and even then may often fail to get to the truth, in part because some of those involved are likely to have powerful reason to conceal or even distort information. Indeed, the advice of lawyers to those involved is usually to refrain from comment, and certainly to avoid self-incrimination. In the legal context, the adversarial process does not always lead to the disclosure of the entire picture; amongst the reasons for this are the rules of evidence and the limitations of expert witnesses. We shall consider the role of the expert in chapter 7.

Compensation

The need to compensate for injury was recognised in the earliest legal systems. Early law favoured a crude system whereby fixed measures of compensation closely linked with the nature of the injury suffered were provided for, purely on the grounds that the defendant had caused injury. Such systems did not concern themselves with blame, and it is only later, with the development of the Roman law concept of *culpa*, that notions of blame came to underpin the duty to compensate. The concept of *culpa* as an abstract legal notion was not developed to any great extent in Roman law itself, but came to the fore in the work of the canon lawyers, who introduced into Western European law strong moral notions of fault as the basis of the duty to provide compensation.[35] By the time of the great

[34] R. K. Webb, M. Currie, C. A. Morgan, J. A. Williamson, P. Mackay, W. J. Russell and W. B. Runciman, 'The Australian Incident Monitoring Study: an analysis of 2000 incident reports' (1993) 21 *Anaesthesia and Intensive Care* 520–8.

[35] J. Gordley, 'Tort law in the Aristotelian tradition', in D. G. Owen (ed.), *Philosophical Foundations of Tort Law* (Oxford, Clarendon Press, 1995) 131–58; R. Zimmermann, *The Law of Obligations: Roman Foundations of the Civilian Tradition* (Cape Town, Juta, 1990), 1033.

codifications of the nineteenth century, a concept of fault had developed which was heavily influenced by the notion of moral blame. A parallel development occurred in English law, where the notion of negligence required that there should be a failure on the part of the defendant to meet an expected standard of behaviour. This failure was inevitably expressed in the language of shortcoming or wrongdoing. As a result, except in those areas where the law allowed for compensation based on strict liability, the law of torts proceeded on the assumption that the duty to compensate was based on a moral duty to provide reparation for the consequences of faulty conduct.

It is significant that, although the law referred to negligence liability being based on fault, the standard by which conduct was judged was an objective rather than a subjective one. Conduct then could be described as 'faulty' or 'wrongful' even if the individual had no intention of behaving wrongfully, and even if he was making his best efforts to avoid harming others.[36] In other words, the external judgement of fault had nothing to do with the internal, subjective mental state of the defendant. In terms of the definition of an accident which we have proposed above, it is the elements of foreseeability and preventability, rather than that of intentionality, that would create liability for compensation. Because it would not be foreseeable, or if foreseeable it would not reasonably be preventable, an accident, as defined above, would not merit compensation.

The objective nature of the concept of negligence, as applied in the law of torts, is absolutely central to our discussion of negligence. In the context of compensation, the law is seeking to establish whether the external features of the defendant's conduct 'fit the pattern' of negligent conduct as defined by the law. For this purpose, it does not matter whether the defendant is morally culpable; all that matters is that the conduct in question was deemed faulty, which is another way of saying that it was deemed to be substandard or inadequate in the circumstances. There is therefore no necessary connection in law between moral culpability and liability for negligence. Such a connection may exist in individual cases (as, for example, in the case of a person who deliberately omits safety precautions for unjustifiable reasons), but this is not essential

---

[36] The use of a masculine or feminine pronoun should be taken to signify someone of either sex when either sex could apply.

to liability. The use of 'fault' in this context is therefore potentially misleading, if one reads into 'fault' any moral significance.

How can this be justified? If a person may be obliged to make reparation for an act which shows no subjective moral fault on his part, then it would appear that the obligation to pay compensation has nothing to do with blameworthiness. This is in fact true (at least in theory – in chapter 5 we shall discuss the extent to which it is or is not true in practice). The objective of the law of torts is to provide compensation to those whose interests have suffered as a result of the act of another. In selecting those acts which will warrant the award of compensation, it identifies acts which unjustifiably intrude upon the interests of others. Such acts cause unjustified harm and our sense of what is fair or just dictates that this disturbance be rectified and the person harmed be put back, as far as possible, into the position in which he or she was before the untoward interference with his or her interests. To give a simple example, if *A* throws an object out of the window without checking whether anybody is in the street below, he is liable for the damage he causes to a passer-by who is injured by it. It may be that *A* believed that there was nobody in the street and that he would not have wished to cause injury. This, however, is not the point. The possibility of injuring a passer-by was foreseeable and preventable, so the law prefers the interests of the passer-by, who has a right to be compensated.

An accompaniment to liability for compensation is the effect it has on the conduct of members of society in general. The risk of being made to pay compensation is thought to serve as a deterrent for negligent behaviour as well as positively encouraging initiatives to reduce risk and enhance safety. Inevitably, but usually not by intention, civil liability also carries an element of punishment. In rare cases, the level of compensation may be fixed at a punitive level to reflect the court's belief that the defendant's conduct merits some form of financial punishment.

The requirement for some element of fault is related to the fact that the right to compensation is exercised against the person who actually causes the damage. There is evidence that this system is quite inefficient. Civil litigation often fails to compensate those who most deserve it and gives money in circumstances that are less appropriate.[37] It is also slow and

---

[37] Localio et al., 'Harvard Medical Practice Study III'; P. Fenn, 'Compensation for medical injury: a review of policy options', in C. Vincent, M. Ennis and R. J. Audley (eds.), *Medical Accidents* (New York, Oxford University Press, 1993), 198–208.

expensive. An alternative is to impose the duty to compensate on the state and extend the right for compensation to all personal injuries arising from 'accidents', whether fault is involved or not. This approach has been tried in a number of countries, most notably in New Zealand. Under this approach, there is not the same need for explanation of how an incident occurred; the important matter is that the incident is confirmed as a non-natural occurrence. An effect of this general approach, of course, is that those who are injured may achieve compensation but may not get a full explanation of what happened. This aspect has also been criticised as resulting in reduced accountability, and the New Zealand scheme at least has been modified to take account of this objection. In chapter 8 we shall return to the difficult question of how injured patients should in fact be compensated, and consider these issues in more detail.

Blaming and sanctioning

The search for explanation is linked to the universal human desire to punish wrongdoing. Wrongdoing gives rise to reactive attitudes; we resent the wrongdoer and feel that a response to the wrongful act is both justified and necessary.[38] This response commonly takes the form of a call for retribution, inspired by a belief that the moral balance, which is upset by the wrong, will somehow be restored through punishment. Retribution has been the subject of immense debate in the philosophy of punishment and, in spite of the objections that it represents a crude, revenge-based approach, it still plays a major role in penology. Moreover, retribution cannot be ignored, however uncomfortable we may feel about it. Its popularity, and the degree to which it accords with the moral feelings of the community, secure for it a central place in our social practices.

There are other theories used to justify the practice of punishment. The declaratory theory, for example, believes that punishment underlines and vindicates the interest which has been wronged by crime.[39] In punishing, then, the courts are seen to be announcing their support for the victim and denouncing the conduct of the defendant. Deterrent theories simi-

---

[38] The role of reactive attitudes in moral philosophy was discussed by Peter Strawson in his paper, 'Freedom and resentment', in G. Watson (ed.), *Free Will* (New York, Oxford University Press, 1982), 59–80.

[39] J. Feinberg, 'The expressive function of punishment', in his *Doing and Deserving: Essays in the Theory of Responsibility* (Princeton University Press, 1970), 95–118.

larly see the good of punishment in the notion that it prevents crime. In this view, the wrongdoer may be expected to make the calculation that committing an offence is simply not worth the risk of detection and punishment.

The declaratory and deterrent views of punishment do not necessarily support the notion that only the deserving should be punished (although they tend to assume that). By contrast, theories of retribution are underpinned by the notion of desert. Retribution is limited to those who deserve to be punished on account of their culpable conduct. Desert requires more than mere authorship of the wrong; it stipulates that the defendant should have acted in a morally culpable state of mind. This close connection between desert and punishment means that blame should only be placed on those who are morally culpable.[40] Strict liability is quite different: it merely requires that the defendant should have acted in a particular way and pays no attention to his or her state of mind at the time of acting. In any developed system of morality or jurisprudence, the impulse to blame will always be subject to the recognition that some persons who cause harm simply are not blameworthy. This is because they either fail some test of responsibility (they are too young, for example, or they are mentally disordered) or because the state of their mind is clearly not blameworthy. The question of which states of mind are blameworthy is contested. We probably all agree on some cases at either end of the spectrum. Between these extremes, however, considerable debate may arise as to the blameworthiness of the individual under the circumstances.

Whether an individual merits punishment is often a complex issue, requiring cautious and well-informed judgement. The desire to blame and punish for misfortune is at times very strong, and concerns have been voiced that blaming behaviour in recent decades has been unduly encouraged by the public media and certain consumer-oriented pressure groups. The idea that life's misfortunes are usually attributable to failure on the part of others to prevent them is a seductive one. Every death in an institution, or every loss of a child at the hands of an abusive parent,

---

[40] Blame is to be distinguished from guilt. We may feel guilty for things we have done, even if we are not to blame: H. Morris, 'Non-moral guilt', in F. Schoeman, *Responsibility, Character and the Emotions: New Essays in Moral Psychology* (Cambridge University Press, 1987), 220. Elsewhere, Morris has drawn attention to the uncoupling of liability and moral culpability: H. Morris, 'The decline of guilt' (1988) 99 *Ethics* 62–76.

raises demands for an inquiry into where fault lies. This culture of blaming has led to a high level of civil litigation in many countries, notably the United States.

In medicine, this attitude has contributed to a marked increase in various types of action against doctors, including civil claims, disciplinary proceedings and criminal prosecutions. The growing frequency with which civil claims are now brought against doctors in many countries points to a much greater willingness of patients to attribute blame for medical misfortune. Many of these claims are, of course, legally justifiable; their significance, however, lies in the fact that they signal the growth of a blaming mentality.

A real danger in this area is an excessive readiness to blame others for events which in fact they might not have been able to prevent. There is a risk that this will give rise to an undiscriminating attitude towards the process of dealing with harmful events and at times with inevitable misfortune. A number of undesirable consequences may ensue. These include increased costs, victimisation and a breakdown in trusting relationships. Blame not only requires genuine moral culpability; it needs cool analysis. A rush to blame, particularly when fuelled by a natural tendency to focus on those aspects of an incident which are dramatic and obvious rather than systemic and underlying, is likely to be counter-productive and obscure opportunities to improve safety. It also creates a serious risk of injustice.

2

The human factor

Our knowledge of the workings of the human brain has progressed enormously over recent decades, not only in respect of the receptors, transmitters and pathways that form the physical matrix of the brain but also in our understanding of human cognition. It is our human cognitive ability that has given us our highly organised and technologically sophisticated societies, with all their advantages and disadvantages. Yet it is precisely these cognitive processes that also make human beings prone to error. To this risk must be added the fact that the technology and complexity which characterise modern life, and which have resulted from our ability to think, have created an environment in which the opportunities for error are numerous and in which serious harm may readily follow if an error is made. Error, then, should be viewed not as an unfortunate frailty on the part of human beings but rather as an inevitable concomitant of the powerful cognitive processes that have permitted us to extend the limits of human achievement.

There have been good observational data concerning human error since the work of Freud first suggested that errors were not necessarily random events attributable to carelessness, but could be meaningful in terms of a person's psychology. Today, cognitive science can provide considerable insight into the workings of the human mind. This knowledge is of more than theoretical significance: a wider understanding of the processes that underlie our decisions and our actions is essential if we are to make progress in improving the safety of complex systems (such as medical practice). This knowledge is, in fact, relied upon by those concerned with designing systems that will lead to the optimising of the human performance of technical tasks. It has proved to be less accessible to those concerned with the judging and regulation of human behaviour – in particular, it is not always considered relevant in a legal context. This is unfortunate: legal inquiries are about justice and social utility, and these goals would be greatly assisted if the law were to pay adequate attention to what this information can tell us about how people behave and, most importantly, how they can realistically be expected to behave.

Error and progress

The remarkable material and scientific progress humankind has made does not reflect a progressive increase in what we might call our raw intelligence. Instead, it is a function of the growth in our language and knowledge, of our ability to communicate sophisticated ideas and co-operate with one another, and of our talent for creating and utilising the increasingly powerful technology which today supports and facilitates our cognitive processes. One might say that it is not the computing power of our brains that has improved, but the software which our brains are using.

Obvious advantages have accrued from our astonishing progress in almost every field of human endeavour. Our ability to organise ourselves into large but coherent functional groups, added to the sophistication and power of our continuously accumulating knowledge and technology, has allowed us to perform numerous complex and useful tasks. Unfortunately, there have also been some less desirable consequences of our increasing reliance on activities based upon ever more complicated technology and dependent upon co-operation within and between complex organisations. Amongst these has been a marked increase in the number of ways in which we can make an error, and in the degree of devastation now possible when accidents occur. Even those human activities which are peaceful and well intended have a tendency to go badly wrong, sometimes with consequences so serious that it might have been better never to have embarked on them in the first place.

Many of our daily activities are highly complicated and depend on the skills, expertise and judgement of a large number of people – either at the time of the activity or before it, by way of design, organisation or other contributory process. The surprising thing is not that something will go wrong eventually. Rather, it is astonishing that we can successfully under-take some of our modern-day functions at all. People's actions must be viewed against a backdrop of this fertile ground for error: it is a fundamental mistake to describe, study or judge people out of context, without considering the social structures, groups, rules (written or simply understood), methods of communication and technologies that form their world. We shall return in chapter 5 to the tendency of the law to make just this mistake.

Iatrogenic harm – a statistical inevitability

Our particular concern is errors in medicine. Medical practice is a good example of the kind of high-level achievement that groups of people are capable of, and that has been made possible by language, technology, research, training and co-operation. It is also highly prone to things going wrong. Two landmark studies, the Harvard Medical Study[1] and the Australian Quality in Healthcare Study,[2] have made it disconcertingly clear that *preventable* adverse events *resulting from medical therapy* are much more common than had previously been supposed. The Harvard study involved structured reviews of 30,121 randomly selected case records from 51 randomly selected acute care non-psychiatric hospitals in the state of New York in 1984. Adverse events occurred in 3.7 per cent of admissions ('hospitalizations') and 27.6 per cent of these were attributed to negligence. Of the adverse events, 2.6 per cent caused permanently disabling injuries and 13.6 per cent led to death. These results were extrapolated to suggest that 27,179 injuries, associated at least in part with 13,451 deaths and 2,550 cases of permanent total disability, resulted from medical care in New York State in 1984. The Australian study was very similar in design, and reviewed 14,179 records from 28 hospitals in New South Wales and South Australia in 1992. The main outcome variable was an 'adverse event', defined as 'an unintended injury or complication which results in disability, death or prolonged hospital stay and is caused by health care management'. Adverse events occurred in 16.6 per cent of admissions, 51 per cent of which were judged to be 'highly preventable' –

---

[1] T. A. Brennan, L. L. Leape, N. M. Laird, L. Hebert, A. R. Localio, A. G. Lawthers, J. P. Newhouse, P. C. Weiler and H. H. Hiatt, 'Incidence of adverse events and negligence in hospitalized patients: results of the Harvard Medical Practice Study I' (1991) 324 *New England Journal of Medicine* 370–6; L. L. Leape, T. A. Brennan, N. M. Laird, A. G. Lawthers, A. R. Localio, B. A. Barnes, L. Hebert, J. P. Newhouse, P. C. Weiler and H. Hiatt, 'The nature of adverse events in hospitalized patients: results of the Harvard Medical Practice Study II' (1991) 324 *New England Journal of Medicine* 377–84.

[2] R. McL. Wilson, W. B. Runciman, R. W. Gibberd, B. T. Harrison, L Newby and J. D. Hamilton, 'The Quality in Australian Health Care Study' (1995) 163 *Medical Journal of Australia* 458–71.

a phrase used to circumvent the debate over what constitutes negligence and to avoid the negative connotations of that term. Death occurred in 4.9 per cent of the patients suffering an adverse event, and permanent disability in 13.7 per cent. Similarly disturbing results have been reported from Utah and Colorado,[3] and from the United Kingdom.[4]

Amongst the dramatic claims which have been made on the basis of these data has been the suggestion that more people die on an annual basis from medical negligence than on the roads. Comments of this type serve to emphasise the magnitude of the problem, but in doing so they tend to reflect only the debit side of the account. They fail to remind us that, in the absence of figures describing positive outcomes to provide balance, the data from these studies do not reflect the *net effect* of medical practice. It would also be wrong to assume that these data mean that the problem of iatrogenic harm is new, or even that it is necessarily getting worse. The exponential rise in the number of aeroplanes in the sky means that, unless considerable improvements in aviation safety are achieved, a stage is likely to be reached in the not too distant future when one major crash will occur per fortnight. It is likely that the public will find it difficult to accept disasters occurring at this frequency, even though this prediction assumes that the level of safety would not have changed from that pertaining today.[5] In a similar way, it may be the *perception* rather than the *reality* which has changed in relation to safety in medicine. Indeed, it is very probable that the increase in data concerning iatrogenic harm reflects a renewed emphasis on safety and a growing commitment to identifying and dealing with problems in the health system. Notwithstanding these caveats, it is obvious from the above studies that iatrogenic harm in general is a significant problem in hospitals, and that it is often the consequence of imperfect practice. It is clear that the situation needs to be addressed. When we are seeking to attribute blame, however, it is important to keep in mind that this iatrogenic harm occurs in the context of a great deal of cost-effective and successful medical treatment. For an

---

[3] E. J. Thomas, D. M. Studdert, H. R. Burstin, E. J. Orav, T. Zeena, E. J. Williams, K. M. Howard, P. C. Weiler and T. A. Brennan, 'Incidence and types of adverse events and negligent care in Utah and Colorado' (2000) 38 *Medical Care* 261–71.

[4] L. B. Andrews, C. Stocking, T. Krizek, L. Gottlieb, C. Krizek, T. Vargish and M. Siegler, 'An alternative strategy for studying adverse events in medical care' (1997) 349 *The Lancet* 309–13.

[5] D. E. Maurino, J. Reason, N. Johnson and R. B. Lee, *Beyond Aviation Human Factors: Safety in High Technology Systems* (Aldershot, Avebury Aviation, 1995).

individual patient during one admission, the chances of suffering an adverse event are actually quite low (although not as low as perhaps they should be); on the other hand, for an individual doctor, working with thousands of patients over a career of thirty or forty years, the chances of accidentally causing such an adverse event are extremely high. The consequences to each are different, of course, since it is the patient, not the doctor, who is injured. Nevertheless, the consequences to the doctor may also be considerable. There are times when this may be perfectly appropriate, but the disciplinary or legal processes which may flow from such events need to distinguish genuinely culpable practices from the human errors which are inevitable in any doctor's career.

Drug administration errors as an example

In the Harvard Medical Practice Study, 19.4 per cent of adverse events involved drug errors. These errors constituted the largest single category, and 14.1 per cent of them led to serious disability.[6] In the first 2,000 anaesthetic incidents reviewed by the Australian Incident Monitoring Study (AIMS), 144 (about 7 per cent) involved the wrong drug.[7] In four American hospitals, voluntary 'critical incident' reporting showed that 6 per cent of critical incidents in anaesthetic practice were wrong-drug errors.[8] In a British hospital, 9.2 per cent of nurses admitted having given the wrong drug to a patient, and 62 per cent admitted errors of omission, while 30 per cent of interviewed anaesthetists had administered the wrong drug at some time.[9] Chopra's group[10] reported 16 drug errors (including 2 which involved giving the wrong blood) out of 148 incidents from 113,074 anaesthetics over 10 years in one hospital in the Netherlands. In an Australian intensive care unit, drug errors were the second most frequent category of incident (after problems with equipment), consti-

[6] Leape et al., 'Harvard Medical Practice Study II'.

[7] M. Currie, P. Mackay, C. Morgan, W. B. Runciman, W. J. Russell, A. Sellen, R. K. Webb and J. A. Williamson, 'The "wrong drug" problem in anaesthesia: an analysis of 2000 incident reports' (1993) 21 *Anaesthesia and Intensive Care* 596–601.

[8] J. B. Cooper, R. S. Newbower and R. J. Kitz, 'An analysis of major errors and equipment failures in anesthesia management: considerations for prevention and detection' (1984) 60 *Anesthesiology* 34–42.

[9] G. D. Smellie, N. W. Lees and E. M. Smith, 'Drug recognition by nurses and anaesthetists' (1982) 37 *Anaesthesia* 206–8.

[10] V. Chopra, J. G. Bovill and J. Spierdijk, 'Accidents, near accidents and complications during anaesthesia' (1990) 45 *Anaesthesia* 3–6.

tuting 122 of 390 reported incidents for 2,153 admissions over 24 months.[11] Eighty-nine per cent of the respondents to a survey of New Zealand anaesthetists reported having made drug administration errors at some stage in their careers, most more than once, and 12.5 per cent reported having actually harmed patients in this way. To place this finding in context, it should be appreciated that most anaesthetists administer drugs at least 250,000 times during their working lives, and for many the number of administrations would exceed 500,000.[12]

To the lay public, a drug administration error is hard to comprehend. It does not seem a difficult matter to give the correct drug in the correct way at the correct time. Yet we can see that the facts belie this understandable assumption. The truth is that errors of drug administration occur in all medical and nursing disciplines in all countries. It is precisely because they are common but not immediately understandable that they are a good example of the type of error that pervades healthcare. In part, the issue is a lack of awareness of the complexity of some of the activities in question. Most people understand that a major surgical operation is a difficult undertaking, but it is perhaps less widely appreciated that an anaesthetic may often involve the administration of twenty, and in some cases more than fifty, intravenous boluses of drug. As with many tasks in medicine, this has to be achieved while the anaesthetist is also attending to a number of other duties. The difficulty lies not in giving the right drug once, but rather in giving the right drug on every occasion, hundreds of thousands of times in a working life, often under circumstances which are far from ideal. A more significant issue illustrated by these drug errors, however, is a widespread failure to understand the nature of human error and the way in which errors may occur even during tasks which are straightforward.

Most drug errors are harmless, and as such pass unpunished and almost without comment. Again, this is typical of many forms of error in healthcare, and goes some way to explaining why, in a system which is often stretched to the limit of its resources and in which many other matters constantly demand attention, they are tolerated. However, harm does occur occasionally. When it does, the severity of the consequences

---

[11] G. K Hart, I Baldwin, G. Gutteridge and J. Ford, 'Adverse incident reporting in intensive care' (1994) 22 *Anaesthesia Intensive Care* 556–61.

[12] A. F. Merry and D. J. Peck, 'Anaesthetists, errors in drug administration and the law' (1995) 108 *New Zealand Medical Journal* 185–7.

may be quite out of proportion to the magnitude of the error, and is usually related to chance more than to the degree of negligence involved. It is therefore worrying, not so much that a tougher approach seems to have been taken by the courts in recent years when harm does follow a particular drug administration error, but more that this tougher approach has tended to focus on the individual practitioner rather than the system. Four of the examples given in chapter 1 are cases in point (those of Drs Yogasakaran and Morrison, of the general practitioner who prescribed a beta-blocker to an asthmatic patient, and of the vincristine administered intrathecally by junior doctors). The prosecution of Dr Teoh in Northern Ireland, following her accidental administration of a drug into the wrong tube while she was fatigued, is also an example of this.[13] It is not our position that these errors should be accepted – indeed, much greater effort is warranted to reduce their occurrence. However, given the frequency of drug errors overall, the conclusion does seem inescapable that the factor which plays the greatest role in the allocation of blame for these errors is their outcome. It is the result that is being judged, not the action. In other words *outcome bias* is compounding the effect of *moral luck* – phenomena to which we shall return in chapters 6 and 7.

Complex tasks

Driving in traffic provides a useful illustration of the interdependence of people and technology, and of many aspects of human cognition and error. This example is especially useful because it is familiar to most people – so familiar, in fact, that we tend to take many quite astonishing aspects of this modern phenomenon for granted.

Consider for a moment some of the steps involved in driving a motor car from one place to another in heavy traffic. The car and all its component parts had to be conceptualised, designed and manufactured, its fuel obtained and supplied, the roads surveyed and built, and a set of rules created and implemented to deal with the ebb and flow of traffic. At the end of all this research and development, the driver had to learn to operate the car, follow the roads and keep to the rules while at the same time avoiding running into other drivers, all of whom are engaged in similar endeavours. As if this were not challenging enough, most people

---

[13] C. Dyer, 'Doctors cleared of manslaughter' (1999) 318 *British Medical Journal* 148.

drive almost automatically, often chatting to a passenger, listening to a radio or talking on a cell phone at the same time as controlling the car. And yet most drivers will almost always see – and respond to – an unexpected event such as a child running into the road ahead. Almost always, but not quite always. Occasionally we fail to respond in time, and a crash results. As human beings we are capable of the most extraordinary feats of individual and collective accomplishment, but, because we are not machines, we are also capable of lapses and failures in performance.

'Normal accidents' and the utilitarian view of punishment

The individual who, after many years of driving safely, eventually makes a serious mistake may not only be punished but is often portrayed as deficient, incapable and worthy of censure or disparagement. This may occur even when the mistake is entirely understandable. The attention paid to the contribution of other people involved in the activity, either at the time or in some antecedent way, is seldom in proportion to its importance. Typically, failure is judged as if the last person in the line were the primary cause of a problem which on closer inspection often turns out to reflect some antecedent failure. The presence of the wrong ampoule in the compartment of the drug drawer in Dr Yogasakaran's case is one example of a *resident pathogen* resulting from a *latent error*,[14] and the fact that the members of the team were chronically short of sleep in the *Challenger* disaster is another. The reality is that accidents in complex systems are not all primarily manifestations of avoidable human misde-meanours. Instead, they are often the result of unpredictable interactions between an error and one or more of the innumerable components and activities that are involved in any sophisticated endeavour within large organisations of people and machines. The idea that such events are inevitable in complex organisations has been developed by Charles Perrow and encapsulated in the title of his study, *Normal Accidents*.[15] Perrow argues that it is not possible to have the benefits of human progress without a certain incidence of failure. In the past this seems to have been quite well appreciated, and people have been willing to accept that things do go wrong occasionally. As our technological sophistication

---

[14] J. Reason, *Human Error* (New York, Cambridge University Press, 1990), 173–216.

[15] C. Perrow, *Normal Accidents: Living with High-Risk Technologies* (Princeton University Press, 1999).

has increased, the risks involved in certain activities have tended to shift. To some degree, it may simply be that one must accept new risks as the price of greater achievement. In addition, however, developments in technology have a tendency to produce hazards which are unexpected, and which in some cases would have been very difficult to predict. Thus aeroplanes are safer today than ever before – but because more people fly further and faster than in the past, the total number of deaths associated with aviation has increased. Medicine, too, is certainly more effective now than ever before, and in general safety has also increased; for instance, anaesthesia has become progressively safer: the risk of dying directly from anaesthesia has changed from 1 in 2,000 cases in the nineteenth century to about 3 per 10,000 anaesthetics in the middle of the twentieth century, to about 1 per 200,000 anaesthetics today.[16] However, the complexity and risk associated with many of the treatments now being undertaken in greater numbers of progressively sicker patients *may* be creating more iatrogenic harm than before. Again, one may find an example in anaesthesia – the filter which became blocked in the Hugel case (see chapter 1) would not have been part of routine anaesthesia ten years earlier. Filters of this type were introduced to reduce a small risk of infecting a patient with a virally contaminated circuit used in a previous patient. In solving one problem (with a sophisticated filter), technology has created a different, rare, but potentially lethal alternative problem. In part, this is because the overall increase in the complexity of anaesthetic equipment makes the identification of a blockage more difficult, particularly in the constrained time limits of a crisis. Unpredicted hazards of improved technology have been referred to as 'revenge effects'.[17] Ironically, the advances in aeronautical, medical and other activities seem to have created expectations that are fundamentally unattainable. The tendency today when there is an accidental death is to call for accountability and compensation with scant regard for the fact that some accidents are inevitable. People seem less willing than before to accept that the occurrence of an accident does not necessarily mean that someone must be to blame. On the contrary, a widely held view in modern society seems

---

[16] A. P. Adams, 'Standards and postgraduate training', and R. F. Armstrong, 'Monitoring in anaesthesia', in J. S. Walker (ed.), *Quality and Safety in Anaesthesia* (London, BMJ Publishing, 1994) 31, 173.

[17] E. Tenner, *Why Things Bite Back: Technology and the Revenge Effect* (London, Fourth Estate, 1996).

to be that safety will only be achieved if we can identify and punish or eliminate all wrongdoers. This idea lies at the heart of utilitarian justifications for punishment, based on the notion of deterrence. However, this concept requires that the deterrent be effective in producing the desired result.

In fact, there is not much evidence to support the view that tort law as a deterrent is effective in producing the desired safer behaviour in medicine. For example, Shuman has reviewed the psychological basis for the belief that tort law will achieve deterrence, considering each school of psychology in turn. He finds little, if any, theoretical basis for believing that the civil law is likely to be effective in this regard.[18] An interesting finding of the Harvard study was that litigation following an adverse event was not closely linked to the presence of negligence. Few of the cases in which negligence was identified by the authors resulted in litigation, and in many of the cases in which litigation occurred the authors could find no evidence of negligence. They concluded that 'medical-malpractice litigation infrequently compensates patients injured by medical negligence and rarely identifies, and holds providers accountable for, substandard care'.[19] As far as the role of the criminal law is concerned in this regard, it is of interest that a recent prospective survey of anaesthetists in New Zealand has revealed that drug errors continue to occur in anaesthesia, with an incidence approaching 1 per 100 anaesthetics.[20] These data do not suggest that the problem of drug administration error has been in any way diminished by the highly publicised prosecutions (reviewed in chapter 1) of Drs Yogasakaran and Morrison for their drug administration errors. Similarly, the case involving Drs Murphy and Lee indicates that the lessons of the very similar earlier experience of Drs Prentice and Sullman were not learned, notwithstanding the considerable publicity associated with their prosecution and initial conviction. Indeed, it was reported that the same mistake (administering vincristine intrathecally instead of intravenously, which is made more likely because it is given

---

[18] D. Shuman, 'The psychology of compensation in tort law' (1994) 43 *Kansas Law Review* 39–77.

[19] A. R. Localio, A. G. Lawthers, T. A. Brennan, N. M. Laird, L. E. Hebert, L. M. Peterson, J. P. Newhouse, P. C. Weiler and H. H. Hiatt, 'Relation between malpractice claims and adverse events due to negligence: results of the Harvard Medical Practice Study III' (1991) 325 *New England Journal of Medicine* 245–51.

[20] C. Webster, A. Merry, L. Larson, K. A. McGrath and J. Weller, 'The frequency and nature of drug administration error during anaesthesia' (forthcoming).

with intrathecal methotrexate) has now occurred ten times in Britain.[21] In chapter 3 we shall discuss an example involving hang-gliding, which illustrates that even the prospect of injury or death is not effective in deterring error.

The fact that deterrence is relatively ineffective in this regard does not imply that nothing can be done about the problem of error. Perrow argues that the most effective approach to minimising the occurrence and consequences of human error lies in considering all the components of the system in question. He lists these, under the acronym DEPOSE, as design, equipment, procedures, operator, supplies and environment.[22] Not only is it too limited to focus on the operator, but in reality the operator is the part of the system most difficult to make error-free, because, of course, operators are human. The development of unit-dosing systems for nursing in the USA has considerably reduced drug error in the ward situation, and a systems-oriented approach to improving the way drugs are given in anaesthesia is currently under evaluation in New Zealand.[23] The addition of anti-hypoxic devices to anaesthesic machines and the widespread adoption of pulse oximetry have been much more effective in reducing accidents in relation to the administration of adequate concentrations of oxygen to anaesthetised patients than has the conviction for manslaughter of an anaesthetist who failed to give oxygen to a child in New Zealand during an anaesthetic in 1982.[24]

Criminal and civil liability can result in pressure on organisations (such as hospitals) to change their systems. However, the facts belie the notion that the elimination of a small number of so-called 'incompetents' or 'error-prone individuals' is likely to improve the performance and safety of an organisation as a whole. This applies most particularly if the individuals concerned are not really 'incompetents' at all, but instead are competent and conscientious practitioners who have simply been unfortunate enough to have made an error that caused harm, perhaps under circumstances which may have been far from ideal.[25] In the airline

---

[21] Dyer, 'Doctors cleared of manslaughter'.   [22] Perrow, *Normal accidents*, 77.

[23] A. F. Merry, C. S. Webster and D. J. Mathew, 'A new, safety oriented, injectable drug administration system (IDAS) and automated anaesthesia record', *Anesthesia and Analgesia*, forthcoming.

[24] P. D. G. Skegg, 'Criminal prosecutions of negligent health professionals: the New Zealand experience' (1998) 6 *Medical Law Review* 220–46.

[25] D. M. Berwick, 'Continuous improvement as an ideal in health care' (1989) 320 *New England Journal of Medicine* 53–6; G. Laffel and D. Blumenthal, 'The case for using

industry the point has been made that a pilot whose error has resulted in a crash is less likely than most to make that particular error again – even assuming he or she survives. In a sense, by virtue of the costs associated with the crash, the airline has invested heavily in this pilot's training. Assuming that the incident was isolated, and in the absence of evidence to show that the individual's performance has been systematically below standard over a period of time, the dismissal of this person from the airline would seem to be misguided.

The unfounded belief that complex human activities can be conducted on an ongoing basis without ever having a significant failure has other important implications. It is very important to realise that human error is, in the end, inevitable. With this in mind, Perrow argues that it is necessary to consider the possible consequences of the accidents that will eventually happen in every branch of human endeavour and weigh these against the social utility of the activity in question. In the case of the nuclear industry, he concludes that the potential consequences of an accident are so serious that its continuation cannot be justified. On the other hand, he suggests that the occasional loss of life, or even the quite serious disasters that occur from time to time in aviation, medicine, shipping and mining, for example, are justified in relation to their magnitude and to the overall benefits to society of these activities. This does not mean that nothing should be done about accidents in these fields of endeavour. Although it has to be accepted that accidents will never be eliminated completely, the focus should always be on improving the system to ensure the greatest possible level of safety. This requires an understanding of how humans co-exist with the machines that provide the advantages which a technological age takes for granted.

Human beings and machines

So much do we interrelate with and depend upon our technology that society needs to be seen not just as a grouping of people but as a highly complex human–machine conglomeration in a world subject to many unpredictable and variable influences, including the effects of chance. The closeness of this relationship between us and our machines (in the widest

industrial quality management science in health care organizations' (1989) 262 *Journal of the American Medical Association* 2869–73.

sense of the word *machine*) is such that it seems to have influenced our expectations both of ourselves and of our machines. To a degree we are starting to expect machines to behave like human beings. We expect increased sophistication, flexibility and the ability to be interactive. The idea that machines may one day be able to think has gained weight with the development of chess-playing devices that outperform the masters (something which was a long time coming), computers which use 'neural nets' and are capable of 'learning from experience', and real progress towards the development of artificial intelligence. In reality, these are very much the exceptions, and any similarities with human beings are still but pale imitations of the real thing and fall within highly circumscribed limits. In fact, the difference between machines and humans underpins a test for artificial intelligence described by Alan Turing. In this test, an intelligent questioner interrogates an unseen human and an unseen machine with a view to telling which is which; if the answers do not permit the one to be distinguished from the other, the machine is deemed intelligent. Although there has been debate about the validity of this test, it provides an intuitive insight into the different nature of the two; to date it would not be too difficult to distinguish even the most powerful of computers from a person. If neural-net technology were to produce a machine so human-like that it was able to respond with both the strengths and weaknesses of a human, then for the purposes of our discussion it would have become a human, and, like us, it would be subject to human error. In the end, an entity not subject to error could not truly resemble a human.

Their lack of humanness is not a reason to denigrate machines. After all, they are not human. Machines can do many things that humans cannot. The strength and the precision of which they are capable far exceeds that of human beings – they can cater for the fine and delicate or the large and brutish with equal facility. They can make possible activities which would otherwise be beyond our capability – prodigious feats of calculation, flight, communication, and all the other things that would have been deemed evidence of magic as recently as a hundred years ago.

Machines are typically very single-minded. Tasks which are boring or repetitive are ideally suited to machines, which, having once been set up properly, will go on doing the same thing over and over again for as long as power and lubrication are provided, with a reliability that we take for granted. Within quite wide limits, it matters not that the clock has passed five, that the tea break has been missed, that the day is hotter than usual, that a distracting story is being recounted by another occupant of the room – the machine will stick to the task in hand, uncomplaining and focused, getting it right.

Regrettably, we have come to expect the same thing of humans, and to see it as a weakness when people prove to be distractible and fail to meet the exacting standards set by their machines in the particular attributes of behaviour which suit machines but not human beings. In fact, some people have learned to do machine-like activities astonishingly well. Traditional production line activities are highly repetitive and tedious. So is sewing, whether by a seamstress or a surgeon closing the skin after an operation. Monitoring a patient during a long anaesthetic in which each successive reading is much the same as the one before is also a task more suitable for a machine – and the same applies to monitoring the instruments in a nuclear plant or on an aeroplane. Human beings are able to do these things very adequately most of the time, but these are not tasks that play to their strengths.

In the same way that we should not denigrate machines for failing to be people, people have no need to apologise for their failure to achieve machine-like standards in those activities for which machines are best suited. They are good at other things – original thought, for one, empathy and compassion for another. It should not be forgotten that one of our strengths is our ability to create the very machines with which we are, increasingly, at risk of being unfavourably compared. It is true that people are distractible – but in fact this provides a major survival advantage for them. A machine (unless expressly designed to detect such an event) will continue with its repetitive task while the house burns down around it, whereas most humans will notice that something unexpected is going on and will change their activity to make an appropriate response. When they are used to monitor routine signals in medicine or industry, machines far excel humans in their reliability in detecting anticipated possibilities – a fall in blood pressure, for example. Humans come into their own in having the flexibility to detect things that were never anticipated, and in their ability to respond in a variety of resourceful and imaginative ways when things do go wrong. Humans can also often tell, in the absence of anything specific enough to trigger an alarm, that things simply don't 'feel' right, that something is going wrong and that further enquiry is needed to diagnose an incipient problem. This form of 'intuition' involves the ability of humans to store vast numbers of mental pictures or patterns derived from previous experience, and to retrieve them when they are needed, not by the relatively rigid and sequential algorithms of traditional machines but by multiple processes operating in parallel, creatively, instinctively, as needed, and, concomitantly, a little unreliably. Human performance can be spectacularly inspiring or terribly disappointing. In the former case the humanness of the achievement is often accepted with complacency – people have done so many astonishing things that one more goes almost without note. In the latter case, however, there is a tendency towards harsh criticism; in many cases people who have made an error are judged as if they were machines.

In his book *Things That Make Us Smart*,[26] Norman has developed these ideas much more fully, concluding that many of today's problems actually arise from a failure to allocate machine-oriented tasks to machines and human-oriented tasks to people. There is often a failure to appreciate that humans have difficulty in adapting to poorly designed machines, whereas it is often possible for machines to be designed to take account of human characteristics and requirements. He uses the term 'soft technology' to describe machines which are designed to facilitate human endeavour by working for and with people, relieving them of the tasks for which they are poorly suited, adding strength to their abilities and protecting them from their human tendency to make certain types of error. He argues, however, that the reverse often happens, and he uses the term 'hard technology' to describe situations in which machines are allocated tasks because they *can* do them rather than because they *should* do them. A prime example of this is the use of recorded messages on answer-phones and automatic switchboards. There may be some financial savings in the use of these devices, but their effect is to increase the difficulties and frustrations of those on the other end of the line who are trying to reach a human being. Taken to absurdity (but not beyond the bounds of possibility), the application of this technology to emergency support services or help lines for people contemplating suicide provides an excellent example of something which a machine *can* do, but which is better left to people. Where the machine might be more usefully employed

---

[26] D. A. Norman, *Things That Make Us Smart: Defending Human Attributes in the Age of the Machine* (Reading, Mass., Addison-Wesley, 1993); see also D. A. Norman, *The Psychology of Everyday Things* (New York, Basic Books, 1998).

is in tracking and recording the source of the call – an application we shall return to the section on skill-based errors in chapter 3.

An understanding of the distinction between machines and human beings, and of the fact that society is in reality an integrated network of many people with many machines, permits us to design systems which are more effective, more satisfying to work in, and much safer. It is also very important in helping to place human behaviour in its appropriate context when the allocation of blame for things which go wrong is being evaluated. It is irrational to judge human actions in isolation or by the standards which we would apply to the functioning of a machine. An individual's actions should be judged in relation to the other people and technologies involved. Such judgements also need to take account of the ways in which the human mind actually works.

Human cognition and performance

Reason,[27] reviewing the development over the last century of the science of human cognition, makes the point that, until the early 1970s, research into human judgement and inference had a markedly rationalist basis. According to the 'Subjective Expected Utility Theory', it was assumed that human beings make decisions in accordance with logical principles, and form judgements by processes analogous to the use of Bayesian statistics. In the same way, much of American economic theory assumed that people actually know what they want and that they typically choose the optimal route to getting what they want. This was a very machine-like model of the human brain. It is interesting to speculate on the degree to which this general view of the mind pervaded the development of legal concepts of responsibility and accountability during the first three-quarters of the twentieth century.

Freud challenged the assumption that humans are rational beings, and psychological research has gone on to make it abundantly clear that human cognitive processes are often far from rational. It is now appreciated that human rationality is usually *bounded*; in other words, human decision making may be severely hindered by restricted or 'keyhole' views of the information in relation to any particular problem. Our rationality is also frequently *imperfect* (that is, not Bayesian at all) and *reluctant* (that

---

[27] Reason, *Human Error*.

is, people prefer to apply a rule, even an imperfect rule, than to think out a problem from first principles). The true motivation behind our actions may at times be subconscious, and there are occasions when human behaviour can only be described as irrational, particularly under the influence of group dynamics. It is hard to ascribe some of the activities associated with war to any plausible rationality, for example. From these insights a much more human-like model of the way in which human decisions are made and implemented has emerged, and, with it, a much more sophisticated appreciation of the nature of human error has been developed.

In any analysis of the ways in which human cognitive processes can go astray, the question of context is very important. Exactly the same external events may represent the endpoints of completely different cognitive processes, and actions cannot be evaluated adequately in isolation. As human beings extend the boundaries of possibility by means of increasingly sophisticated systems of organisation and technology, hitherto unattainable standards of quality and safety are achieved. Unfortunately, as we have already noted, one result of this is to create expectations amongst the population of near-infallibility. Infrequently, but inevitably, these systems fail. They do so because their design and operation depend on human beings. When such failures are being judged, whether to reduce the likelihood of their recurrence or in the interests of justice, it is very important that we see beyond machine-like models of human cognition and retain a human-oriented perspective based on a proper understanding of the basic concepts of modern cognitive psychology.

Pattern recognition vs. deliberation

A fundamental theme pervades many different views of human behaviour – namely, that there is more than one type of cognitive function commonly employed by humans, and furthermore that more than one type of cognitive processing may operate at any given time. There is also general agreement that two basic types of cognition can be identified, perhaps distinct, perhaps as two ends of a continuum within which subtypes can be discerned. This view is supported by experimental data in which images of the brain obtained by positron emission tomography during the performance of a cognitive skill change before and after practice. This implies that there are differences in the neural circuitry supporting performance of tasks in the naïve and practised states.[28]

At one end of this continuum is the slow, active, effortful thinking by which we solve problems which are new to us, or to which we do not already know the answer. At the other is the automatic, effortless, rapidly responsive processing by which an action is performed or a decision made virtually instantaneously. There are various terms for these processes. Norman has referred to them as *reflective* and *experiential* thinking respectively. Reason, following Rasmussen, refers to the first, effortful type of reasoning as *knowledge-based*, and divides the effortless processing into *rule-based*, in the case of decision making, and *skill-based* in the case of actions. There is general agreement that the latter, more automatic processes tend to be used by default. This has been expressed by Rouse's statement that 'humans, if given the choice, would prefer to act as context-specific pattern recognisers rather than attempting to calculate or optimize'.[29]

The mind's eye – mental models of the real world

Our relationship with the 'real world' is an indirect one. We depend on a conceptual 'map' of our surroundings – what one might call our *internal environment*. The correspondence between our internal and external (or 'real') environments is usually close enough for all functional purposes, but the internal map is always different from the real world in at least some details. If one closes one's eyes and tries to enumerate as much detail as possible about one's immediate surroundings, it is very unlikely that even all the main features will be accurately recalled. This is particularly so in situations that are transient and novel – at a restaurant or in an airport lounge, for example. In a reasonably crowded room it is very unlikely that one would be able to say, after closing one's eyes, how many people were present; one person's best guess is likely to differ from another's, even though they may be sitting next to each other and conducting the experiment at the same time. Similarly, details such as the clothes other people are wearing, the colour of their hair, the pictures on the wall, and so on are likely to be recalled inaccurately and to different

[28] M. E. Raichle, 'The neural correlates of consciousness: an analysis of cognitive skill learning' (1998) 353 *Philosophical Transactions of the Royal Society of London B* 1889–1901.

[29] W. B. Rouse, quoted in Reason, *Human Error*, 44.

degrees by different individuals. This phenomenon is well known and very important in relation to the testimony of witnesses at the scene of an accident or crime – at times the accounts of what happened are so different that it seems the individual witnesses must be describing different scenes. The success with which we can perform this type of recall, whether in an experiment or in the context of providing an account of some important event, will vary from person to person, and for the same person at different times depending on the degree to which his or her attention has been focused on other things. Nevertheless, we seldom, if ever, know more than the broad outline of our surroundings at any given time, and this is actually a good thing. It is only by filtering, ordering and interpreting the barrage of incoming information that we are able to function efficiently. Failures in these processes may contribute to certain forms of mental disorder.[30] The mind operates from a set of facts that may have been assimilated in the order of their salience but are only understandable after they have become organised in a way that takes account of their pertinence, their significance and their interrelationships.

One reason why we do not have to have every detail of our surroundings clear in order to function adequately is that much of the information is accessible – 'in the world' as Norman says – if we need it. This idea, that we operate on the basis of *information in the world* and *information in the head* is very important when it comes to design. If a thing is well designed we should not need much instruction in its purposes and uses, because they will be obvious from its *affordances* – the applications to which it lends itself, in other words. For example, a chair (even a chair that we have never seen before) is easily identified as a chair, and it is possible for us to sit on it quite easily, but rather difficult to use it to cut up a piece of steak. Many other things are also easy enough to sit on, but for some of these this affordance is misleading, and the object may turn out to be poorly constructed to support the weight of a person. In the same way, a steak knife in a restaurant may look a little different from one's familiar cutlery at home, but it is more likely that one would recognise its function as a knife than that one would try to sit on it, even in the absence of any instruction in its use. Many things have more than one affordance – knives and forks lend themselves to being poked into things, for example.

[30] D. J. Siegel, 'Perception and cognition', in H. I. Kaplan and B. J. Sadock (eds.), *Comprehensive Textbook of Psychiatry* (6th edn, Baltimore, Williams and Wilkins, 1995), vol. 1, 277–91.

This can be very useful but also very dangerous in uneducated hands, such as those of a child, particularly in the presence of another device whose own affordances create the possibility of an inadvisable application of the former implement. Electric toasters, for example, lend themselves to being poked, particularly if the toast becomes stuck. The consequences of this particular juxtaposition of the unintended affordances of two commonplace things whose primary uses are entirely benign is potentially lethal. Norman's book *The Psychology of Everyday Things*[31] discusses in detail how the good and bad design of things used in daily life can influence the ease and safety of human experience. Our primary interest at present, however, is in the fact that we routinely function on the basis of mental maps, and that this is made possible because we are able to check, modify and refine our internal representation of our surroundings by reference to the information that resides in the world about us. In addition, we may refer to knowledge stored in our brains. These two sources of information together form our *knowledge-base*. Thus, for example, if we really needed to know how many people were in the room, we could count them, provided the number were not too large. If it were a very large number, and the reason for knowing were important, then, as humans, we would find a way of estimating the number to a reasonable degree of accuracy. We might do this by reference to a previously learned rule stored in our brain, or we might derive a novel approach working from first principles. One of our strengths is that we can find new and imaginative ways to solve problems.

Unfortunately, this mechanism of regularly reviewing our internal map by reference to our surroundings and our interpretation of this information in relation to the knowledge stored in our memories is subject to failure. Numerous examples have now been published of cases where a mismatch develops between the external or 'real world' situation and its internal or mental representation. The starting point of such a dichotomy is often one erroneous piece of information which is either presented incorrectly (a wrong name on a map, for example) or which is incorrectly perceived (a correct name, misread).

Perrow reports in detail a truly illuminating example of this, in which the initiating event involved a mistake by the captain of the coastguard training vessel *Cuyahuga* in 1978, in Chesapeake Bay. He saw only two of

---

[31] Norman, *Psychology of Everyday Things*.

the lights being carried one night by another ship, when in fact there were three. This led him to believe that the ship was sailing away from him, when in fact it was approaching. Once a firm, but incorrect, interpretation has been made in any set of circumstances, the stage is set for the gap between perception and reality to widen. This undesirable dichotomy is contributed to by a phenomenon called *confirmation bias*. The effect of this is that, having once formulated an idea of events or of their surroundings, people have a strong tendency to interpret other information in such a way as to confirm or strengthen their initial interpretation of circumstances. In Perrow's example, two more bits of information were available to the captain: the image on the radar which appeared to be that of a small object, and the fact (presumably also derived from the radar) that the two ships were closing rapidly. Instead of interpreting this last point correctly as a *countersign*, the captain took from it the inference that the other ship was very small and very slow, and that his own ship was therefore overhauling it rapidly, thus adding to the conviction with which he held his incorrect internal view of the world. His first officer – who understood the real situation – could see that the captain was attending to the pertinent information but, in the absence of explicit communication, he had no way of knowing that the captain's picture of the world differed from his own, and therefore saw no need to comment. As a result of this, the captain, just at the moment when (by virtue of his internal scheme of things) he believed that his vessel was about to overtake the 'smaller' boat, 'realised' that in doing so he would cut it off from the entrance to the Potomac river. He therefore ordered a sudden change in direction to allow the 'fishing boat' better access to an entrance to the harbour. This was an entirely well-intentioned man-oeuvre, based on a now fairly detailed but seriously flawed idea of what was happening. The result was a last-minute swerve by the captain's ship under the bows of a large vessel sailing in the opposite direction and a disaster ensued in which eleven people died. On superficial inspection, the captain's actions were bizarre and inexplicable. They were certainly unexpected. Interestingly, Perrow makes the point that this example is not exceptional but in fact typifies the way in which ships tend to collide (which, apparently, they do disconcertingly often).[32]

Perrow's example is particularly graphic, but the underlying principles

[32] Perrow, *Normal Accidents*, 215–24.

illustrated by it are very common in medicine. In the case of Dr Hugel, for example, which we outlined in chapter 1, it is clear that a contributory equipment-related problem from a blocked filter did develop at some time during the crisis. Dr Hugel, however, had been presented with a clear, patient-related problem at the outset of the incident, manifest as difficulty in breathing. This was followed by pulmonary oedema, which continued to froth from the lungs very dramatically, continuing to suggest that something was seriously wrong with the patient. The fact that the patient's lungs became progressively more difficult to ventilate was therefore attributed by Dr Hugel to an ongoing problem within the patient himself, and taken as confirmation of the presence of serious spasm within the lungs. At some stage in the proceedings this perception changed from being an accurate description of what was happening to being an outmoded and seriously wrong one. Whether or not the filter took over as an important cause of the obstruction to ventilation at a point early enough to have made it a leading cause of the patient's ultimate death is pure conjecture, but by the time useful help (in the form of a second anaesthetist) arrived, the filter was completely blocked. Dr Hugel (now beside herself with desperation) was still convinced that she was dealing with a patient-related problem, and was continuing to interpret all the signs of obstruction to ventilation as pointing to a problem within the patient's lungs. The fact that a second anaesthetist was able to identify the blocked filter almost as soon as he arrived made Dr Hugel's failure seem very incompetent. In reality, several factors contributed to the speed with which the problem was discovered when help arrived. Simply having two people instead of one was very valuable – Dr Hugel actually handed the rebreathing bag to the new anaesthetist for him to hold while she disconnected the anaesthetic circuit and suctioned out the lungs; holding the bag with the circuit disconnected made it obvious that there was a problem with the equipment – the answer was literally handed to the newcomer. However, it is very likely that his perspicacity was also attributable to the fact that he was bringing a fresh mind to the situation, without the confounding influence of having partaken in an unfolding sequence of events in which the salient signs were highly misleading. For Dr Hugel, all the information could be explained in a way which supported her original interpretation of the situation. For example, the event had occurred at the end of an anaesthetic during which the filter had given no trouble. Also, she had checked the anaesthetic circuit (including the filter) at the outset and had found it to be in working order. More than one person had noted that air entry into the chest was diminished but present – and this too could be fitted into her concept of a patient-related problem. Each fact would have been added to the previous ones to build a convincing but incorrectly evolving mental picture of events. This kind of incorrect mental image of the environment can underlie or initiate any of the error types we shall discuss in chapter 3.

A more mundane example of how information can be misinterpreted or variously interpreted is found in many books of psychology. A very well-known picture can be seen as either a beautiful young girl or an ugly old woman. Even those who have seen it before often find it quite difficult to switch between the two, and tend to favour one or other interpretation quite strongly. There are many other puzzle-pictures of this kind.[33] The printing of the the same word twice (as in this sentence) often goes unnoticed, particularly if the repetition is split by the end of a line. Anyone who has undertaken the proofreading of a manuscript will know how difficult it can be to detect certain errors, and it is often harder to see one's own mistakes than those of someone else. The reason for this is quite simple – one tends to see what one expects to see, rather than what is before one's eyes. Thus if a writer used a word similar but not identical to another (intended) word, it is quite likely that he or she would subsequently also read it as the intended word. A second person, having no preconceptions, would be more likely to detect the error.

These trivial examples become very important when applied to reading drug labels or prescriptions. Dr Yogasakaran may or may not have looked at the label on the ampoule of dopamine. It was said in court that he did not, but it is far more likely that he did at least glance at it (his memory for an event of that sort would be unreliable, and very probably overwhelmed by the subsequent tragic events). If he did glance at it, it is not at all surprising that he would have read the word 'dopamine' as 'dopram' – the drug he expected to be in the ampoule. This type of misreading has been reported on a number of

[33] E. G. Boring, 'A new ambiguous figure' (1930) 42 *American Journal of Psychology* 444–5.
[34] M. R. Cohen, 'Drug product characteristics that foster drug-use-system errors' (1995) 52 *American Journal of Health-System Pharmacy* 395–9; B. A. Orser and D. C. Oxorn, 'An anaesthetic drug error: minimizing the risk' (1994) 41 *Canadian Journal of Anaesthesia* 120–4.

occasions[34] and probably represents a major factor in the causation of drug administration errors. The particular example of giving the wrong drug, if undetected, may be compounded by subsequent errors of interpretation based on the unexpected response or lack of response that ensues from the given rather than the intended drug. For example, some years ago a junior anaesthetist failed to realise that the device for administering the anaesthetic vapour was not properly attached to the anaesthetic machine, with the result that a patient who had received a muscle relaxant, and who was therefore unable to move, was awake during a surgical operation. The anaesthetist attributed the failure of increasing doses of the agent to control a rapidly rising blood pressure to the elderly patient's age and pre-existing hypertension – another example of confirmation bias reinforcing an incorrect mental image of events. Only on the arrival of a supervisor (one of the authors) was her *mindset* broken and the real problem identified, regrettably too late. The correct diagnosis was more obvious to the newcomer not only because of his greater experience but (as in the case of Dr Hugel) also because of his fresh perspective on events. He was not nearly so strongly influenced as the first anaesthetist by the way in which events had unfolded. A variation of this problem is that doctors faced with a particular set of signs and symptoms have a strong tendency to make a diagnosis that falls within their own field. Thus, consulting a series of specialists from different fields about the same symptom may at times result in being given a different diagnosis by each of them. In each case the diagnosis would be of a disease process commonly seen in the particular doctor's own speciality. This illustrates once more the way in which people tend to see what they expect to see: they interpret information to fit the 'diagnosis' with which they are familiar. Any new information is also interpreted in this way, if at all possible, so that the practitioner's conviction becomes progressively stronger under circumstances in which, to a fresh and more objective observer, the correct diagnosis might appear increasingly obvious. Behaviour which is completely bizarre and inexplicable from the perspective of the real world – particularly when interpreted with hindsight – may become understandable if seen in the context of the individual's internal representation of events. The potential gap between the world and one's mental picture of it is a very dangerous force in the generation of errors.

Cognition: chunking, processing and responding to information

We have seen that the human brain is capable of dealing with a large amount of information at one time. This ability can be enhanced by training and experience. As we have already observed, driving a motor car in traffic provides a good example of an ordinary activity which is, on reflection, an impressive accomplishment. This is true in the broader sense of the way in which society works as a whole, but also in the individual sense of the highly efficient way in which our minds are capable of functioning, particularly with the benefit of practice. A novice, placed at the wheel of a car and launched into the rush-hour traffic of a large city would be overwhelmed by the range and subtlety of physical actions required to guide the vehicle successfully to its destination. He or she would struggle with the gear changes, the need to use the clutch properly, the nuances of acceleration and braking, and even with the relatively straightforward matter of steering the car. These activities are essentially a matter of skill, and this requires time and practice to build up. For an expert, on the other hand, many of these processes have become highly integrated and are mostly automatic. Accelerating, changing gear and steering are done by experienced motorists largely subconsciously, not as individually planned actions but as unified sequences, conceptualised at a subconscious level as quite large *cognitive chunks*.[35] In effect, as tasks become more routine they are incorporated into reflex-like action sequences which can be executed as integrated conceptual units, rather like subroutines in a computer program. This is Rasmussen's *skill-based* level of human performance. Although it is necessary for an experienced person to disassemble these cognitive units or chunks into their individual components only when something slightly unusual causes an interruption in the automatic sequence, it may then sometimes be quite difficult to resume from exactly the place in the sequence where one left off, such is the fixedness of the chain of actions in which the individual task is embedded.

For the novice driver, lack of skill would be only part of the problem. It

---

[35] G. A. Miller, 'The magical number seven, plus or minus two: some limits on our capacity for processing information' (1956) 63 *Psychological Reviews 81–97*; A. M. Graybiel, 'The basal ganglia and chunking of action repertoires' (1998) 70 *Neurobiology of Learning and Memory* 119–36.

is obvious that the need to interact with other traffic, respond to road signals, deal with lane changes, avoid running over pedestrians, and at the same time stay within the limits of the law would present an overwhelming task to the beginner. He or she would need to process far too much information at one time. Decisions which, for the novice, would necessitate detailed and careful thought would have to be made rapidly. Even the preliminary matter of assembling the pertinent facts in the forefront of the mind, while at the same time setting aside the other myriad of salient but unimportant bits of incoming information, would be very difficult, particularly if this had to be done at the same time as the skill-based activity of actually driving the car. The novice has no choice but to think through the implications of each successive situation and work out logically, from the facts, what to do in every circumstance. This is the type of effortful thinking which Rasmussen (and Reason) call *knowledge-based* reasoning.

Although the Reason/Rasmussen nomenclature is widely accepted, this name is not very descriptive of its key feature – the effortful, deliberative aspect of solving a problem from first principles. We propose to use the term *deliberative reasoning*, or *deliberative cognitive processing*, or simply *deliberation* for this, and suggest that our term is more intuitively understandable and less likely to cause confusion in respect to the processes which underlie the errors associated with it.

The expert driver in the same situation would function quite differently from the novice. The mass of irrelevant detail would automatically be filtered out by the mind. The name of the streets he is driving along, the name of the last intersecting street, the corresponding features on the map and the details of the intended route, the position of other cars, the rules of the road and the presence of various signs and signals are all examples of facts relevant to the driver trying to find her way in traffic. These facts would need to be selected from the barrage of other information competing for attention at the same time – the colour of the buildings, the details of pedestrians' clothes, the type of clouds in the sky, the music on the radio, and so on. Again, the expert will have an advantage over the novice. This is because the vitally important process of rejecting information likely to be unhelpful in the resolution of a given problem, while at the same time focusing on the key facts that actually are pertinent rather than simply salient, is more instinctive to an experienced person than to a beginner. The complex mass of facts which actually were relevant would be recognised by the expert as corresponding to a small number of distinct patterns stored in the memory on the basis of previous experiences. These patterns might themselves be synthesised into larger coherent wholes which could be combined into an essentially unified picture. These stored patterns or templates are called *schemata*. In much the same way as our minute by minute appreciation of our surroundings tends to be an approximate rationalisation of what is really there, these schemata are not thought to be exact representations of previously encountered individual situations but are considered more likely to be conceptualisations of the essential features of idealised versions of various similar situations. Thus a room may be conceptualised as having four walls, a ceiling, doors, windows and so forth. This view is supported by evidence that memories of briefly seen objects tend to be recalled in an idealised rather than an accurate fashion. Thus, for example, a clock on the wall of a room to which a subject in an experiment has been briefly exposed will often be recalled as having hands even if the hands have in fact been removed from it. At the subconscious level this reworking, or ordering and simplifying of the information stored in our memory is a very powerful mechanism for rapidly making sense of complicated situations. Schemata may be refined, so that increasingly more specific versions of a general situation may be stored in a sort of hierarchy, to cope with the variety of situations that characterise our existence. Even these lower-level patterns or templates will tend to be conceptualisations of the important (possibly the exceptional) features of a given place or event rather than photographically accurate representations of them.

To return to our expert driver: a schema would usually be available which would correspond, at least approximately, to situations seen before. The driver would therefore know what to do on the basis of a previously learned 'rule', or response, which he or she knows has worked well before, in similar circumstances. It would not be necessary to analyse the problem in detail. The process would be on the basis of: if situation x, do action y. This is known as *rule-based* performance, and requires far less effortful processing of information than deliberative reasoning. The given situation would be identified as approximately equivalent to a particular conceptual representation already stored in the mind. The expert has a large store of such patterns and a similarly large store of rules that are known from experience to produce a satisfactory result if applied in the presence of the corresponding schema. All that is required is to recognise the pattern and respond by applying the most appropriate rule – a rule known to have worked previously on similar occasions. Only when an unfamiliar situation arises must the expert resort to more effortful deliberation. Expert chess players are able to reconstruct complex positions from real games with ease, but interestingly they are no better than novices at recalling the positions of pieces placed at random about the board.[36] Again, this reflects the way in which meaningful information can be brought together and retained within one's store of knowledge as unified blocks, while meaningless patterns are less readily remembered. Similarly, in finding his or her way, a driver will follow a familiar route with ease, and with little need for conscious thought, but, once hitherto unexplored territory is entered, it becomes necessary to rely once more on the slow and deliberate process of identifying relevant facts and then working out from first principles how they should be interpreted. In practice, people switch from rule-based to deliberative processing and back again as the evolving circumstances demand. Decisions made deliberatively may be implemented by sequences of actions that are largely automatic – the application of a rule, the use of a skill. Often it is necessary to continue to operate at a skill-based level, without conscious thought, using rule-based responses to keep the activity on track, while at the same time processing information actively to specify the next major task. In this way it is possible to do several different things simultaneously – so-called *multi-tasking*.

Earlier theories of human behaviour presumed that human cognition was essentially rational. As we have already observed, humans seem to have a stronger preference for responding to situations by using a pre-formulated rule than by thinking things out from first principles – the phenomenon known as *reluctant rationality*. It may be thought that the application of pre-formed rules to situations identified as corresponding to appropriate schemata is rational enough, but in fact the process of retrieving a schema or selecting a rule to apply in a given situation is not necessarily either logical or rational. The relatively subconscious choice of a particular rule is strongly influenced by factors such as how recently the rule has last been used successfully, the frequency with which it has worked before successfully, and the strength of the emotional experience

---

[36] F. Gobet and H. A. Simon, 'Expert chess memory: revisiting the chunking hypothesis' (1998) 6 *Memory* 225–55.

associated with its previous use. Even at the deliberative level, decisions seldom follow rational lines in the Bayesian or statistical sense. One major reason for this is that the set of facts available for making decisions – the *problem space* – is often incomplete or inadequate. This applies both to the information in the world and to the information available from memory. In a medical example, there may be a very large number of facts relevant to a patient's condition, available as information in the world (which includes information in other people's minds and information stored in books), but some of these might not be provided for a doctor or be readily available to him or her. The history of a relevant previous illness or allergy may be forgotten by a patient, for example. In order to manage the patient's problem properly, the doctor must rely on a great deal of information stored in his or her memory, some of which may be missing, inaccurate, or difficult to retrieve at the time required. He or she may have forgotten one of the side-effects of a drug in question – an example of a failure very common in medicine. The solution to a problem may be logically sound even with incomplete information – such a solution is sometimes referred to as *satisficing*. Clearly, however, the lack of a complete set of pertinent facts and the incorrect nature of some of the information which is available militate against the making of an *optimal* decision. Furthermore, there is a problem in assembling the pertinent facts in the front of the mind – our ability to think of all the various aspects of a complex problem at once is quite limited. If the problem space is thought of as a blackboard full of facts, then for human beings it is a blackboard illuminated by a narrow beam whose movements from one place to another are largely random and only partly responsive to voluntary control. This feature of the human condition is known as *bounded rationality*.

Expertise

There is, of course, a gradation between the complete novice and the inveterate master, and people cope with activities (including driving) by using different levels of skill and experience. Each individual's store of retained patterns and rules will also differ, both in its size and in the precise nature of the conceptualisations and corresponding pre-formu-lated responses. A major objective of training a person to be competent at a particular activity is to create greater conformity of the schemata and rules in the individual's store to those known by the teacher to be relatively reliable. Rules need to be matched to their appropriate schemata, and they need to be sound, robust and (so far as possible) capable of working in all the circumstances to which they are appropriately applied. The expert who has benefited from a well-designed and administered training programme is more likely to have sound conceptual patterns and robust rules than the self-taught person. The expert will have to resort to active deliberation less often than the novice, and he or she is also likely to have a more comprehensive store of sound basic information for use when this type of first-principles approach actually is needed.

It follows that expertise is highly desirable. The ability of human beings to undertake complex activities is only possible because of the inherent properties of the human mind which facilitate the filtering and processing of information, and allow rapid and skilled responses to difficult and dynamically changing challenges. Equally, many contemporary human activities are only possible on account of the social fabric of human society, which permits co-operation between individuals and allows knowledge and skill to be passed from one person to the next. These factors are manifest to a very high degree in an activity such as the practice of medicine. It would be quite impossible for doctors to function in their various and often concurrent roles as diagnosticians, advisers, technicians and counsellors if it were not for the way in which the human mind works, the way in which people interact, and the technology with which they can enhance their abilities. If the doctor had to start afresh from first principles every time a procedure was undertaken or a patient examined, little would get done. Some practitioners have honed their psychomotor and analytical skills to very high levels in order to undertake extremely difficult operations or other procedures on, for example, tiny babies or infirm elderly patients. In doing this, they are in no small way like professional sportsmen whose natural ability has been developed by training and practice to produce a very high level of skill, although the range of activities and the theoretical knowledge involved in medical practice exceeds that in most sporting activities. Even top batsmen (for example) do get bowled out from time to time, and in the same way doctors occasionally fail to achieve the outcome they intended for a patient, sometimes to the extent that injury or death is the result, instead of healing. We shall discuss these failures in chapter 3, under the heading 'technical errors', but, as in sport, perhaps the most surprising thing in medicine is that some of the more difficult procedures are possible at all.

The price of success

This chapter has stressed human abilities and achievements. The way in which our minds work has permitted us to develop a highly technological society, and to function within it. Many of the cognitive processes which have allowed humans to function successfully in the world are so successful precisely because of our flexible, distractible and interpretative nature. These attributes are the ones that also underlie the predisposition of human beings to error. The technology and complexity which we have created in our modern society have increased the demands on our abilities to reason accurately, respond promptly with the correct rule for any given situation, and carry out actions requiring considerable skill. They have also produced scenarios in which the consequences of error may be very serious indeed; we have reviewed data confirming that accidental harm is a major problem in modern healthcare.

The informed response to harm from error does not lie in a denial of the existence or nature of human error, and it is therefore worrying that medical practitioners and the courts often take a view of error that sits more readily with a model of people as machines than with the insights of contemporary psychology. Justice and safety would both be better served by a more sophisticated appreciation of the relationship between the highly desirable achievements of today's society and its inherent vulnerability to accidents. In particular, the inevitability of human error should be seen not so much as evidence of a primary human weakness, but rather as an inevitable concomitant of our impressive cognitive ability and evolutionary success.

3

Errors

We all know that everyone makes mistakes – but are everyday mistakes (misplacing a household item or misdialling a telephone number) really equivalent to inadvertently administering the wrong drug to a patient? There is an understandable view that professionals are trained and paid precisely to ensure that they do in fact do the right thing. The problem of iatrogenic harm in healthcare described in chapter 2 demands a response. The first reaction to accidents in medicine is often punitive, and based on a denial of the nature of human error. The culture of clinical practice is in general one of relentless dedication to high achievement and the medical profession is the foremost culprit in perpetuating the myth of professional infallibility. It is not surprising that the courts and disciplinary authorities have taken their lead from doctors themselves and have at times seemed to treat any kind of failure in medical practice as unacceptable.

In chapter 2 we discussed some of the processes involved in human cognition and described the way in which the mind may mislead an actor and create a situation in which bizarre and apparently inexplicable actions become perfectly understandable. We now attempt to distinguish between different types of error and investigate whether it is possible to predict which type of error is most likely to occur in a given situation. We shall discuss reasons for believing that errors (in contrast to violations) are both understandable and inevitable, even for a highly trained and regulated professional. However, not all unsafe acts are errors. If we are to gain any useful insights into the issue of blame from our consideration of the ways in which human cognitive processes can fail, it is essential to distinguish unintentional *errors* from deliberately unsafe acts, or *violations*. Violations will be the subject of chapter 4, and the distinction between errors and violations will be important to our discussion of blame in the rest of the book.

Definition of error

In his book *Human Error*, Reason defines 'error' as a generic term encompassing '*all those occasions in which a planned sequence of mental or physical activities fails to achieve its intended outcome, and when these failures cannot be attributed to the intervention of some chance agency*'.[1] Reason's book provides an authoritative account of error, but it is explicitly not concerned with blame, and consequently this definition does not fully delineate the characteristics of error which are important for our purposes.

Error can only be understood in relation to an intention to achieve a particular result or outcome – automatic acts are excluded. However, an error may be made in which the intended overall *goal* is still successfully achieved. The appropriateness of an act or decision cannot be reliably assessed on the basis of its outcome or result. In general, errors tend to reduce the chances of achieving a given outcome or they reduce the margin of safety associated with a particular activity. We would probably have little interest in errors which had neither of these results, but these are not the critical aspects of the definition of an error. As we have said, the concept of a happy accident makes this clearer – for example, the possibility that one might misread a timetable and erroneously miss a flight which subsequently crashes. In this case the error would actually lead to a safer and more desirable outcome, but it remains an error. In error, the failure lies in some aspect of a particular *act* or *plan* which is part of the process of achieving a goal. To qualify as an error, this failure in planning or acting must be unintentional. If the act or decision knowingly falls short of a reasonably expected standard, we would classify the act in question as a *violation*, even though there may be no intent to cause harm or to jeopardise a particular goal. Knowingly exceeding the speed limit is a violation even if a driver believes this will get him to his destination sooner, with no loss of safety. Giving the wrong drug to a patient is almost always an error because the intention of the practitioner includes giving the right drug as well as achieving a therapeutic goal. There can be no suggestion in the case of an error that the faulty action or decision was undertaken in the knowledge that it was faulty, but in the belief that this faultiness did not matter. Indeed, the actor is often

[1] J. Reason, *Human Error* (New York, Cambridge University Press, 1990), 9.

completely unaware at the time that the error has occurred – a salt-for-sugar substitution is often only identified on tasting the tea, for example, and many drug errors go completely undetected by the person concerned, to be identified later by their consequences, or perhaps by a second practitioner (such as a supervisor) who notices the empty ampoules. When we are evaluating events for the purpose of attributing blame, these are important points, because our focus needs to be on the actions and thought processes themselves, not on their results. For these reasons we propose the following definition:

> *An error is an unintentional failure in the formulation of a plan by which it is intended to achieve a goal, or an unintentional departure of a sequence of mental or physical activities from the sequence planned, except when such departure is due to a chance intervention.*

This definition retains the principle that errors are not associated with automatic actions, and that there must be some intended aspect of the act or plan which 'goes wrong', although the error itself is unintentional; it explicitly shifts the focus from the outcome of an act or plan to a failure in the act or plan itself.

Taxonomy of error[2]

There are various ways in which errors may be classified, but for evaluating events with a view to the possible attribution of blame, there is great value in an approach which draws on the principles of cognitive psychology which we have discussed in chapter 2. In this approach errors are classified on the basis of the type of cognitive processing involved at the time they were made. Thus Reason, in describing a 'Generic Error Modelling System', refers to *skill-based, rule-based* or *knowledge-based errors*. Skill-based errors involve actions and are usually the result of *distraction*. Rule-based and knowledge-based errors are problem-solving failures, or planning failures, and may be grouped together under the heading of *mistakes*. As we explained in chapter 2, we shall use the term *deliberative errors* to mean exactly the same thing as *knowledge-based errors*. We shall also discuss two sub-classes in our overall analysis of error types, both of which are widely and intuitively recognised in medical practice, namely: *technical errors* and *errors of judgement*. Two other

---

[2] Ibid.

concepts are important, but they are best used to refine our understanding of the cause of an error within each individual class rather than as the basis for identifying error types in their own right: *mindset* refers to the process, discussed in chapter 2, by which there may be a mental misinterpretation of external events which underlies and explains an error – a process that may play a role in the genesis of any of the three main categories of error; *knowledge failures* are those situations in which the fault lies in the information recalled from the individual's internal store of knowledge. This may reflect a *memory failure* or it may imply that the individual has never known the fact or principle in question. This type of failure may also underlie any form of error and it may contribute to the development of an erroneous mindset.

An important feature by which error types can be distinguished involves the focus of attention at the time the error occurred. In skill-based activities, attention is consciously directed towards the task or sequence of actions only from time to time – particularly at the initiation of the sequence or at key points within it when decisions are needed. In most rule-based and in all deliberative errors, attention is actually focused on the task in hand.

Skill-based errors

Slips and lapses

Skill based errors may be *slips* or *lapses*. It is useful to refer to them collectively as *slip/lapse errors*, to stress that they are of the same general type. They occur as a result of *attentional capture* or distraction – which may be momentary. Thus a lapse involves a failure of attention which results in the omission of some intended action, whereas, in a slip, something is done which was not intended, also because of a failure in attention. Both are typical of learned or familiar sequences of actions which are usually carried out more or less automatically. Forgetting to switch off the house alarm on returning home is an example of a lapse. Typically this might happen if some minor but unexpected distraction diverted one's attention during the critical period between opening the front door and going to the alarm keyboard. Driving through a stop sign would be a more serious example of a lapse, and again, this would usually be attributable to a moment of distraction in which one's attention was captured by something else. Failing to give a drug that one had intended to administer is an example of a lapse and, giving an unintended drug, perhaps in substitution for the correct one, is an example of a slip. In the case of Dr Yogasakaran,[3] for example, the error may have been a lapse – one explanation for his having given the wrong drug is that he unintentionally omitted to check because his attention was distracted by the developing emergency.[4]

Inadvertently adding milk to one's tea a day or two after deciding to give up this practice provides a trivial example of a slip. The tendency to revert from an exceptional or new way of doing things to a well-established routine is a very powerful force in the generation of skill-based errors. Human beings are very inclined to run on automatic pilot whenever possible, operating by the exercise of learned sequences of skilled actions in response to context-specific patterns in their surroundings. Driving home from work after moving from a long-established residence makes this clear – there is a good chance of finding oneself back at the old house without much idea of how one actually got there. Typically, the new route will begin along the same route as the old and well-established way home, but at a particular point it may turn away and proceed along new, unfamiliar roads. A point such as this, in which an active decision needs to be taken, may be thought of as a *decision node*. Driving a car along a well-known route really involves a combination of skill-based and rule-based activities; most of the time the skills and rules are used automatically, in response to situations recognised as corresponding to pre-stored schemata, but when a decision node is reached, focused attention is required. Thus a moment of distraction at a decision node will often lead to an error – typically a lapse.

The distraction, or *attentional capture*, which is a characteristic feature in the genesis of these errors can involve over-attention as well as inattention. Checking is a process that can break into a sequence of events and cause an operator to lose his or her precise place, with the result that a particular step that may well have been undertaken correctly if the routine had simply been allowed to run as usual is either missed or repeated. This can occur with drug administration errors, particularly in certain branches of anaesthesia where, at times, over forty drug adminis-

---

[3] See chapter 1.

[4] An alternative explanation discussed in chapter 2 is that in reading the label he saw the name he expected to see rather than the one that was actually there.

trations need to be given in one anaesthetic. It is quite possible for one drug to be missed or given twice because the doctor, in pausing to check, loses track of his or her place in a well-established sequence of administrations.

It follows that slips and lapses are not necessarily manifestations of carelessness – although they may be. A resolve always to pay close attention to the many routine but dangerous tasks that form part of one's regular duties is a commendable attempt to respond to the obvious need to take care, but such a resolve is doomed to failure over any prolonged period of time. We noted in chapter 2, that human beings are distractible by nature, and indeed need to be to survive. Distractibility is a requirement if we are to notice when the house is on fire or when some unexpected event occurs during a surgical operation, and at some stage in any prolonged or often-repeated activity distraction is inevitable – and may occasionally result in an error.

A hang-gliding lapse

Several features of slips and lapses are graphically illustrated by an event reported in a daily newspaper.[5] As a Christmas present from his partner, a man had been given an introductory hang-gliding lesson. While the instructor was getting ready, he was momentarily distracted by a puff of wind and failed to secure his harness properly. Putting on his harness would have been, for the expert instructor, an automatic sequence of events, and the effect of a momentary distraction in producing a break in this sequence and precipitating a subsequent failure to complete it properly is typical of a lapse. On launching, the instructor fell some distance, injuring himself – and leaving his pupil to soar out into the sky, alone, on his first ever flight. Fortunately, he too survived, with relatively minor injuries.

This example illustrates several points. The first is the role of distraction in the generation of lapses – the puff of wind in this case. The second point is that these errors do not necessarily represent *carelessness*. It is inconceivable (short of suicidal intention) that the instructor would not have cared about securing his harness. Similarly, it is reasonable to

---

[5] A. Horwood, 'Hang this gliding lark says novice after solo flight', *New Zealand Herald* (16 March 1996), s. 1, p. 1.

presume that airline pilots care about avoiding crashes in which they will be leading participants. If care were all that were needed, airline pilots would never make slips or suffer lapses – but they certainly do. Obviously carefulness and attention are distinguishable from care in the sense of concern about consequences, but the important conclusion from this example is that deterrence cannot eliminate this type of error. Another example illustrating this point is to be found in the case of the observer on a police traffic-spotting plane who walked into a spinning propeller during a fuel stop.[6] There is no suggestion other than that this action on the part of an experienced professional was a lapse. The idea of walking into a propeller on a light aircraft is particularly unpleasant and the hazardous nature of a propeller is very obvious. It is not possible to avoid slips and lapses by choice, by good intention, by strict regulation combined with draconian punishment, or by the risk of harm inherent in a dangerous situation; the remedy has to be sought elsewhere, notably in the way systems are designed.

The third point is that slips and lapses are characteristic of experts – in the hang-gliding case it was the instructor, not the pupil, who was subject to the lapse. This point is counter-intuitive, and it often leads to much misunderstanding, especially in the legal and disciplinary proceedings which may follow such errors. It is often said that the person responsible for a slip or a lapse was trained in the field and therefore could have been expected not to make an error, particularly of the very basic sort typical of slips and lapses. Giving a wrong drug is a good example – on the face of it, it seems ridiculously easy to give the right drug and it is difficult to see why a competent and careful professional would fail in this elementary aspect of the job. It is sometimes even suggested that the money paid to professionals justifies the expectation that errors of this type should not be made, and this view is understandable. It is based, however, on a misconception: namely that expertise or incentives or threats create a situation in which an individual can suddenly stop being human and, on the basis of choice alone, avoid unintended actions (such as slips or lapses) that occur independently of choice. Experts may reasonably be expected to remain sober and to be attentive, but it is not reasonable to suggest that they should somehow become superhuman and thereby never make an error. Thus in chapter 1 we were able to make a distinction between the deliberate

---

[6] 'Propeller kills traffic observer', *New Zealand Herald* (17 February 1996), s. 1, p. 1.

neglect by one expert anaesthetist (Dr Manjanatha) of his responsibility to attend to his patient and the accidental administration of the wrong drug (almost certainly a slip/lapse error) by another (Dr Yogasakaran).

It is expertise which makes a difficult and dangerous task possible at all – the instructor was capable of flying a hang-glider, the novice was not. The expert's knowledge is deeper, and more robust, than the novice's, and expertise reduces the likelihood of error overall; there are many reasons for this, but a particularly relevant one is that an expert would have a large number of well-practised rules at his or her disposal and so would be less reliant on error-prone deliberation than a novice; he or she would also have a better understanding of the fundamentals of the subject if active deliberative reasoning actually was required. In addition, one component of the development of expertise involves the learning of techniques which counter the risk of particular skill-based errors – the use of a double-checking protocol as advocated after the case of Dr Morrison, for example. In fact, for many competent experts the overall likelihood of making a mistake is so low that part of the problem lies in the fact that expectations have become unrealistically high. However, the fact remains that skill-based errors are impossible to eliminate completely; it is unrealistic to assume that, simply on the basis of good intentions, anyone can successfully avoid ever making a slip/lapse error again. These errors are inextricably linked with the way in which the multi-tasking and distractible human mind works. It is the nature of expert activity to rely heavily on automatic skills for the undertaking of several activities simultaneously, while counting on human distractibility to identify and respond to unexpected or new developments. It follows that expert or highly skilled activity actually *predisposes* to slips or lapses at the same time as it reduces the chances of other types of error.

Finally, this example clearly illustrates the very powerful influence of outcome on the judgement of an action. Because nobody was seriously injured, the matter was treated as worthy of little more than an amusing newspaper article. Had the pupil died, it is very likely that the instructor's lapse would have been subject to much stronger criticism. There may be a pragmatic justification for reserving the resources needed to undertake a detailed investigation of an event for those situations in which serious harm has occurred – but there is no rational justification for judging the culpability of an act by the severity of its unintended consequences. On the contrary, the argument that dangerous activities warrant a high level of care – which we fully accept – is in fact a reason to investigate those 'near misses' in which the outcome is fortunate just as closely as those in which it is disastrous.

Calls for help

Slips and lapses are not only the province of the professional – they are a feature of everyday life. This is made clear in another example from the daily papers. It was reported that the fire brigade was receiving a surprisingly high number of calls to burning houses in which the wrong addresses were being given. It transpired that the callers were people who had recently moved home and that the wrong addresses were in fact those of their former residences. This is very similar to the example of driving home to a previously occupied house and not knowing how one has got there. As with the hang-gliding story, however, it does make clear the fact that this type of error does not represent carelessness. These people must have cared – that was why they were telephoning for help. It is even harder to construe their failure in terms of carelessness than in the case of the hang-gliding instructor. These were people whose whole attention was focused on communicating their need for help – and yet they were getting the information wrong. The deterrence of losing their house by failing to give the correct address did nothing to prevent their error and, from the opposite perspective, the possible reward of saving their home was equally ineffective in modifying their behaviour. Again, a systems-oriented approach would be more likely to produce an effective solution than simply trying to modify people's behaviour. For example, advances in technology have made it possible for emergency services of this type to obtain and record automatically the locations from which callers are telephoning. This is an effective response to the problem, using tech-nology to compensate for the failings inherent in human cognition.

Technical errors

Runciman and his colleagues have delineated a particular variation of error common in medicine which they have called technical errors.[7]

---

[7] W. B. Runciman, A. Sellen, R. K. Webb, J. A. Williamson, M. Currie, C. Morgan and W. J. Russell, 'Errors, incidents and accidents in anaesthetic practice' (1993) 21 *Anaesthesia and Intensive Care* 506–19.

These are probably best seen as a type of skill-based error distinct from slips and lapses. These authors give the example of failing to place an epidural catheter correctly, in such a way that the needle is inserted too far, causing the complication of a dural tap, or in such a way that the correct space is not entered and no block results. The plan and choice of technique are appropriate, no slip or lapse occurs, and there is also no suggestion of a violation – but there is a failure to carry out the intended action successfully.

Two factors contribute to these errors. The first is patient variability. Runciman's group refers to this problem as 'underspecification of the task', by which they mean that any abnormality in the anatomy of a patient may be unknown and unknowable. If every practitioner produced the same result in the same circumstances, then one would have to conclude that the adverse event was due to circumstances beyond their control.

This is not the case, however, because of the second factor, which is the variability of the skill and knowledge of individual practitioners. This applies both from one practitioner to another, and also to the same practitioner on different days, or perhaps at different times of day and night and at different levels of fatigue. For example, the incidence of dural taps differs between anaesthetists. In general, the frequency of this complication diminishes with the increasing training, experience and skill of the operator. It is never possible to eliminate the problem altogether, and some practitioners do better than others even when they are all fully trained and equally experienced.

An example from sport may help us to understand the issues involved with technical errors. A weekend golfer will set out to drive the ball straight down the fairway, but will often fail to achieve this goal. The failure will generally occur despite an appropriate decision, and in the absence of a slip or a lapse. The task is just too difficult. Note that it is not too difficult for even an average golfer to hit a good drive occasionally. The difficulty lies in doing it over and over again. This point was well illustrated in a recent series of tests undertaken for an article in a golfing magazine. A professional golfer, a player with a handicap of seven (a strong amateur player) and one with a handicap of fourteen (an average golfer, who was said to play twice a week) were asked to perform the same tasks. In the driving test, the first drive of the fourteen-handicapper was accurate (landing on the fairway) and very nearly as long as the professional's. However, the professional hit only one out of ten drives into the rough, against four out of ten on the part of each of the amateurs.[8] In this analogy, doctors are, of course, more like *professional* golfers, especially in the context of specialist practice. Because of their greatly enhanced skill, the success rate of professional golfers is very good, but even professionals fail to hit the fairway on occasion – as demonstrated in the above test. There is also a difference between professionals. A few stand out as more consistently successful than the majority, even though the majority perform very well indeed. To return to epidurals: some anaesthetists experience more dural taps than others. Can these extra taps be characterised as errors? An alternative view might be to treat them as evidence of technical incompetence. In either case it is generally agreed that, if an individual practitioner's rate of any complication is 'too high', some intervention is called for, such as additional training or redeployment into a less technically demanding field. The difficulty lies in knowing where to draw the line – an issue we shall consider further in chapter 7.

Apply these thoughts to surgery. Many cardiac surgical units experience a 2 per cent mortality rate for first-time coronary artery surgery. In some the rate is higher; in some it is a little lower. Part of this variation relates to differences in the characteristics of the different patient populations, but at least some of it relates to factors other than casemix. Clearly, a major contribution to the incidence of the complication of death in these patients comes from the skills of the surgeon, the anaesthetist, the intensive-care specialists, and from the overall standards of the unit in which these specialists work.[9]

In the recent highly publicised Medical Council proceedings involving cardiac surgery in Bristol, the performance of the surgeons concerned seems to have fallen below an acceptable standard, although questions have been asked (reasonably enough) about the possible contribution to the Bristol unit's results of other members of the team. The surgeons were criticised on other grounds as well.[10] It is only fair to the surgeons to note

---

[8] P. Masters, 'How much better are the pros?' (2000) 41 *Golf World* 112–21.

[9] G. T. O'Connor, S. K. Plume et al. for the Northern New England Cardiovascular Disease Study Group, 'A regional prospective study of in-hospital mortality associated with coronary artery bypass grafting' (1991) 266 *Journal of the American Medical Association* 803–9; A. F. Merry, M. C. Ramage, R. M. L. Whitlock, G. J. A. Laycock, W. Smith, D. Stenhouse and C. J. Wild, 'First-time coronary artery bypass grafting: the anaesthetist as a risk factor' (1992) 68 British Journal of Anaesthesia 6–12.

[10] See chapter 1.

that the technical skill associated with the successful conduct of paediatric cardiac surgery is very high indeed. Nevertheless, it seems probable that poor results in this type of situation would be attributable, at least in part, to inadequacies of technique. However, the inadequacies can be judged only in relation to the performance of other cardiac surgeons undertaking the same work. If the results of all units in paediatric cardiac surgery had been similar to Bristol's, the same level of performance would have to be accepted as the best that could be done.

It can be seen, then, that technical errors are an important category of error in medical practice. Given that specialists are being called upon to undertake increasingly difficult and hazardous procedures, often in association with excessive workloads and limited resources, it is likely to be an even more prominent problem in the future. It is likely to be very difficult to evaluate the degree of blame due when a generally competent individual who tries conscientiously to undertake a technically challenging procedure fails to succeed in an individual case. This situation may be highly analogous to that of a golf shot which an otherwise very successful professional golfer just happens on one occasion to hit out of bounds – but while the golfer is judged on his total score for the competition, and indeed on his overall performance over many years, the doctor faced with a dead or injured patient may (understandably) have a hard time explaining what went wrong. In particular, any action for negligence would focus on the isolated failure and discount the doctor's many previous successes.

Rule-based errors

Rule-based errors involve some failure in the process by which a set of circumstances is recognised and an appropriate rule applied. This failure might occur because the pattern of events is incorrectly recognised, and is matched to an inappropriate mental schema, or it might involve the application of either the wrong rule or an inadequate rule to a correctly matched schema. One important factor which can contribute to the former situation, which is quite common in medicine, is the process called *frequency gambling*, which, like skill-based activity, is typical of experts, often in the context of heavy workloads. The essential idea expressed by this term is that people tend to choose a rule known to have worked on many previous occasions in more or less the current circumstances, without necessarily establishing beyond doubt that the circumstances really are equivalent to those in which the rule was previously applied. Doctors are actually taught to work in this way and the concept has been encapsulated in the adage 'When you see hoof prints, think of horses, not zebras.' The difficulty is to know precisely when to look more closely in case the animal actually *is* a zebra! Thus a general practitioner faced with a pyrexial and unwell patient might diagnose influenza on the basis that he or she had seen ten cases of this illness in the previous two days, in all of whom the same salient features were present. In doing this, the doctor runs the risk of missing a more pertinent but less obvious feature – neck stiffness, for example, which might warn of the possibility of the more serious but less common condition of meningitis. An excessive amount of work may create pressure to resort to frequency gambling; thus a usually conscientious practitioner, exhausted by the demands of an influenza epidemic, might be tempted to provide advice over the telephone, late at night, in the belief that he or she is dealing with yet another case of 'flu, instead of insisting on seeing the patient in order to undertake a full physical examination. Frequency gambling usually works, and may allow a practitioner to cope with a heavier load than would otherwise be possible. Indeed, to some degree most medical diagnosis involves frequency gambling – the main variable being the depth of enquiry which precedes any decision. In this example, a careful practitioner would formally eliminate neck stiffness to rule out meningitis, and might perhaps also look for specific signs of various other conditions. Blood tests and a chest radiograph might be considered, as well as a lumbar puncture. At some stage, however, a halt must be called, and a diagnosis made on the basis that any alternatives not yet fully eliminated are too unlikely to warrant the expense and additional risk to the patient entailed in the further investigations that would be required to rule them out completely. The precise point at which this halt is called will depend on the circumstances, but also on the training and experience of the individual practitioner. Typically, it is the more experienced doctor who does the fewer tests, but it is also the more experienced doctor who knows precisely when the extra test is indicated. For most doctors the response to a given clinical situation will involve the use of a rule or set of rules, but the complexity and robustness of the rules, and the degree to which their use is reinforced by deliberation, may vary substantially.

The types of error possible in rule-based processing are relatively limited in variety and reasonably predictable from identifiable inadequacies in the rules themselves and in the ways in which rules are selected. We have already discussed the fact that the strength with which a rule is likely to present itself for selection depends on a number of factors, some of which do not necessarily promote rational decision making. Rules which have been used frequently and recently will be more attractive than those which have lain dormant for a long time. A rule which has produced an unusual but highly adverse result may be eschewed, quite irrationally, on an emotional basis; thus doctors often change their practice because of one bad experience with a certain treatment, even though the logic of the situation might suggest that this experience was a rare event unlikely to be repeated.

The control of rule-based activity is referred to as *feed-forward*; this implies that rules are applied with objectives in mind, on the basis of previous experiences in similar circumstances. Thus situations may arise in which it is believed that a particular objective (the patient's safety, for example) will be achieved by the use of a particular rule – but in which the conviction with which that rule is selected is quite misplaced; this phenomenon is referred to as the application of a 'strong but wrong' rule.

Experts are not immune from making rule-based errors, but rule-based errors become less likely with increasing expertise, because experts develop better and more comprehensive sets of rules with a wider range of stored patterns (based on experience) to use in selecting the appropriate rule. This process of acquiring a larger repertoire of more robust rules also increases the possible range of activities. In the end, the only way many activities can be carried out at all is by the use of rule-based performance. One aspect of expertise lies in reducing the need to resort to deliberative cognitive processing by having rules for almost all circumstances – it is this that permits doctors (and other experts) to cope with heavy workloads in reasonable time.

Rule-based cognitive processing seldom takes place in a pure way, isolated from skill-based and deliberative processes. Rules are usually developed by the passive mechanisms associated with experience, but they may be improved, added to and even generated by deliberative processes. Thus, at one end of the scale, deliberative reasoning may be used to varying degrees to develop rules and to select, check and support the application of the best rule, and at the other, rules may be applied 'on the fly' to direct and control skill-based activities. In the former case, deliberative processing may go wrong because the rule selected in this way is a flawed rule, while in the latter case, one possible manifestation of a lapse is the failure to apply a rule at the right time. A moment's distraction, for example, might lead the normally careful practitioner to omit one step of his usual examination without realising it, and as a result he might miss information that he would normally elicit (neck stiffness in meningitis, for example).

Knowledge-based errors – errors of deliberation

In deliberative cognitive processing progress is tentative and controlled by feedback from the results of each action, iteratively, on the basis of trial and error. This is in contrast to rule-based reasoning, in which (as we have seen) control is feed-forward and goals can be achieved fairly assuredly on the basis of applying a rule known from past experience to be correct.

Many rules used in everyday life concern exceptions that simply don't make sense from a logical perspective. Much of the physical world is relatively resistant to logic, or to the process of arguing from first principles to a conclusion which ought to be right. To a large extent this reflects limitations on the information that is available to any individual at any particular time. This is the concept of bounded rationality, discussed in chapter 2. Typically, the information available for solving a problem is incomplete, the facts to hand may not be the most useful, and some may not even be correct. The deficiencies may lie in the knowledge stored in the memory or in the knowledge available from the events and circumstances of the situation. The analogy of a blackboard full of facts but only partly illuminated was used in chapter 2 to illustrate this idea. It is because of the importance of deficiencies in knowledge in the generation of errors during active, deliberative reasoning that the term 'knowledge-based errors' has been applied to them, but in fact problems with the 'knowledge-base' are just as likely to contribute to a rule-based error. In this way, a person whose perception of a situation is inadequately informed is equally likely to apply a rule (which will probably be the wrong rule), as resort to deliberative reasoning to reach a solution (which is also likely to be the wrong solution in the circumstances). Thus an incorrect internal representation of a situation may be as important in the generation of a rule-based error as in the generation of a knowledge-based error. The key feature of knowledge-based errors as described by Reason, following Rasmussen, is the slow, deliberative, feedback nature of the processing involved. This type of reasoning is a powerful but slow process by which even extremely difficult problems can be solved, but only if there is adequate time, and only if a trial-and-error approach can be tolerated. The process involves formulating an idea, testing it, finding it to be imperfect (or in error), modifying the idea, re-testing it and so on. Because it is an *error-driven* process, it follows that deliberative reasoning will inevitably be prone to error, especially at an early stage in the iterative process of working towards a satisfactory solution to a problem, and particularly in unfamiliar circumstances. The implications of this for the management of a crisis are very important, and will be considered below.

Scientists have recognised the difficulties of finding correct answers to problems on the basis of theoretical reasoning alone. They have developed the process known as 'scientific method' to allow for the inconvenient intrusions of what *does* happen into what *ought to* happen. Scientific method is a highly developed and formalised example of deliberative (or knowledge-based) reasoning, illustrating particularly well the feedback nature of this type of cognitive processing. This method involves stating a hypothesis derived from logical interpretation of the observed facts which form the knowledge-base at that point in time, and then testing it by experimentation. The feedback from these experiments either supports the hypothesis or adds new information to the knowledge-base which allows the hypothesis to be refined and then tested again. This process produces an increasingly useful hypothesis, but few hypotheses explain all the observed data in all situations, and so, as new facts continue to emerge, the process of iterative refinement continues to be needed. In this way science has developed from Newton's observation of a falling apple to modern theories of nuclear physics.

In the same way, but less formally, a decision or plan formulated in daily life by effortful reasoning from known facts and principles will be tested against the results of its implementation, and then refined and tested again. One of the results of such activity is an increase in an individual's store of rules. Iterative deliberation adds knowledge that we can formulate into schemata or heuristics, to which we can return in the future without the need to repeat the processes by which they were derived.

Much has been made in recent times about improving the quality of decision making in medicine by applying Bayesian principles in a formal way.[11] This usually involves subjective assessments in relation to the importance placed on various possibilities. How does one quantify the difference between losing a limb and losing one's life, for example? Applying decision theory might involve allocating ten points to the former and a hundred to the latter, and then multiplying each by the probability of its occurrence, assuming one or other of two different methods of treatment is used. In this way an attempt is made to be systematic in decision making. Decision theory is not used very widely in medicine and this may simply reflect the fact that humans prefer to work by rule-based pattern matching rather than by effortful deliberation – in effect people are not naturally Bayesian in their decision making. Another difficulty relates to knowing how far it is valid to apply the results of studies of groups of patients to the management of particular individuals who may or may not have much in common with the sample studied. There may well be a place for such techniques, but very often the information concerning the chances of an event occurring is inadequate to make this approach meaningful, and in reality these methods often rely on much that remains subjective.

Knowledge failures

In the previous section we have seen that deliberative errors are often attributable to problems in the so-called knowledge-base. Intuitively the term 'knowledge-based error' suggests failures in the knowledge stored in the memory. Many errors in medicine are of this type. The doctor simply doesn't know some fact relevant to the problem. However, not all errors generated by a doctor's ignorance are deliberative – many will involve applying a poor rule (perhaps an incorrectly learned rule) or a rule inappropriate to the situation. For example, giving the wrong dose of a drug may involve what Reason would call a knowledge-based error if the mistake lay in an effortful part of the process, such as the calculation of the dose, or a rule-based error if it simply reflected the fact that the doctor had learned the wrong dose in the first place (a poor rule). Furthermore,

---

[11] D. L. Sackett, W. S. Richardson, W. Rosenberg and R. B. Haynes, *Evidence Based Medicine* (New York, Churchill Livingstone, 1997), 99–104.

both knowledge-based and rule-based errors are just as typically generated on the basis of inadequacies in knowledge derived from the world as in knowledge stored in the mind – an example of this would be if a patient's weight was incorrectly recorded in the notes and formed the basis of the incorrect dosage calculation. We think this problem is best resolved by recognising that problems in the knowledge-base are not the key distinguishing factor in the classification of error types. The term *deliberative* is more descriptive of errors associated with so-called knowledge-based reasoning, and we think it is preferable to refer explicitly to failures or inadequacies in the individual's knowledge or to the fault in the information available in the world as the factor underlying the error, and to define the particular type of error as a separate exercise.

Errors of judgement

When things go wrong in medicine it is quite common for a mistake to be called an error of judgement. In order to exercise judgement, it is necessary to think about a problem, so errors of judgement are clearly a subset of deliberative errors. If one is simply applying a rule automatically or responding at a skill-based level, then no judgement is involved.

In the most common scenario, the term is used when the decision in question might have produced its desired goal, but didn't. However, outcome is a poor guide to the quality of a decision. A perfectly rational decision on the basis of the facts known at the time may not prove to be the correct one in terms of the result. The question should be, could the person reasonably have been expected to have made a better decision? If, when asked to choose between heads and tails on the toss of a coin, one chooses heads, it can hardly be called an error simply because tails comes up. Many decisions in medicine are essentially of this type, in that they contain an element of uncertainty and that their outcome is to some degree unknowable. The phrase 'error of judgement' has much currency in common parlance and is often used normatively to suggest that an individual's judgement tends to reflect a level of willingness to take risks different from those thought appropriate by the commentator.

Given our definition of the term 'error', a decision should be called an error only if it can be shown to have been unsound, perhaps because of a fault in logic or because of a deficiency in the information available to the individual making the decision. In an error of judgement the decision is tested against normative rather than objective standards. If the decision was objectively faulty, there would be no distinction from any other deliberative error. Somewhat circularly, an error of judgement is designated an error primarily because it is *judged* to be an error by those who believe they would have done something different. Typically, it may be felt that, although either of two choices was sustainable, the vast majority of practitioners would have chosen the alternative. The *Bolam* principle (to which we shall return in chapter 6) allows for differences in opinion between doctors, but (as we shall see) more recent decisions by the courts in Australia and the United Kingdom have set limits to the principle that it is a sufficient defence to have the support of a body of medical opinion (regardless of the size of that body). The courts have asserted their right to determine, not what *would* have been done by a reasonable practitioner (or even the majority of reasonable practitioners), but what *should* have been done. In other words, decisions taken by medical practitioners have been judged to be wrong even though they have had the support of other doctors. Thus, in *Rogers* v. *Whittaker* (a case involving an ophthalmologist and informed consent), for example, in awarding damages against the doctor, the court could be said to have concluded that he had made an error of judgement in failing to inform the patient of a material risk.[12] The point that defines the doctor's decision over what to tell the patient as faulty is that it was faulty in the court's judgement; the point that defines it as an error is that the doctor believed it to be a sustainable decision at the time it was made (that is, the doctor thought that his practice in this matter was right, or at least reasonable – the decision was not a deliberate violation); the point that defines the error as an error of judgement rather than a standard deliberative error is the fact that the doctor's decision does seem to have had a sustainable basis at the time it was made[13] – so much so that its faultiness remains a matter of debate, and there are still those who think that it was the court that made the error of judgement. In fact, it may be very difficult to distinguish between a matter which is no more than a difference of opinion and one that can justifiably be called an error of judgement. For this reason it is relatively

---

[12] [1957] 2 All ER 118; the *Bolam* principle is discussed in more detail in chapter 6.

[13] Given that the *Bolam* principle was accepted at the time, and that the level of information provided was supported by other ophthalmologists, the sustainability of the decision when it was made seems hard to dispute, even if one holds a different opinion about informed consent.

unusual for a true error of judgement to create major legal difficulties for a medical practitioner, but (as in *Rogers* v. *Whittaker*) not unknown.

The exercise of judgement plays an important role in medicine. Soundness of judgement is one of the attributes by which peers are evaluated. Comments intended to reflect on an individual's overall exercise of judgement should do so explicitly. In the evaluation of judgement on an individual event, it is essential that the decision is considered on the basis of the facts available at the time. As we shall see in chapters 6 and 7, there is a high risk that such judgement will be influenced by outcome bias.

Variations, gradations, overlaps

We have described the different types of error in such a way as to emphasise the distinguishing features and the underlying cognitive processes involved. However, the external features of an event may reveal little about the underlying mechanisms of an error, and differentiation between classes of error may be made more difficult by the way in which humans switch from one type of processing to another, conducting several activities at the same time.[14] Thus the classification of an error may depend on the honesty of the account of his or her mental processes given by the person concerned.

Consider Perrow's ship's captain, whose disastrous collision with another ship is outlined in chapter 2. What type of error was involved in this accident? It is tempting to suggest a lapse, but in fact the evidence suggests that he was not distracted and actually had his mind focused on the task in hand and was thinking about his actions quite carefully. The fundamental problem was a flawed mental representation of events. This was precipitated by a failure in the information on which he was basing his analysis of the situation (the incorrect perception that there were only two lights instead of three). The final decision was the result of effortful deliberative thinking, operating from first principles. As with most experts, even this deliberative reasoning would have involved the use of pattern recognition and rule-based responses; it would have been a synthesis of the two cognitive processes. Thus the captain recognised the significance of the lights (rule-based) but with the wrong visual information (seeing two when there were actually three); he analysed the data

---

[14] See chapter 2.

on the radar screen (deliberation), with correct logic but faulty information, the faultiness being reinforced by confirmation bias. Finally, he made a wrong decision and turned, possibly on the basis of a deliberative analysis but equally likely by applying a rule at a more subconscious level – a rule that would have worked adequately had the real world corresponded with his 'internal map' of things.

Obviously any *post hoc* analysis of this type must contain some judgements and be to some degree a matter of opinion. As with any attempt to classify and name phenomena, distinctions are difficult at the margins. This does not matter. Perrow's example illustrates perfectly how behaviour which, on the face of things, is inexplicable and apparently seriously negligent, may start to look very understandable given an appropriate framework for the analysis. For the purposes of assessing blame it is not the precise category of error that matters, and considerable overlap may occur. The important thing is an appreciation of the mental processes involved and an understanding of the ways in which well-intentioned, competent and sober professionals can sometimes do astonishingly inadvisable things.

If we look at a medical example, it can be seen, then, that the administration of a wrong drug could be the result of a deliberate and careless failure to look at the label – which would be a violation (see chapter 4). More commonly, however, it would be due to a skill-based error – a slip or a lapse. However, the same event may equally well represent a failure to understand the properties of the drug. In this case it would be a rule-based error if little active thought had gone into the decision and the mistake simply reflected the lack of the right rule in the doctor's armamentarium. On the other hand, it would have been a deliberative error if the doctor had actively attempted to work out the best choice from a range of possibilities, taking account of the patient's medical condition and his knowledge of pharmacology, but had come to the wrong conclusion either because of flawed reasoning or because of inadequate or incorrect (including incorrectly perceived or remembered) information. In both rule-based and deliberative errors the failure may arise from a deficit in the doctor's knowledge, but the cognitive processing involved is different. Thus events which are superficially identical, contextually may represent quite different error types on closer analysis of the underlying cognitive processes. It is important not to attribute an event to the most culpable option available without a proper consideration of the alternatives.

Crises and the 'catch-22' of human monitoring

We have seen that deliberative cognitive processing is effortful, time-consuming, unpredictable in its results and error-driven by feedback of the information that may be derived from the results of iterative decisions. This is in contrast to rule-based processing, which is fast, relatively predictable and controlled (or driven) by feed-forward considerations – that is, by the objective in mind. The typical occasion on which a doctor is required to abandon rule-based processing and resort to deliberation is in a crisis – when the store of applicable rules has run out; this is also the very situation in which deliberative processing is least likely to be successful.

The problem of bounded rationality or keyhole vision of the problem space is also at its most serious in a crisis. In a routine situation, a great deal can sometimes be done to improve the quality of deliberative decision making by the allocation of adequate time to the task, by the use of a pen and paper to write down the information in such a way that it can be reviewed, by reference to textbooks which contain the required information, and so on. Co-operation in the form of consultation with a colleague may be a powerful tool for improving performance, particularly for inexperienced practitioners. However, in a crisis, time is limited and decisions must be made without the benefit of this type of support.

Every doctor will eventually meet a case with features not typical of his or her pre-stored patterns. In these circumstances, taking a gamble that a rule will work which has been satisfactory in a more or less similar and relatively frequently occurring condition is very dangerous. Given time, a better response would be to resort to deliberation and consultation. In a crisis, however, the choices are often stark. An anaesthetist facing a hypoxic patient may have only two or three minutes to prevent irreversible brain damage. Very often the most attractive option (if not the only option) is to resort to frequency-gambling. In the case of an expert, this will often work, but problems arise when decisions, taken under intense pressure to act, lead to bad outcomes and are subjected to unsophisticated analysis with the benefit of hindsight.

In some areas of medicine, notably anaesthesia, and also in many areas of industry (including aviation and the nuclear industry), people may be required to monitor relatively stable situations in anticipation of the rare occasion in which a crisis might develop. Reason has referred to this as 'the catch-22 of human supervisory control'.[15] Machines are, in general, better at monitoring routine data, such as blood pressures and pulse rates, than humans are. Modern alarms are very reliable, but one valid function of the human is to back up the monitors in case they fail; thus an anaesthetist may check a suspect pulse rate on an automatic monitor by feeling for the patient's radial or temporal pulse. The main reason for retaining a human in the system, however, is for his or her ability to do what machines cannot do: that is, to identify, analyse and cope with the unexpected – in other words, to manage a crisis should it occur.

The catch-22 lies in the fact that endless hours of watching normal blood pressure provide little chance to develop experience in handling an emergency. The safer the system, the more infrequent the crises, the less chance for experience in handling problems. In addition to this, the fear and emotional stress associated with a crisis often inhibit calm and rational thought.

Add to that the fact that humans are not good at prolonged monitoring, suffer tedium poorly, and have a tendency to see what they expect to see, and you have a situation tailor-made for disaster. It is asking a great deal to expect a human being to stay alert for extended periods, notice the earliest signs of something going wrong, evaluate them correctly, and then remain calm, skilled and effective while treating a life-threatening problem seldom if ever seen before, often without the benefit of help, and at times when he or she is significantly fatigued. Given the feedback, error-driven nature of deliberative cognitive processing, it is a testimony to the quality of human performance that professionals handle crises successfully as often as they do.

When we are evaluating the moral culpability of apparent failures to do the right thing in an emergency (such as in the case involving Dr Hugel, described in chapter 1), it is essential to take into account the available alternatives (or lack of alternatives), the time frame in which decisions had to be made, and the limitations of the cognitive processes involved.

---

[15] Reason, *Human Error*, 182–3.

The egregious error

Should errors ever be considered morally culpable? Given that our strict definition precludes any deliberate element to an error, it might seem that the answer should be 'no'. Consider, however, the doctor who has been lazy throughout his or her training and has thereby failed to acquire the knowledge and skill that could reasonably be required of a medical practitioner. Such a doctor might make an error (by our definition) which quite clearly ought to be avoidable. Thus, failing to check for neck stiffness in a case of possible meningitis through a lack of awareness that this examination is mandatory in the presence of certain signs and symptoms would be unacceptable, even if it was technically an error – although the same failure by a generally competent practitioner on account of a lapse might, under some circumstances, have quite different connotations. We shall see in the next chapter that the antecedent failure in application to training would be a recognisable violation, and it seems straightforward that culpability should apply in such circumstances.

What if the underlying problem were not laziness but simple inability on the part of the individual concerned? Perhaps the doctor in question is congenitally incapable of the cognitive or motor skills required of his or her particular speciality. This might well apply in a case involving technically difficult surgery. Alternatively, age or illness might lead to an impairment in performance, perhaps without any appreciation on the part of the doctor that this has occurred. The test, as we shall see in chapters 6 and 7, is an objective one. If such a person falls below the standard of the reasonable practitioner, then liability may apply, appropriately, even if the failure is subjectively a genuine error. It is quite possible, however, that the true responsibility relates less to the individual and more to those responsible for poor training, or for a failure of the examination system and other mechanisms for screening incompetent doctors before they reach a position to cause harm.

The key lies in the application of the test of what is reasonable, and in chapter 7 we shall discuss the importance of recognising that the reasonable person is human. There is a difference between a single slip or lapse in an otherwise competent practice and a repeated failure to achieve a required standard. Similarly, there is a difference between a genuine mistake generated by a misunderstanding, or by a failure to appreciate subtle nuances of a situation, and one generated by a lack of knowledge so basic that the vast majority of doctors would view the information as fundamental. Thus errors may constitute negligence, and if the departure from the expected standard is major, they may constitute gross negligence. Analysis along the lines proposed in this and the next chapter is not in any way aimed at exonerating all human failures; it is simply intended to bring a greater sophistication to the process of ensuring that blame *is* attributed where it is deserved, but *only* where it is deserved.

Error, safety and blame

Modern authorities on the psychology of human behaviour are virtually unanimous in saying that certain types of error are inevitable in any human endeavour and in the technological systems devised by people. This is not the same thing as saying that error should be tolerated. Every effort should be made to reduce the occurrence of error to the lowest level possible. The prevailing failure in medicine (and other activities) to appreciate the need to engineer systems (in the widest sense) to facilitate human function and compensate for its weaknesses is no doubt one reason for the number of preventable adverse events which occur every day. There are exceptions, but in part this is the result of an attitude of denial of the limitations of human cognitive performance and of a culture which too readily asserts that the solution lies in employing the right type of individuals and getting rid of the others. Attitudes of this sort prevail not only in medicine but in many organisations.

Further progress towards greater safety in medicine (and other activities) will be greatly facilitated by a better understanding of the ways in which human cognitive processes can fail. The law has an important role to play in this. It is basically counter-productive to respond in a harsh and ill-informed way to the inevitable failures of well-motivated, well-trained and competent individuals who have been required to deal with situations of enormous difficulty in which there has been little time for response. Investigative approaches which delve beyond the 'smoking gun' into the antecedent and underlying causes of adverse events make better sense in the promotion of safer practice. Appropriate legal signals may provide pressures for organisational change and promote a culture of safety.

When accidents result in harm or the loss of life, it is understandable that there will be blame. Individuals who have contributed to any such accident must expect to be called to account for their role in its generation. However, the degree to which such a person may be considered morally culpable will vary greatly depending on the circumstances involved. An appreciation of the processes which underlie human errors and contribute to many modern-day disasters is essential to any meaningful analysis of blame.

4

Violations

It is not only error that contributes to the failure of human endeavour. People drink, drive and wreak havoc on the road. Substandard structures are erected, and collapse, with loss of lives. Doctors in intensive care units fail to wash their hands between patients, and contribute to the problem of cross-infection. There are many situations like these in which harm flows from an action which, in contrast to an error, is quite deliberate in its conceptualisation and execution, even though no harm was intended. We have said that errors are entirely involuntary. The moral implications of an injury are quite different if some element of choice by the actor was involved in the actions which led to its causation. A mistake (mistakes being that subset of errors in which the flaw lies in the decision or plan) is defined as an *error* precisely because the actor believes that the action is an appropriate way of achieving an objective safely. He or she is acting in good faith, trying to do the best possible thing, but failing. A decision or plan can no longer be considered a mistake (or any other kind of error under the definition in chapter 3) if the person concerned *knows* that there is a more acceptable alternative, or an alternative more likely to achieve the given objective safely, and yet *deliberately chooses* the less satisfactory alternative. This element of choice in relation to the action (but not in relation to the outcome) defines an action which falls short of some identifiable standard as a violation rather than an error.

Distinguishing violations from errors – definition of a violation

Reason defines violations as meaning 'deliberate – but not necessarily reprehensible – deviations from those practices deemed necessary (by designers, managers and regulatory agencies) to maintain the safe operation of a potentially hazardous system'.[1] Elsewhere he defines the term more simply as 'deviations from safe operating procedures, standards or rules'.[2] This second definition would permit the inclusion of some errors into the category of violation, and in fact Reason makes the point that '[t]he boundaries between errors and violations are by no means hard and fast, either conceptually or within a particular accident sequence'.[3] We have acknowledged the possibility of an egregious error, but even in these the culpability usually lies not so much in the error itself as in some antecedent factor which made the error more likely. In order to be able to discuss an action or decision in the context of blame, we need to be able to identify the degree to which its generation has included the element of choice. Therefore we do need to be able to distinguish clearly between errors and violations. There seems to be little value in introducing an additional term to cover the overlapping category that consists of errors which unintentionally break rules, although such actions clearly exist.

In this book we are concerned with the underlying cognitive processes that have led to particular actions. Reason's first definition is cognitively based, the second contextually based. In chapter 2 we made the point that a given action described contextually, on the basis of its external features, may represent any of the different error types, or may be a violation. Distinguishing a lapse from a rule-based error or a deliberative error depends on knowing the cognitive processes involved. Exactly the same applies here. There is both theoretical and empirical evidence that errors and violations are mediated by different cognitive processes. Even the demographic profile of the individuals concerned may be different – violations decline with age, while errors do not, and violations are more common in men than women at all ages.[4] The key cognitive factor distinguishing errors from violations is the element of choice.

The emphasis in Reason's definitions of violation is on the breach of rules related to safety. Our conception of violations is broader than that and also embraces breaches of rules or established procedures which have nothing to do with safety. We suggest, furthermore, that the concept of violation should be broad enough to include acts which knowingly

---

[1] J. Reason, *Human Error* (New York, Cambridge University Press, 1990), 195.
[2] J. Reason, *Managing the Risks of Organizational Accidents* (Aldershot, Ashgate, 1997), 72.
[3] Reason, *Human Error*, 195.
[4] Ibid., 197.

jeopardise the achievement of a goal which the act is intended to achieve. So, for example, where a manufacturer sets out a correct method for the successful use of a product and where these instructions are deliberately ignored, any failure of the product must be said to be due to a violation of appropriate use. Similarly, inadequate preparation of a wall before painting would probably result in failure to achieve the objective of a satisfactory and long-lasting surface covering. If this lack of preparation was deliberate, but undertaken in the hope that the result would still be acceptable, it would be a violation. In the same way, parking in a tow-away zone is a violation, which, while not necessarily hazardous, may jeopardise the objective of finding the car at the same place after an undisturbed period of parking. In this example, however, the violation may also interfere with the functioning of the complex system of traffic flow, which was probably the reason for the regulation. Thus the violation may jeopardise the integrity of a system of rules, the principles of safety, the objectives of an undertaking or the ongoing function of a system or organisation. We are prepared to take as granted that all systems and all things are potentially hazardous.

In general, violations are defined in relation to established rules. The existence of the rule makes the violation clear. In terms of our broadened conception of violation, however, it is not essential that the rule be formalised in writing or in any other way for an action to be categorised as a violation rather than an error. It is enough that some identifiable principle has been knowingly breached. This principle may take the form of a broad legal proposition – for example, that one should not act in such a way as to cause foreseeable damage to others – or it may take the form of a rule which follows from scientific fact. Take the case of riding a motor cycle without a safety helmet. In some countries this will be a violation of a specific law requiring that such headgear be worn. In other countries there may be no such legal rule. Nevertheless, it is an accepted fact that head injuries are a common consequence of riding motor cycles, and that helmets provide worthwhile protection against them. If, therefore, one wishes to avoid a head injury then one should not violate the obvious requirement to wear protective headgear. If, as a consequence of not wearing a helmet, a person suffers a serious head injury, it is only reasonable to attribute this to a violation, not an error.

There are a number of common-sense rules that must be observed if one is to survive unharmed and without harming others. The violation of one of these common-sense rules is enough to define an unsafe act as a violation rather than an error. The importance of this distinction lies in the fact that errors, being entirely involuntary, should not be a matter of moral culpability, although antecedent actions which predispose to errors (such as drinking before driving) might well be culpable. A key point about violations is that they tend to make errors more likely and more dangerous when they do occur. This is usually the reason for the rule in the first place. Thus excessive speed on the road increases the chance of an error and makes the consequence of any error much more serious. Violations, in contrast to errors, are a matter of choice. It is therefore quite appropriate to hold the violator morally responsible for the consequences of his or her violation.

Indeed, Reason makes the following point about violations: 'violations can only be described with regard to a social context in which behaviour is governed by operating procedures, codes of practice, rules and the like'.[5] We have extended the definition of violations to include situations where the rule which has been broken may be simply a matter of common sense, but even then the concept of violation implies some form of moral assessment, and therefore some social context. Violations and blame are linked concepts. However, the degree of culpability attached to any given violation varies, as we shall discuss in some detail below.

For our purposes, therefore, we offer the following definition, modified from that of Reason:

A violation is a deliberate – but not necessarily reprehensible – deviation from those practices appreciated by the individual as being required by regulation, or necessary or advisable to achieve an appropriate objective while maintaining the safety of people and equipment and the ongoing operation of a device or system.

Recklessness and violations

The fact that a course of action constitutes a violation does not necessarily mean that it amounts to recklessness. Recklessness is a term which carries a considerable measure of moral opprobrium. To describe an action as reckless is usually (if not inevitably) to censure the actor. Many acts will involve a risk to others, but this risk may be thought to be justifiable on

[5] Ibid., 195

the grounds of social benefit derived from the conduct in question. If the risk is outweighed by the social value of the conduct, the action will not be reckless, nor will it usually be a violation.

Recklessness implies knowing that an action or omission will involve an unacceptable level of risk to someone or something, and deciding nevertheless to take that risk. Violations involve a decision to do something in the knowledge that the given action or decision will place at risk some aspect of safety or of the system. However, some violations constitute recklessness, while others do not. Few people would describe it as reckless to exceed the speed limit by 1 mile per hour, although it would be a violation. Most would say that exceeding it by 50 miles per hour would be seriously reckless. Defining the point at which an action may be called reckless comes down to a matter of judgement as to the acceptability or otherwise of the level of risk involved, and needs to take account of all the circumstances of the particular instance.

Distinction between violations and skill-based errors

Because violations always involve a decision, they most closely resemble mistakes. However, a violation could very easily masquerade as a lapse if the decision involved the omission of an important step in a procedure. For example, the failure to check an anaesthetic machine could be a lapse, but equally it could be a violation. These two categories of unsafe act are quite distinct, and the difference is very important. We have seen in chapter 2 that a lapse is something to which all human beings are liable at some time, on account of the phenomenon of attentional capture. People do not choose to have lapses – they can occur even when every effort is being made to avoid them. On the other hand, a violation involves an active choice. Violations are therefore, to a greater or lesser extent, avoidable, and this raises very different moral questions, to which we shall return in the next chapter.

One clue to distinguishing between the two is the track record of the individual concerned, if this is available. If a person is known to be a meticulous checker of anaesthetic machines, then the chances are that a single failure in this process would be a lapse. The other features which would support the diagnosis of a lapse would be the presence of some unusual distraction – the fact that a colleague had interrupted the preparatory process just before the point at which the check would normally have been undertaken, for example. Even more convincing would be a sudden crisis at the critical moment – for example the sudden onset of a seizure in a patient about to be anaesthetised might lead the anaesthetist justifiably to omit the check, and subsequently forget to perform it later.

The picture of the typical violation will become clearer as we describe the different types of violation below, but the majority of violations tend to be habitual. Unfortunately, there may be atypical examples of both lapses and violations, and in many cases making the distinction may depend on the honesty of the individual concerned.

Actions – correct or appropriate?

We have discussed the concept of the 'happy accident' in chapter 3, and seen that it is even possible for an error to be life-saving. In the same way, an action that is clearly a violation may have very satisfactory consequences. Reason discusses this issue, and introduces the idea of *correct* violations.[6] This approach allows us to distinguish actions or decisions on the basis of their outcome and is intuitively obvious. If we bet on a horse and it wins, we have backed the right or correct horse. Similarly, if we buy a raffle ticket, and win the prize, we have been fortunate enough to buy the correct ticket – and so on. If someone drives home at excessive speed while under the influence of alcohol, he may succeed in his objective, and indeed may get home sooner than his companion who chooses to take a taxi in the same circumstances. He might well argue that he made the right (or correct) decision. From the perspective of result on that occasion, his action was successful.

The *appropriateness* of the action is a different matter. There may be circumstances in which all reasonable choices constitute violations. For example, in certain fields of medicine, notably anaesthesia and surgery, it is often necessary to act quickly and decisively, and a failure to do anything may be the most certain route to disaster. It is possible to encounter a situation of this type which involves choosing among several courses of action, none of which is safe. It may be that all available options are violations; there may be no choice by which an important goal can be achieved safely and within the rules. The tendency in such

[6] Reason, *Managing the Risks of Organizational Accidents*, 75.

circumstances is to praise a decision if it proves successful and to call it 'an error of judgement' if not. As we emphasised in chapter 3, in the context of errors, the result of a decision or action does not necessarily justify any firm conclusions about either the quality or the moral implications of the decision or action concerned.

If an individual in such circumstances makes a justifiable decision in good faith which, although it breaks a rule, is a decision which at least some other appropriately qualified individual would have made in the circumstances, then the best way of classifying the action is to call it an *appropriate violation*. For the purposes of evaluating the quality of the decision, the concept of appropriateness is much more useful than the concept of correctness. Another way of looking at this is to ask whether a different person in the same circumstances, and with events unfolding in the same way, would have been likely to behave any differently, assuming that this hypothetical person came from the same general field of activity and had similar experience, abilities and qualifications. This is the basis of the Johnston 'substitution test'. If the answer is not in the affirmative, then, according to Johnston, there can be no justification for apportioning blame to the individual concerned, and indeed to do so simply creates a risk that any underlying contributory or systemic factors will be obscured.[7]

Obviously the individual may need to face the regulatory or legal consequences of any rules which have been broken; in law the defence of *necessity* may well be available (see p. 105 below). There are very strong arguments for other relevant authorities to take all circumstances into account in evaluating such situations, but of course there is no guarantee that they will exonerate an individual simply because he or she has acted in good faith. As we shall discuss in chapters 5 and 6, the factor most likely to influence the result of any investigation or trial that ensues from an unfortunate accident is the outcome of the course of action pursued. Success is its own justification; failure needs a great deal of explanation.

The appropriate violation may turn out to be an error. If logical arguments or empirical evidence can subsequently be advanced to demonstrate that a better decision was possible at the time, without the benefit of hindsight, then the judgement was an error. In this case the cause of the error would lie with the inadequacy of the knowledge-base or reasoning of the individual at the time of the action, and we would be

---

[7] Johnston, quoted in ibid., 208.

dealing with a deliberative error. If the criticism of the decision was based on normative rather than objective criteria, then this would be called an error of judgement. If no logical, empirical or normative evidence can subsequently be advanced to demonstrate that a better decision was possible, then the judgement was sound, not an error, and the violation was appropriate whatever the outcome.

There are other situations in which an individual may elect in good faith to violate a rule. Many rules are poorly conceived or have lost their rationale and become outmoded. One position is that any violation of a rule is wrong because organisations and complex systems need rules and it cannot be left for an individual to pick and choose between those which need to be observed and those which can be ignored. In this view, such laxity would import a dangerous subjectivity and would compromise the efficiency and indeed the safety of the organisation. Such an argument is at its strongest when applied to the law of the land in a democratic society. In general, it is not possible to justify the selective observance of the law in this context. If a law is thought to be wrong, then procedures exist in most countries to seek its repeal or reform. An expectation of technical adherence to the letter of the law is therefore justified. In exceptional circumstances, such as those discussed above, the law recognises that an overriding principle may justify violating a legal rule. The defence of *necessity* is based on this premise. This defence may allow a person to break the law in the interests of protecting human life or limb from an otherwise unavoidable threat.

In the context of bureaucratic organisations the reality is often different. Again, this has been recognised by Reason. In such organisations there is often a tendency for the promulgation of excessive numbers of rules, and frequently these are simply added to existing ones rather than substituted for those which have become obsolete. This process may be well intentioned, but it may also be motivated by a perception that such rules provide protection for senior management or directors, who may be held liable in the event of an accident. Reason makes the point that continuously adding to the number of safety regulations tends to reduce the scope of action permissible for performing the required tasks successfully. Thus, ironically, a situation may eventually be created by the very process of regulation in which violations become necessary, either routinely or in exceptional circumstances when operational conditions make this unavoidable.

The important thing is not just the existence of a rule; it is also necessary that the rule be generally accepted as well founded, and also that it should apply in the circumstances of the particular case. It is thus quite possible for a poor rule to be violated appropriately in a technical sense in the interests of safety, or in order to reduce the risk of an adverse outcome. Reason has gone so far as to say: 'The important issue in many hazardous technologies is not *whether* to violate, but *when* to violate – or perhaps, more importantly, when to comply.'[8]

Categories of violation

As with error, some classification of violations is possible. The primary division is between routine and exceptional violations.

Routine violations typically involve the cutting of corners in everyday tasks. They reflect the natural human tendency to take the path of least effort, and are made more likely by designs or procedural requirements which are perceived as unnecessarily cumbersome or restrictive. This is graphically illustrated by an example from landscape architecture. If a path takes a longer route around a lawn rather than simply going straight across it, perhaps for aesthetic rather than utilitarian reasons, there is a high probability that pedestrians will choose to take a short cut across the grass rather than follow the pathway around the perimeter. If a procedure is perceived as unreasonably arduous, there is a good chance that people will find ways to shorten it or to leave it out altogether. The literature is replete with evidence that health professionals routinely flaunt the rules in respect to handwashing between patient contacts, in intensive care units and other situations where cross-infection is a known risk.[9] Another example of a violation of this general sort is to be found in anaesthesia. The anaesthetic machine should be checked before every anaesthetic to ensure that it is properly assembled and safe to use. Several protocols are available for this, notably one promulgated by the Australian and New Zealand College of Anaesthetists, which has been revised twice. This protocol was originally too long, and it took an anaesthetist several minutes to work through all

---

[8] Ibid., 51.

[9] D. Pittet, P. Mourouga and T. V. Perneger (and the members of the Infection Control Program), 'Compliance with handwashing in a teaching hospital' (1999) 130 *Annals of Internal Medicine* 126–30; N. El. Mikatti, P. Dillon, and T. E. Healy, 'Hygienic practices of consultant anaesthetists: a survey in the North-West region of the UK' (1999) 54 *Anaesthesia* 13–18.

the prescribed steps. Doing the full check before every case might add nearly an hour to the time needed to anaesthetise a list of seven or eight patients. The protocol was often shortened by individual anaesthetists to a greater or lesser degree. Sometimes this was done in a well-thought-out way which retained the most important steps; sometimes it was done more sporadically and on occasion the check was omitted altogether. The likelihood of a prescribed task of this sort being omitted is increased if the individual's workload is high, inadequate time is available for the completion of the task and the organisational culture values productivity and efficiency more than safety. Often the violation results in only a slight reduction in the margin of safety associated with a particular procedure or situation, and an adverse result is indeed quite unlikely. This is true in the case of the anaesthetic machine check, for example. It is common for the individual concerned to believe that the violation is actually a good thing, on grounds of economy or efficiency. The individual may believe that the organisation could not continue functioning if the proper procedures were followed, and it may be true that the organisation would at least face increased costs on account of conscientious and scrupulous compliance.[10] The latest version of the protocol is vastly improved and differentiates between three levels of checking, depending on whether the machine has just been commissioned or serviced (very detailed), is to be used for the first time at the beginning of a session (reasonably detailed) or is to be used for subsequent cases on the same list (brief, and focused on essential points).[11] Thus practices that would have been construed as violations under older versions have now been endorsed as appropriate in the revised document.

A good non-medical example of a violation (or violations) which reflected a genuine effort to make a system function in the absence of adequate resources concerns the tragedy that occurred at Cave Creek in New Zealand. The construction of a viewing platform above a cliff was carried out with limited resources and almost entirely by volunteers. Little if any supervision was provided, council approval for the plans was not

---

[10] To a degree this is borne out by the notion of 'work to rule' as a means of industrial action.

[11] 'Protocol for checking the anaesthetic machine. Policy document review PS31' (Melbourne, Australian and New Zealand College of Anaesthetists, 1997). This document was originally promulgated in 1984, with revisions in 1990 and 1996. See also 'Checklist for anaesthetic apparatus and checklist for anaesthetic apparatus 2' (London, Association of Anaesthetists of Great Britain and Ireland, 1997).

obtained and no inspections were conducted (all obvious violations of good building practices). A procedural violation involved the use of nails instead of nuts and bolts in certain critical positions. After some years of apparently satisfactory function, the structure suddenly collapsed under the weight of a number of students on a field trip, with considerable loss of life. The actions which led to the construction faults precipitating this disaster were entirely well motivated. It would have been believed, perhaps correctly, that only by means of such voluntary work could platforms (and many other necessary structures) be erected at all. Clearly, the most fundamental violation was committed on behalf of the government department involved, in permitting the unsupervised construction of a structure whose potential dangerousness was foreseeable. Even this was probably quite well motivated. It might have been thought fundamentally unhelpful to place excessive restrictions on voluntary activities of this type.

There are many other examples of routine violations in medical practice. These include: providing patients with less information than certain regulatory bodies have prescribed for the purpose of obtaining informed consent; failing to check results of clinical investigations (such as blood tests) in a timely manner; eating and drinking within areas in which food is prohibited, such as intensive care rooms and operating rooms; wearing jewellery in the operating room; taking medical histories from patients in open ward situations which fail to provide adequate privacy; filling in labels incompletely; completing case notes inadequately. A specific instance of the last example is provided by a study related to the accuracy of anaesthesia records. The records of anaesthetists were compared with those of an observer, present throughout the procedure, with the sole purpose of documenting perioperative events. Eighty-six items of information were analysed for accuracy from 197 records. Information was omitted from the record in respect of a mean of 35 per cent of the items, and 3.4 per cent of recorded items were incorrect. Inaccuracies were common for the majority of sites on the record, irrespective of whether or not they reflected on the anaesthetist's performance. The authors concluded that the inadequacies in the anaesthetic records were not related to any defensiveness on the part of the anaesthetists, but instead probably reflected their attitudes to the value of the record and their response to possible deficiencies in the record's design. There has been much interest in recent years in the development of electronic methods of anaesthetic record keeping. This approach is not without its difficulties, but in the long term it is likely to provide an answer to what at present is an endemic problem, which even the obvious medico-legal risk associated with poor record keeping has done little to correct.[12]

An important characteristic of routine violations is that they often become a matter of habit and are repeated without much thought whenever the violation is committed; the element of choice is often essentially historical – the choice was made at the time the violation was first committed. Nevertheless, these violations do involve an ongoing deliberate infringement of appropriate practices, and it would be physically possible for the doctors concerned to avoid them, although a sudden change in the practice of one individual might create pressures which might be very difficult for that individual to handle.

The fact that routine violations are daily occurrences is one factor which helps to distinguish them from most errors. Errors are nearly always exceptional events, although it is possible to make an error of judgement about a common situation, obtain no negative feedback from the action, and therefore adopt a faulty rule into one's repertoire of schemata without realising that it is faulty. In these circumstances an individual might repeat the same error many times. A variation on this theme is that one might learn the wrong way of doing something from a senior colleague for whom a particular method of carrying out some procedure is a violation which he or she has long since come to think of as acceptable. In this way a trainee anaesthetist might learn an inadequate method of checking an anaesthetic machine from a consultant, for example, and might not realise that the procedure he or she has been taught is in fact in violation of the college protocol.

Exceptional violations are quite different from routine violations. They occur in situations which are themselves exceptional and which create conditions in which some rule which is normally accepted as appropriate cannot easily be followed. The *appropriate violations* discussed above are typically exceptional violations, but the exceptional violation will not always be the best thing to do. Typically, but not always, they are well intentioned. Exceptional violations are quite likely to occur in emergencies. For example, in an emergency an anaesthetist might elect not to

---

[12] L. Rowe, D. C. Galletly and R. S. Henderson, 'Accuracy of text entries within a manually compiled anaesthetic record' (1992) 68 *British Journal of Anaesthesia* 381–7.

expend resources on keeping an adequate anaesthetic record, a surgeon might omit to carry out a full hand-washing procedure, or the process of obtaining informed consent from a patient may be reduced to take the least amount of time possible.

Having distinguished routine from exceptional violations, one can identify several subsets of violation that may fall into either of these two main categories.

Necessary violations are violations created by unexpected and unpredicted situations (in the exceptional category) or by what may be called *system double-binds* (in the routine category). The examples given above, concerning the anaesthetic record and surgical hand-washing in an emergency, would qualify as necessary violations in the exceptional category if the patient's situation was so urgent and demanding of immediate attention that neither of the tasks mentioned was reasonably possible. In New Zealand the law currently prohibits the use of 'standing orders' by which doctors can leave instructions for nurses to follow in certain circumstances. This law is routinely violated because of the inordinate difficulties of operating a hospital without a mechanism of this type. The fact that this law is now under review is an indication of the extent to which it is seen as unworkable.

Another interesting example of a systems double-bind which produces routine violations involves the excessive hours regularly worked by many doctors. There is now considerable evidence to support the contention that fatigue contributes to errors and to diminished performance in general. The impact of fatigue on performance has been compared with that of alcohol.[13] However, many doctors find themselves in a situation where they are required to work for 24, 32, or sometimes even more hours at a time, often at high levels of intensity. An example of this is given in chapter 1, in which a coroner actually commented on how long a surgeon and anaesthetist had been working without a break at the time an accident occurred. He indicated that he considered the hours the doctors had worked at the time of the event to be unacceptable. At the same time, this coroner also recognised that these individual doctors were not primarily or solely responsible for the situation; the hours had not been worked by choice but had been forced on them by the system. He

---

[13] D. Dawson and K. Reid, 'Fatigue, alcohol and performance impairment' (1997) 388 *Nature* 235.

recommended that the hours doctors work in general should be re-examined.

Optimising violations are violations for the thrill of it. Driving in excess of the speed limit would be an example if the motivation was the pursuit of excitement rather than the desire to get somewhere more quickly.

A characteristic of all the above forms of violation is that there is no actual intention to cause harm. In general, the perpetrator believes that the consequences of the violation will be neutral at worst, or even beneficial – in terms of greater efficiency, for example. Actions deliberately aimed at causing harm can be described by easily understood terms such as *sabotage* or *fraud*.

Violations as antecedent actions to errors

Violations often create an increased risk of error and make the consequences more serious when an error does occur. Alternatively, like errors, they may make it more difficult to detect or deal with a problem which subsequently arises spontaneously. This is a very important aspect of violations, and a major reason why it is so important to take them seriously. Thus speed itself may not cause motor accidents but it reduces the time available for the driver to react to new situations and increases the chance of a mistake. If a mistake is made and an accident occurs, the energy associated with the crash increases in proportion to the square of the speed, so that the chance of serious injury or death is greatly increased.

A medical example of this principle is to be found once again in a case relating to an anaesthetic machine.[14] At the beginning of an operating session, a machine check identified a problem with part of the breathing circuit. The relevant piece of apparatus was dispatched to a technician for a small repair, while the surgeon proceeded with a number of minor operations under local anaesthetic. The proper technician was temporarily absent, but he shared a workshop with another technician who worked in a slightly different field. This second technician, with the best intentions, to save everyone concerned the delay and trouble of finding the appropriately trained and qualified person, took the initiative of doing the job himself. He did this in the belief that the matter was very straightforward

[14] C. Du Chateau, 'Some deaths are never the end', *Weekend Herald* (3–4 October, 1998), A15.

– which on the surface it appeared to be. Regrettably, because of an arcane quirk in the design of the apparatus, his method of repair created an invisible but lethal fault. Owing to a subsequent lapse, the apparatus was not properly rechecked before use. An independent problem subsequently developed in ventilating the first patient to be anaesthetised with the repaired apparatus. This, combined with the fault in the apparatus, caused considerable difficulties for the anaesthetist and the patient actually died. The degree to which the fault in the apparatus contributed to the cause of death was disputed, but clearly this fault was not helpful to the anaesthetist dealing with a difficult clinical situation. This example provides a good illustration of the way in which a sequence of minor events can lead to disaster. The first violation involved the well-motivated but inappropriate assistance of the wrong technician. There is a similarity between this and the antecedent cause of the Cave Creek example discussed above. It really is very dangerous for people to undertake tasks for which they are not trained in the absence of supervision or instruction – as Lord Finchley found to his cost.[15] The violation was followed by an error – failing to recheck the machine. Although it might be argued that this was also a violation, it is obvious that the machine had been checked at the beginning of the day, and it seems at least likely that the omission of the recheck was a lapse precipitated by the break in the normal sequence of the day's events. At any rate, the violation and error together had created a situation in which it was much more difficult to deal with a completely independent problem when one arose.

The use of a power tool or outdoor appliance without the precaution of an isolation transformer or equivalent safety device provides another example of the way in which errors and violations may interact to cause harm. In itself, failing to use an isolation device should not be dangerous, but the ability of the system to tolerate subsequent errors is clearly reduced by this violation, with a consequent reduction in safety. Recently, the children of one of the authors offered to clean the family car. Fortunately, this author decided to check on progress fairly early in the proceedings and discovered the children hard at work – one with a vacuum cleaner cleaning the inside of the car, the other with a garden hose washing the outside. This was an error – a rule-based mistake; the

---

[15] H. Belloc, 'Lord Finchley', in *Hilaire Belloc's Cautionary Verses* (New York, Alfred A. Knopf, 1941), 268–9.

children did know the rule concerning the relationship of water and electricity, but only vaguely, and had not appreciated that it would apply to the activity in question. The vacuum-cleaner cord was plugged into an extension wire, and this pair of connected plugs was lying in a pool of water made by the hose. The combination of a violation (failure to use the isolation transformer, which was available and part of the normal routine of the household in respect of out-of-door appliances) and an error (by which water and electricity were unthinkingly allowed to come together) had created a potentially lethal situation. The proper procedure on the part of the parent in checking on his children's progress offset *his* earlier violation of not supervising the initial steps of the process and ensuring that the isolation transformer was in use. The fact that a disaster was averted was mainly a matter of good fortune. It is interesting to speculate on the analysis of blame that would have ensued if five minutes' additional delay in checking had resulted in the death of a child. The implications of this element of moral luck, sometimes referred to as an outcome lottery, will be discussed in greater detail in chapter 7. The point at present is to emphasise that the outcome of most violations and most errors is strongly influenced by random combinations of subsequent actions, events, latent pathogens in equipment and in the system, and the prior state of health of the individuals concerned. An important ground for objecting to even minor violations is that they weaken one layer of the defences that exist in any system, and reduce the margin of safety.

Working while fatigued – an example of violation?

Writing in *The New Yorker*, Atul Gawande observed that 'The real problem isn't how to stop bad doctors from harming, even killing, their patients. It's how to prevent good doctors from doing so.'[16] Until relatively recently most people declined to take the elementary precaution of wearing seatbelts in motor cars. This did not imply that the majority of the population were intellectually or morally deficient. In chapter 2 we advanced data which suggest that there is an unacceptable level of avoidable harm occurring in hospitals at the present time, probably world-wide. We referred to the claim that more people die from iatrogenic harm than from road accidents. A problem of this magnitude is

[16] A. Gawande, 'When doctors make mistakes', *The New Yorker* (1 February 1999), 40–55.

unlikely to involve only a minority of practitioners. If it is the case, as it seems to be, that most doctors cause avoidable harm to a patient at some stage in their careers, this cannot mean that the majority of doctors are incompetent or habitually careless. It must mean that Gawande is correct – this is a problem which is affecting the 'good' doctors as well as those who may be less competent or conscientious.

In chapters 2 and 3 we have argued that every human being is inevitably subject to error at some stage. Can it be that all people are also guilty of violations of one sort or another, from time to time? We turn now to consider in greater depth the issue of doctors (and others) who undertake hazardous activities after working for excessive hours. We suggest that this is an example of a routine violation, made by most practitioners at some stage. It is a violation which has been essentially eliminated from commercial aviation, and it is one which provides interesting insights into some of the reasons why iatrogenic harm is endemic in medicine, and illustrates the importance of addressing systemic issues if any worthwhile improvement is to be made in safety in medicine. This example also illustrates the diffuse nature of responsibility in relation to certain types of violation.

In a recent survey of New Zealand anaesthetists, 71 per cent of trainees and 58 per cent of specialists reported that in the preceding six months they had worked longer hours than they considered safe, while 63 per cent and 40 per cent respectively had worked longer hours than they considered compatible with their own personal well-being.[17] In 1984 Libby Zion, an eighteen-year-old woman, was admitted to the emergency department of a New York hospital. She died without having been seen by any senior member of staff, and having been in the care of junior doctors who had all been on duty for more than 18 hours continuously at the time. Recommendations for reform of the hours worked by junior doctors in emergency departments were made as a result of this case. Amongst these, a 12-hour limit was placed on emergency room shifts; residents in acute care specialities were to work no more than 80 hours a week averaged over a 4-week period,[18] and no more than 24 consecutive

[17] P. H. Gander, A. Merry, M. M. Millar and J. Weller, 'Hours of work and fatigue-related error: a survey of New Zealand anaesthetists' (2000) 28 *Anaesthesia and Intensive Care* 178–83.

[18] This still implies some very long weeks indeed. In order to have one week of, say, 40 hours in a four week cycle, the hours worked in the remaining three would need to exceed 90 hours per week, for example; more probably the hours worked in at least one week in the cycle would be in excess of 100.

hours, and no moonlighting was to be allowed! Obviously, the hours worked previously were even longer, but even the recommended hours of work are hardly compatible with safe practice. Astonishing as it may seem, five years later many hospitals in New York had failed to implement the recommendations on economic grounds. After considerable wrangling over who should pay the increased costs of compliance with these recommendations, many emergency department doctors continued to work hours which by any reasonable standards must be considered excessive.[19]

Anecdotal accounts of heroic feats of endurance are part of the folklore of medicine, and most doctors can recall periods of their training and of their subsequent careers when they have worked 48 or more hours on continuous duty with little or no sleep. In a war, many people are called upon to perform marathon efforts of this sort. There may be no alternative. In the past, when there was a world-wide shortage of doctors, such hours may have been justifiable on the grounds that it was better for patients to be seen by a tired doctor than by no doctor at all. In peacetime, in most of the western world today, neither justification applies. In particular, there seems to be a relative oversupply of doctors, and even if there are specialities or regions which remain short of manpower, it would not take long to address these shortages if there was a genuine will to do so. The problem lies in the culture of medicine, in the need to gain enough experience to become and remain competent, and in some instances in the relationship between hours worked and money earned. It also lies in the difficulty of demonstrating that fatigue really does make a difference to performance.

There are certainly data to show that fatigue has an adverse effect on performance in the laboratory.[20] It is not entirely clear that impaired performance on a psychomotor test can be extrapolated to the clinical situation. A number of studies have gone on to examine the question of the impact of fatigue on the performance of doctors in real life, but the results have often been equivocal.[21] Against this background, and in the

---

[19] US Congress, Office of Technology Assessment, *Biological Rhythms: Implications for the Worker*, OTA-BA-463 (Washington, D.C., US Government Printing Office, 1991), 168–70.

[20] J. J. Pilcher and A. I. Huffcutt, 'Effects of sleep deprivation on performance: a meta-analysis' (1996) 19 *Sleep* 318–26.

[21] V. Narang and J. R. D. Laycock, 'Psychomotor testing of on-call anaesthetists' (1986) 41 *Anaesthesia* 868–9; E. E. Christensen, G. W. Dietz, R. C. Murry and J. G. Moore, 'The effect of fatigue on resident performance' (1977) 125 *Radiology* 103–5.

face of the attitudes of many senior doctors whose entire career has been built around a culture of denial of human weakness, it is hardly surprising that change has been slow in coming.

Some of the problems associated with studies of fatigue in medicine include the confounding influence of practice effects on psychomotor testing, the influence of circadian rhythms and the fact that different tasks may be impaired to different degrees. Effective monitoring by an anaesthetist may be more at risk than the technical activities of a surgeon, although all doctors depend heavily on certain common requirements such as the exercise of judgement. Recently, Gaba's group in San Francisco published results which place many earlier studies in a very interesting light.[22] Traditionally, studies of fatigue in medicine have compared junior doctors who have been on duty the night before with those who have not. In Gaba's study a third group was added to these two traditional samples. In this group rest was actively promoted for several days. Not only were the junior doctors relieved of night duty, they were permitted to arrive later than usual for work, and their early morning duties were covered by seniors. The results were striking, particularly in regard to sleep latency. This test measures the time taken for a subject to fall asleep in a quiet and darkened room with his or her eyes closed. A value of five minutes or less is typical of patients with sleep disorders such as narcolepsy. A normal time is in the order of twenty minutes. In Gaba's study, both the traditional groups had sleep latencies of about five minutes (i.e virtually pathological), with no difference between them, but the third or rested group had significantly longer sleep latencies, much closer to those of normal subjects. The implication is that a single night off duty was not enough for these sleep-deprived doctors to catch up. It is quite likely that the two groups compared in many previous studies have both been sleep deprived, and the failure to show clear differences between them is therefore understandable.

It has recently been shown that the degradation in performance associated with fatigue is progressive and takes place in much the same way as that seen with increasing levels of alcohol in the blood.[23] In the New Zealand survey quoted above, 86 per cent of respondents reported making an error that they attributed to fatigue, at some stage in their

---

[22] S. K. Howard, M. R. Rosekind and D. M. Gaba, 'Improving daytime alertness in resident anesthesiologists: the effects of sleep extension' (1996) 25 *Sleep Research* 468.

[23] Dawson and Reid, 'Fatigue, alcohol and performance impairment'.

careers.[24] It is likely that certain types of error are more influenced by fatigue than others. For example, in the Australian Incident Monitoring Study, fatigue was overrepresented in drug administration errors.[25]

Fatigue has been cited as a contributing factor in a number of major disasters, including the *Challenger* explosion.[26] Medical cases have also been reported. Dr Teoh, who was found not guilty of manslaughter after making a drug administration error which led to the death of a patient, had worked 110 hours in the preceding week.[27] We referred above (pp. 22–4) to the coroner's case in Rotorua in which fatigue was cited as a factor contributing to suboptimal aspects of care in the management of an emergency case in the early hours of the morning. Both the anaesthetist and surgeon had been working since early morning, and by the end of the case had been on duty for over 24 hours. Doctors frequently find themselves in a position such as this, in which they may have to drive home while fatigued or face some inconvenience and expense in relation to getting themselves home while leaving their car at the hospital. This is a typical situation for a violation – the pressures to do the wrong thing and drive while very tired are strong, but could be overcome if the individual were convinced that the violation was truly dangerous. To make matters worse, insight tends to be less acute in the presence of fatigue. As always, an organisational solution would probably solve the problem – a policy, backed up with a taxi service paid for by the hospital and proper arrangements for the car which must be left behind. As it stands, the situation is one which will obviously add to the hazards that the doctor's fatigue may already have created for others. The question of driving while fatigued by long haul truck drivers and by the public in general has been the subject of a recent editorial which compared this problem to that of drinking and driving.[28]

Taken collectively, the weight of evidence is now sufficiently convincing to suggest that carrying out elective work while excessively fatigued should be viewed as a violation of a good practice principle. To

---

[24] Gander et al., 'Hours of work and fatigue-related error'.
[25] A. L. Garden, M. Currie and P. H. Gander, 'Sleep loss, performance, and the safe conduct of anaesthesia', in J. Keneally and M. Jones (eds.), *Australasian Anaesthesia* (Melbourne, Australian and New Zealand College of Anaesthetists, 1996), 43–51.
[26] S. Coren, *Sleep Thieves* (New York, Free Press, 1996).
[27] R. Savill, 'Tired doctor cleared over patient's death', *Daily Telegraph* (20 May 1995), 3.
[28] W. C. Dement, 'The perils of drowsy driving' (1997) 337 *New England Journal of Medicine* 783–4.

continue with current medical attitudes to fatigue is to flaunt the emerging message that the safety record in medicine is not as good as it should be. The importance of fatigue to safety has long been recognised in the aviation industry, and applies in trucking and many other dangerous occupations. The flying hours of commercial pilots have typical monthly limits similar to those worked by some doctors in a week.[29] It is not quite clear how to define the exact level at which one would draw the line, but it is fairly obvious that many doctors often exceed any reasonable level of fatigue by a substantial margin. The coroner in the Rotorua case recognised this, but also recognised that the system was more to blame than the individual doctors. He called for the matter to be reviewed by the relevant colleges. Such reviews are being undertaken, notably by the Australian Medical Association.[30] It is likely that in years to come people will look back on the hours worked by doctors in amazement. However, if they are surprised at all by the number of accidents which have occurred in association with fatigue, it may be because they are fewer than one might expect. Working while fatigued is an example of a violation. So far from the notion that violations imply laziness or carelessness, this violation is a manifestation of excessive commitment to one's work and goes hand in hand with extraordinary levels of motivation. People seem capable of remarkably successful performance while very tired – most of the time. However, medicine has reached a stage where a more mature approach to working hours is overdue. An interesting innovation would be to include hours worked in the preceding days in the information required as part of informed consent. What would a patient who was presenting for routine rather than emergency surgery say if he or she was told that the surgeon or anaesthetist had not been to bed in the preceding 24 hours? Of course, there is more involved in the generation and management of fatigue than hours of work alone. Circadian factors are very important, and sleep may be lost at home as well as at work. Fatigue counter-measure programmes have been described which seek to work around the difficulties which

---

[29] The actual hours worked exceed the hours of flying, and there are big differences between pilots flying long haul for major airlines and those working for smaller companies flying light aircraft over short distances with frequent stops and a greater proportion of other duties. Nevertheless, the limits described above in relation to the Libby Zion case are not unusual for doctors, and in general are far in excess of the hours which would be required of a commercial pilot.

[30] AMA Safe Hours Project, *National Code of Practice – Hours of Work, Shiftwork and Rostering for Hospital Doctors* (Kingston, Australian Medical Association, 1999).

confront industries that are committed to providing service 24 hours a day. Doctors are notoriously unwilling to take sick leave. Improved safety may depend on a cultural change which results in individuals being willing to admit when they are too tired or too ill to work. Who should be held responsible for harm attributable to fatigue in the meantime is far from obvious.

Design and violations

In chapter 2 we discussed the way in which inferior design may predispose to error, and this is equally true for violations. Conversely, good design is a major force in the reduction of violations. We have discussed Norman's concept of the affordances of things in the context of error. If something is designed in such a way that its correct use is obvious and easy, while at the same time undesirable practices are difficult, the likelihood of its being used in the appropriate way is greatly increased. If the design of something permits dangerous practices, it is probably only a matter of time before these occur, whether deliberately or in error. The ferry *The Herald of Free Enterprise* sank in 1987 with the loss of 188 lives when it sailed with both its inner and outer bow doors fully open. In that the order to sail was given in the belief that the doors were closed, this was technically an error, although it was obviously an error that violated an important rule. The assistant bosun whose job it was to close the doors was actually asleep at the time, and no one else in the chain of command conducted an explicit check of the doors. There were a number of organisational factors and deficiencies in communication which contributed to this failure, but aspects of the ship's design were also highly relevant. In the first place the very concept of bow doors which could be flooded if left open is questionable. However, given that such doors have particular advantages and that it had therefore been decided to incorporate them into the design of the ship, it would seem obvious to include within the design of the doors some mechanism to ensure that the ship could not set out to sea unless they were properly closed. At the very least, there should have been an automatic warning system, with indicators on the bridge, to ensure that the master of the boat was aware of their state of openness or otherwise. Neither of these features was present. Apparently bridge indicators of an appropriate type would have cost only about £500 to add to the completed ship, but the real question is why they were not incorporated from the beginning.[31] This was a situation in which simple design improvements would have been far more effective in ensuring proper practice than any number of rules or procedures, although the rules and procedures associated with this disaster seem to have been seriously deficient as well.

A very good example of the same principle is to be found in the design of anaesthetic machines. We have noted that the pre-anaesthetic check of these machines is not always undertaken in the prescribed way, and not always even in an adequate way. In the past there have been several tragic deaths associated with failures to deliver oxygen to patients, either because of an undetected fault in the machine or in the arrangements of the pipes carrying different gases to the machine, or because of a failure by the anaesthetist to understand fully the functions of an unfamiliar machine.[32] This was a serious risk, and many more near misses occurred than actual disasters. Reducing this risk has involved several initiatives, but the most effective developments have been in the design of anaesthetic equipment. Today's anaesthetists take advantage of a number of techno-logical developments to make sure that they deliver adequate amounts of oxygen to their patients. Most notably, these include devices which simply will not permit a hypoxic mixture to be delivered from the machine. In general, no mixture of gases with a lower oxygen content than air can be specified by the anaesthetist. As well as this, it is now routine to analyse the composition of the gas mixture coming from the machine and to display it continuously, with alarms set to warn the anaesthetist if certain predefined limits are crossed. As a third tier in this safety network, pulse oximetry is used routinely to monitor the percentage of oxygen in the patient's bloodstream.

We touched on the issue of preventing hypoxia in anaesthesia in relation to error in chapter 2. The violation of failing to check a machine may be as important in the generation of problems of this type as any error in the conduct of the anaesthetic. In the case of violations there is an even stronger tendency to approach problems of this type by focusing on the operator, by exhorting people to behave better, threatening them with harsh punishment if they fail to meet expected standards and by writing increasingly prescriptive regulations to define acceptable procedures. This

---

[31] Reason, *Human Error*, 193, 256.

[32] P. D. G. Skegg, 'Criminal prosecutions of negligent health professionals: the New Zealand experience' (1998) 6 *Medical Law Review* 220–46.

is not entirely without justification – violations are certainly more amenable than errors to control by initiatives to modify the way in which people carry out their duties. However, taken collectively (and in conjunction with proper standards in relation to the gases which are supplied to the machines and with devices that make incorrect attachments of pipelines and cylinders difficult if not impossible), these safety innovations in respect to anaesthesia have achieved far more to prevent disasters than would any amount of regulation or exhortation. As with errors, the key is to engineer human failure out of the system wherever possible.

Promoting compliance

Systematic and design factors are very important in ensuring that an activity or environment is inherently safe. Unfortunately, safety devices may fail, may generate new problems of their own, or may be circumvented by ingenious individuals who consider them a nuisance. The technology exists to limit the speeds on cars, and even to respond to different speed limits in different geographical zones. Devices to measure the alcohol in expired breath can be attached to the ignition systems of cars to prevent the cars from starting until the driver has provided an acceptable sample of breath. Such technology has failed to achieve widespread use. Instead, devices continue to be sold to detect traffic officers' radar equipment and thereby facilitate the optimising violations of those who choose to drive at unlawful speeds. Each new generation of cars is faster than the one before. Very recently there has been a widespread increase in the interest in passive safety features in the design of cars, and there is clear evidence that these make a considerable difference to outcome in road traffic accidents.[33] Even today, however, features other than those related to safety are deemed more important in the marketing of a new model. The magazines in which motor cars are reviewed devote considerable resources to evaluating their performance. Top speeds ludicrously in excess of any legal limit are extolled as virtues. The road toll is one of the major health problems facing modern societies, and yet our culture is one of denial and of complicity with violation.

---

[33] NCAP data are available from *http://www. nrma. com. au. index. html*, from *http://www. nhtsa. dot. gov. /ncap/ncap. cfm*, and from other sites. Interestingly, safer cars may result in greater risk-taking on the part of drivers – a recognised revenge effect, called 'risk homeostasis'; see E. Tenner, *Why Things Bite Back* (London, Fourth Estate, 1996), 261–8.

Increasing the number of rules, and of the signs or other notices which promulgate them, is likely to have limited effect on reducing violations unless it is widely perceived that the chances of being apprehended are high and that some punishment will result. The likelihood of routine violations is increased by an environment which seldom identifies and punishes inappropriate behaviour, and which rarely rewards observance of the rules. Commonly, the violators do not believe any harm will flow from their actions, either to themselves or to other people. Many violations in medicine may be understood on the basis of this insight. The practitioners concerned are simply not convinced that the rules which they violate on a routine basis are important. Their day-to-day experience reinforces the perception that they can get away with these violations. They believe that the risk of harm from such violations to their own patients is negligible. In the same way, the reduction of excessive speed on the roads is more likely to be achieved by ensuring that speeding is highly likely to result in apprehension and a fine than by the thought that it might cause a terrible accident, because most drivers believe the chances of such an accident to be relatively low.

In New York a stricter approach to policing in respect of minor violations appears to have paid dividends in reducing major crime. Most people are more readily influenced by the perception that a moderately undesirable event is likely than by the perception that a terribly serious event is remotely possible – although the factors that lead to an individual's evaluation of any given risk are often far from rational.[34]

At Green Lane Hospital in Auckland, two innovations have improved performance with the checking of anaesthetic machines. First, a revised, simpler protocol which focuses on key items has been developed, with input from all participants. This is in accordance with the principle of facilitating compliance by making it easier for people to comply with what is important and removing irritating rules which will never be seen as worth following. Secondly, a checklist has been introduced which must actually be signed. This was done to increase the chances of detection when violations occur. Failing to sign the checklist is fairly likely to be detected because copies of the anaesthetic record (into which the list has been integrated) are kept and reviewed for various purposes. Previously,

---

[34] K. Petrie, 'Sum of our fears a bit over the odds', *New Zealand Herald* (17 October 1997), A13.

the most likely way of identifying a violation of the checking rule was by virtue of a problem manifesting during a case. This was relatively uncommon and an anaesthetist who was found (by virtue of the development of such a problem) not to have checked a machine could quite easily pass this failure off as a lapse. It is much harder to argue that a procedure has simply been forgotten if one has completed and signed a relevant checklist. Signing in the absence of compliance would be a very clear and wilful violation, and would be viewed by all members of the department as a rather serious one. Perhaps the most important aspect of this initiative has been the promotion of cultural change. The process of developing the checklist and modified protocol involved meetings, presentations of previous problems, discussions of the possible consequences of inadequate checking and so forth. To return to the road traffic problem: many countries in recent years have run publicity campaigns to try to change the cultural approach to driving, both by reinforcing the consequences of accidents and by promoting safer behaviour on the roads. In both examples, improved performance is more easily obtained than sustained – ongoing effort is required to avoid a gradual drift back to widespread routine violation. It is also important to recognise the extent of the challenge associated with attempting to improve safety; checking the anaesthetic machine is but one of a myriad of requirements, each vitally important.

Violations and the culture of organisations

It is natural to expect that properly trained professionals would know the rules and obey them. Examples taken from everyday life, it might be said, have little bearing on the work of a specialist doctor, electrician, airline pilot or other professional. There is much truth in this, and it is reasonable to expect a high standard from trained individuals. Indeed, it is accepted in law that the standard of care expected of people undertaking dangerous activities is higher than in other circumstances. There is no doubt that much of medical training, particularly at a specialist level, is aimed at ensuring that the rules are known.

Violations can be due to the carelessness or laziness of individuals, but most professionals are well motivated and there are probably greater differences between institutions or organisations in the prevalence of certain routine violations, and in the degree to which they are tolerated, than between most well-trained and highly qualified members of a trade or profession within a single institution. A great deal depends on the culture of the institution or organisation. In some surgical units shortcuts are common in the precautions taken to ensure sterility. In others, meticulous attention is always paid to sterile technique, even in emergencies, to the degree that many of the precautions are probably without scientific foundation. For example, a restriction on the wearing of jewellery in the operating room makes sense if applied to rings for staff who are actually scrubbed and operating or assisting with the operation. It makes less sense if applied to a neck chain worn by an orderly (which would be unlikely to contaminate a sterile field), and even less if an exception is permitted for wedding rings but not for other types of ring. At least one British unit has, in the past, gone to the lengths of requiring all staff to undergo a full shower with liberal use of antiseptic soap solution before entry into the operating suite. This rule applied even to people whose function, once in the operating room, had nothing to do with the sterile procedures being undertaken. Other units have a much more casual approach. What is standard practice in the latter would be considered a violation in the former. The case for the more rigid approach is that it results in the important things being done, even if this means a great deal of effort is also expended on relatively unimportant activities. A similar justification can also be advanced for the more relaxed approach – that the best way to make sure the important things are done is to concentrate on those and not waste effort on trivial issues. Another slant on this dichotomy arises from the lack of certainty of much medical knowledge (which we shall discuss in chapter 7). Those in the former camp may say that, although only half their effort is of value, they do not know which half.

Individuals within an organisation or community may have only limited ability to influence standards, even in the case of those in relatively senior positions: the *culture* of the group or organisation as a whole tends to be more influential than the advocacy of a minority. This is very clear in the case of road traffic accidents. When responsibility for accidents is being evaluated, these factors ought to be considered. A well-motivated individual in an organisation whose culture is not strongly oriented towards the promotion of safety is at a considerable disadvantage compared with his colleague in a sister organisation in which the culture is very safety-conscious. While it may be difficult for a court to take such matters into account in relation to the responsibility of an individual, there should at least be some effort to examine the wider picture and to look at the contribution of factors within the organisation to the generation of any accident.

Violations and blame

The distinction which is proposed in this and the previous chapter is that between errors, which we regard (in general) as unavoidable and non-culpable, and violations which are, by contrast, avoidable, and which therefore involve at least some degree of culpability. The basis of culpability within a violation is the fact that a choice has been made to depart from a rule or principle which the actor either knows as an explicit rule or knows to be appropriate in the circumstances. Because of this element of choice, the actor must accept moral responsibility for the consequences of the action. Not all violations are equally culpable. We have identified violations which are appropriate in certain circumstances and which are therefore justifiable. The person who commits such a violation has the defence that it was the best thing to do – a defence which can, if necessary, be translated into the legal defence of necessity.

All other violations involve culpability but it is important to note that this culpability may rest, at least in part, on persons or organisations other than the individual who performed the act in question. We have seen that there are many cases where violations are made almost inevitable by aspects of the system, and we have discussed the contribution of organisational culture to their generation. If it is impossible for an employee to achieve work targets without committing a violation, the issue of responsibility for this violation becomes a complex one. The employee may well deliberately choose to violate but may only do so because he feels unable to carry out his duties in any other way. This does not necessarily exonerate the employee, but it is certainly a mitigating factor. More importantly, it implies a definite responsibility on the part of the employer for the consequences of the violations. For this reason any allocation of blame should ensure that *all* those involved in the generation of the violation should be answerable and share the liability. Too often the finger of blame is pointed at the individual, who is often relatively junior within the organisation. This has been noted in particular in the prosecution of individuals within corporate bodies in which the relatively junior member of the organisation who actually commits the violation may be blamed while those at a higher level, who bear an overall responsibility, escape liability, on the grounds that they were not directly involved. We are not suggesting that the true responsibility is always to be located in the higher echelons of an organisation; in many organisations directors and managers make considerable efforts to ensure safe practice. Our point is that this broader aspect of responsibility must be taken into account.

Even when we have identified a culpable violation and tied it to an individual, it is important to recognise that there may be degrees of blameworthiness. Our discussion of the context in which violations occur and of all the factors that may contribute to their generation reveals that culpability will vary. In a situation in which compliance with regulations or principles of good practice is made difficult by limited resources or other operational factors, the violation may be understandable. This is quite different from a situation in which it is simple laziness or disregard for the safety of others which has led to the violation.

The commission of a violation is a clear wrong in respect of the rights of those affected by it. While we have argued that errors should be accepted as an inevitable concomitant of any complex human under-taking, the same does not necessarily apply to violations. We have indicated that certain violations ('necessary violations') might be imposed upon individuals by the system, but a person who suffers as a result of a violation has every right to assert that the violation constitutes a direct wrong against himself or herself. How this is translated into rights of complaint, or the right to seek compensation, or even a call for criminal or disciplinary sanction, will depend on the circumstances. In this respect society must seek a delicate balance of rights and interests. This process involves the elaboration of an acceptable and realistic standard of care, and, in the context of criminal liability, the identifica-tion of that point of deviation from acceptable conduct which is sufficient to trigger a criminal-law response.

5

Negligence, recklessness and blame

We have argued that certain incidents which lead to harm and attributions of liability may, in fact, reasonably be regarded as accidents – in the sense in which we have defined accidents – and not as occasions for blame. We have also suggested that error is an inevitable concomitant of human activity, particularly in complex systems. In practice, however, when things go wrong, there is often a call by the community, or by the injured party, for an explanation, and this is frequently accompanied by pressing demands for the attribution of blame. In some cases these demands are justified, but the justification lies not in the mere fact that harm has occurred, but in the fact that it has been caused in a culpable manner.

Theories of moral responsibility based on free choice have traditionally stressed the inextricable link between blame and culpability. Yet this connection has been weakened by the tendency to assume that if there has been a harmful outcome then there is a strong possibility of blame. This claim may be made in the name of accountability and is a concomitant of the policy of dismantling elitist patterns of professional privilege. The consumerist movement has encouraged this view, arguing that more strenuous efforts to uncover responsibility for mishaps will ensure better protection for the public. There is, of course, some merit in this: it is clearly not in the interest of the public that those providing public services should be able to conceal incompetence or deliberate wrongdoing behind institutional or professional shields. Complaint is an essential part of the process of maintaining quality. The right of reasonable complaint is important. Yet the excessive encouragement of complaint may promote the belief that the attribution of blame, and the identification of a particular offender, whether an individual or an institution, will normally be possible. This leaves little room for acceptance of accident, or, more generally, of less than perfect outcomes (which, as we have argued, may not necessarily be a matter of blame). In such a climate, there may be excessive blaming, with serious consequences for safety and at a high personal cost for those involved in useful but inherently hazardous activities.

The connection between blame and moral culpability has also been undermined by the positivist contention that the law can function as a value-free, mechanistic regulator. In this view, utilitarian considerations allow the invocation of the criminal law as a means of social control irrespective of the moral status of the targeted offender. What matters in this analysis is that breaches of the criminal law are discouraged by the application of criminal sanctions, even if the offender has not deliberately sought to offend against the law or indeed has been unable to avoid non-compliance. Such a model of criminal justice allows extensive room for crimes of strict liability, in which the moral innocence of an individual transgressor is subservient to the perceived social value of conviction and punishment.

This demotion of culpability is also evident in the therapeutic approach to crime, which inclines to view criminal offending as a matter of psychopathology rather than individual choice. While sensitivity to the psychology of offending furnishes useful insights into crime and offers, in the long run, considerable possibilities of enlightened crime prevention, the abuse of psychiatric or psychological explanations threatens to destabilise notions of individual responsibility which lie at the heart of the criminal law and indeed of our everyday morality. Herbert Morris has raised objections to this position, which he sees as leading to a demotion of the importance of human agency.[1] Guilt plays a central part in our social lives: without inferences of guilt, moral rules are deprived of their effect and are indistinguishable from other, lower-level, precepts or exhortations.

While the role of reason in moral agency should not be discounted, other explanations of moral action stress the role of learned rules, moral metaphor and, indeed, intuition. The sense of guilt plays a part in some of these, not only helping us to identify our own moral failures but also sharpening moral intuitions. Guilt, of course, is capable of being both subjective and objective. We feel it, or we attribute it to others who we

---

[1] H. Morris, 'The decline of guilt' (1988) 99 *Ethics* 62–76.

consider *should* feel it. To be guilty, then, is to stand in relation to some act or state of affairs that would normally give rise to punishment. But if punishment is visited upon those who are not deemed to merit guilt in this sense, then the moral defensibility of punishment is weakened and, with it, the authority of the criminal law. In such circumstances, the strongest, most practical grounds for obedience to law – our sense that the law represents *fairness* – stands to be undermined. This alone provides adequate reason for preserving the connection between moral culpability and the attribution of liability. Yet, as we have seen in chapter 4, determining precisely which categories of behaviour are culpable may not be simple. Behaviour which is intended to cause harm needs little discussion. On the whole there is agreement that acts of deliberate wrong-doing are culpable; the debate tends to focus on the scope of what conduct is legitimate. These are debates about values; what concerns us is the culpability of particular states of mind in situations in which the values at stake are not the issue. At what point does innocent (even if faulty) behaviour become culpable? At what point does culpability (in the moral sense) become sufficiently serious to merit a criminal sanction? These are familiar issues in criminal law theory yet there still exists surprising uncertainty as to the relationship between these questions and the question of legal liability. At least some of this uncertainty may be because of an insufficient understanding of human cognition and its relevance to the analysis of human action. We address these problems below, starting with an enquiry as to the essential ingredients of a blame-worthy state of mind.

Blame

There are two senses in which a person can be blamed for a state of affairs. In the first of these, blame is a matter of mere causal responsibility in which the person who has caused the state of affairs to come into existence is held accountable for it. Conclusions of causal responsibility of this sort – or causal blaming – are reached on the basis of what we understand about the world and its workings. These judgements are not necessarily normative; causal judgements are compatible with the absence of moral culpability, as in a case where damage is caused accidentally. *A* trips over a concealed obstacle and knocks over *B*'s property. The damage to *B*'s property is caused by *A* in this simple, physical sense, but this does not necessarily mean that *A* should be blamed for it in the moral sense. In fact, if there is nothing which could have been done to avoid the obstacle, then it would be quite wrong to blame *A* in this way.

In legal theory this form of causation is referred to as *causation in fact* or *factual causation*.[2] The process of establishing a causal link of this sort between conduct and consequence is usually based on the conclusion that the conduct is sufficient to result in the consequence and that – and this is crucial in legal tests of causation – without the conduct in question the consequence would not have occurred. A factual cause in the law is thus often referred to as a cause *sine qua non*. If the consequence would have occurred without the conduct, then it is not produced by that conduct, and the actor is not to blame (in this causal sense) for what has happened.

Legal causation is something quite different. Its first requirement is factual causation but, once this has been established, it proceeds to a normative evaluation of the conduct in question. The question which underpins this evaluation is this: does the actor *deserve* to be held accountable – to be blamed, in the normative sense – for what has happened? The causal question at this level thus often becomes indistinguishable from the moral question.

We suggest that it is possible to classify blame into five levels. The first level is pure causal blame, where the agent is identified as the physical cause of an event, but has acted reasonably, has broken no rules and has done nothing wrong in moral terms. The second is blame attributed for an action which unintentionally deviates from or falls short of what can *normatively* be expected of the actor (that is, the way of doing things prescribed in the textbook – the 'theoretical norm'), but where, as we argue below, no moral culpability exists. This may be construed as negligence if conduct is measured against an absolute standard and fails to take account either of the fact that the reasonable person is a human being, with all the limitations that this status implies, or of the state of mind of the individual at the time. The third level is blame attributed for an action which deviates from or falls short of what can *reasonably* be expected of the actor (that is, the way things *are* done by people of reasonable competence in the field – the 'empiric norm'), and where, as

---

[2] The issue of legal causation is discussed extensively in H. L. A. Hart and T. Honoré, *Causation in the Law* (2nd edn, New York, Oxford University Press, 1985). See also M. S. Moore, *Placing Blame: A General Theory of the Criminal Law* (Oxford, Clarendon Press, 1997), 333–62.

we shall argue, moral culpability may exist, even though there is no intention to cause harm. We would argue that people can only be morally accountable for those acts which they have chosen to perform; things which they could not reasonably have avoided doing should not be laid to their moral account. The fourth level of blame is appropriate for situations where the actor knows of the existence of a risk and nevertheless proceeds with the action. This is recklessness. Finally, the fifth level (which we have already alluded to above) entails an unambiguous intention to cause harm.

In distinguishing these levels, we must take into account antecedent activity. The conduct of a person prior to the making of an error or the manifestation of other failure may have an important bearing on our moral assessment of the error or failure. Antecedent liability, which focuses on the background to an event rather than on the actual event itself, may be based on either a prior act (such as the consumption of alcohol before engaging in a dangerous activity) or a prior omission (such as a failure to attend a safety training session).[3] If something were to go wrong, in a situation where there has been a failure to take all reasonable steps to ensure the safety of a procedure or to minimise risk, culpability may exist, even if the causative action itself fell into category 2 above.

First-level blaming

To illustrate the first level of blame, we might consider the familiar example of a person who fails to see a child behind him when he reverses a vehicle. He had no reason to believe there might be children in the vicinity. He may have looked in his rear-view mirror and may have taken all the precautions expected of a driver in the circumstances; the child, however, has strayed into the road completely unexpectedly and cannot be seen from the driver's position. The driver in this case may be expected to say of himself: *I am to blame for the child having been run over.* It makes sense for him to say this, even if he understands that the incident is not his *fault* – in the sense that, because there was nothing he could reasonably have done to avoid this event, he is not morally culpable. It is interesting to observe here that such a driver may well feel *guilty* about what has

---

[3] A state of mind may also be culpable because of past conduct, as in a failure to acquaint oneself with the facts. See H. Smith, 'Culpable ignorance' (1983) 92 *The Philosophical Review* 543–71.

happened and may reproach himself for the child's injury. Indeed, not to feel remorse about such an incident would be unnatural and would reveal an astonishing lack of sympathy or ordinary human feeling. But we would be inclined to urge the driver not to reproach himself and not to fall prey to feelings of guilt; and we would do so for the precise reason that we understand that what happened to him is independent of moral fault on his part. There is therefore no sense in which moral opprobrium is appropriate.

The feelings of regret which the driver would experience in respect of the child's injury are very likely to be mirrored in the hostile reactive feelings of the child's parents. Their initial response to the incident is likely to be that the injury is, in all senses, the driver's fault. They may well not distinguish at this early stage between strict causal fault and moral culpability. Again, their feelings of anger are entirely understandable. Indeed, many parents may continue to feel angry and to demand punishment and compensation in the face of a convincing body of evidence as to the driver's lack of *moral* fault, but at least some would be capable of progressing from the crudely reactive state to a more subtle understanding of the issues. At this point, they might accept that the incident is one in which the attribution of blame is simply inappropriate. Whether or not the aggrieved person makes this transition, it is essential that the law should do so. In fact, the ability to distinguish between purely causal blame and morally culpable blame is a phenomenon which appears at a fairly primitive level of the development of a legal system. Of course, there may be attributions of blame involving other people in this particular case. For example, others may blame the parents for failure to supervise their child, the manufacturer of the vehicle for poor design in respect of visibility, or the city authorities for failing to fence off dangerous roadways.

This example also illustrates the general difficulty of distinguishing the various senses in which the terms *blame* and *fault* are used. There is a sense in which the driver *is* to blame, just as there is a sense in which the incident is his fault. But we suggest that if these terms are used in this context it should only be in the minimalist sense of *causal* blame and *causal* fault. There is no justification for their use in any moral sense.

In the medical context, examples would come from adverse events caused by patient-related factors. One example would be a patient who, in the absence of a history of allergy, suffers an unforeseeable anaphylactic reaction to a drug and dies in spite of all reasonable efforts being made to resuscitate her. It could be said that the doctor who administered the drug is causally to blame because if it had not been administered no reaction would have occurred. Few, however, would draw any inculpatory conclusions from that.

Second-level blaming

At this level of blaming, conduct is measured against a standard which sets out what *ought* to be done in the circumstances in question. The standard which is set is not intended to be an unrealistic one, and in general it will not be impossible to attain it. It should also take into account the circumstances in which the action takes place, and the economic and logistic constraints. If conduct fails to reach this standard, then it will commonly be described as negligent. This form of negligence is objective; it does not take into account the subjective state of the actor's mind at the time of the act. Furthermore, it fails to allow for human fallibility. What determines negligence, then, is a disparity between the actual conduct of the actor and the standard of conduct expected.[4]

The prime example in medicine is that of a drug administration error. We have seen that a wrong drug may be given as a result of a momentary lapse caused by distraction. We have also seen that most if not all practitioners make these errors from time to time – they are in effect inevitable in the statistical sense; they are entirely analogous to the various slips and lapses made by all people in everyday life. Assuming that there are no contributory or antecedent factors, and that the doctor has indeed been trying his or her best to give the right drug, how is such an error to be judged?

A great deal depends on the question upon which the test relies. If the question is: is it reasonable to give the wrong drug? the answer to that would seem to be no. No expert could ever say that giving the wrong drug is the appropriate thing to do, that is, the expected or standard thing to do. The conduct is therefore, in this sense at least, wrong. If, instead, the question is: *could* this have been done by a reasonably skilled and competent practitioner? then the answer, as we have seen in chapters 2

---

[4] H. M. Hurd, 'The deontology of negligence' (1996) 76 *Boston University Law Review* 249–72; S. Sverdlik, 'Pure negligence' (1993) 30 *American Philosophical Quarterly* 137–49.

and 3, must be yes. In fact, the empirical and theoretical data both lead us to believe that all practitioners make this type of mistake at some time even when trying their best to avoid errors. Phrasing the question in this way places the act in its statistical context as something which is inevitable on an occasional or infrequent basis. The focus is not on the act in isolation from other acts of its type, but on the act as one of a large number of similar events. Thus one might go one step further and phrase the question as follows: is it reasonable for a practitioner to make one mistake in (for example) one thousand drug administrations? On this basis, it is hard to conclude that such an act should be construed as negligent.

The question, as it is posed in the legal inquiry, is often none of these. In determining whether there has been negligence, the courts may ask the question: *would* this have been done by a practitioner who, at the time of the action, was manifesting a reasonable degree of competence? An important feature of this question is that 'reasonable degree of competence' means that degree of competence to which the practitioner might reasonably be expected to aspire. In other words, it is the *standard* or *recommended* degree of competence or the *standard* or *recommended* way of doing things.

This standard is clearly not unattainable on a single occasion. However, it would be impossible to meet it on *every* occasion over an entire working lifetime in the same way, for example, that it would be impossible for a professional golfer to score par or better on every round of golf. In the case of the doctor, he should certainly try his best to meet the standard on every occasion, but, as we have seen in chapters 2 and 3, it is inevitable that at some point he will be subject to a slip or a lapse on account of a momentary distraction and will be unable to do so.

Even if it is agreed that some deviation from the standard is inevitable, this may in practice have little effect on the legal inquiry for the reason that the law is primarily concerned not with overall patterns of behaviour or sequences of acts but with one particular act. This means that the legal assessment of behaviour is artificially detached from the behaviour's context in relation to many similar acts which have been undertaken over a long professional career. In a medical negligence action, the issue before the court is not whether the practitioner is, in general terms, a negligent doctor (that is, it is not whether he could, on the whole, be described as negligent) but whether *on a particular occasion* he manifested negligence.

For this inquiry, questions of statistical likelihood appear irrelevant. A very clear statement of this position was made in the case of Dr Yogasakaran, discussed in chapter 1. The judge observed that the issue was not whether Dr Yogasakaran was a negligent doctor in general but whether he had been negligent on the one occasion before the court.

The concern of the law with single, isolated events is particularly evident in the way in which criminal law functions. Under current theories of criminal liability, it is the defendant's act rather than his character which comes under the scrutiny of the court. Proponents of character-based theories of liability would argue that we should attribute liability to a defendant on the basis of his general disposition rather than by what he has done on an isolated occasion.[5] In practice, this is not the way in which criminal justice operates. The fact that the act is isolated and 'out of character' does not constitute a defence although it may mitigate the severity of the sentence. Provided mitigation of sentence is a possibility, the pragmatic requirement for single act-based liability is acceptable in the case of criminal acts proceeding from a deliberate choice on the defendant's part. Even the criminal law recognises circumstances in which the act is more 'understandable' and less clearly a product of deliberation. It is this that underlies the defence of provocation, a defence which applies where the defendant has been so provoked by the victim as to lose his power of self-control.

An objection to the application of this 'snapshot' view of action to errors of the type inevitably made by all human beings is that it tends to create an undue risk of liability for those who are professionally required to engage in skilled and hazardous activities. This level of liability may be seen as unreasonable by those upon whom it is imposed, given the inevitability that they will eventually make exactly this type of error. This raises fundamental questions as to the principles underlying civil liability. The question of whether conduct at the second level of blame should be regarded as negligent depends *on the purpose for which one is making the assessment*. If liability is imposed purely for loss-adjustment purposes, and no element of moral culpability is implied, then the single-act approach is

---

[5] An example of a theory of liability which would give greater weight to character is that supported by N. Lacey, *State Punishment: Political Principles and Community Values* (London, Routledge, 1988). For further discussion, see P. Arenella, 'Character, choice and moral agency: the relevance of character to our moral culpability judgments', in E. F. Paul (eds.), F. D. Miller and J. Paul, *Crime, Culpability and Remedy* (Cambridge, Mass., Blackwell, 1990), 59–83.

appropriate. If, however, the basis of liability includes a moral component, or if there is an element of punishment in the process, then there is an objection to the adoption of this approach at this level of blame. We need, therefore, to examine civil liability with a view to ascertaining the degree to which the objectives underlying the whole system of tort law dictate the grounds upon which such liability will be attributed.

Blame and the purposes of tort liability

The primary purpose of tort liability is to ensure that those who suffer injury, whether to their property or to their person, are compensated and, in so far as is possible, returned to the position they were in prior to the injury.[6] This is a system of loss redistribution: where appropriate, loss is not left to lie where it falls – but is transferred by the law to the person who caused it, provided, of course, that he *deserves* to bear it. This is clearly the main function of the law of torts, but, in addition to this compensatory goal, the law of torts is widely credited with a deterrent role. In this view, the prospect of legal liability has the effect of discouraging unsafe practices across the whole range of human activity. It is argued, for example, that the degree of caution exercised by manufacturers would be considerably reduced if they were not faced with the possibility of substantial damages claims in respect of faulty products. In the medical context, the argument is that hospitals and individual doctors would place a lower priority on patient safety – and patient interests in general – if the threat of legal action were removed. Would the medical profession have given so much attention to the need to obtain informed consent if this had not been brought home by a number of high-profile civil suits? It is impossible to say, but it seems likely that litigation acted as the spur in this area, although other devices might have been equally effective. In New Zealand, for example, the role of the Health and Disability Commissioner and her Code of Patient Rights, backed by disciplinary sanctions, seems to have achieved much the same result.

A further function served by the law of torts is that it provides access,

---

[6] For discussion as to the objectives of tort law, see the illuminating treatment of the topic by J. L. Coleman in his *Risks and Wrongs* (New York, Cambridge University Press, 1992), especially chapter 10: 'The goals of tort law', pp. 197–211.

effectively of right, to a forum in which an injured person can obtain a thorough airing of his or her complaint. Almost all other systems of redress, including criminal and disciplinary processes, involve some screening as to merit. In the latter case, the possibility exists of 'professional capture' at the screening stage. Even if this does not occur, the perception that it might do so is a major drawback. There are various reasons why people take an issue to court, but a powerful one in this context is the need for explanation and, in many cases, for tangible acknowledgement that something went wrong. For some, an explanation and an apology is all that is wanted. Others appear to be searching for retribution or even revenge, in the sense that they either want the wrong 'annulled' by punishment or, in the case of revenge, they seek the satisfaction of seeing the wrongdoer suffer.

It is important to acknowledge that all these objectives are, to a greater or lesser extent, achieved by tort law, and indeed this is one of its attractions and strengths. However, many of these objectives are secondary or are achieved as incidental effects. The support that they lend to the case for the continuation of the traditional system is, however, weakened by the fact that some of these purposes could be more reliably achieved by other means. For example, safety objectives may be met by the implementation of regulations designed to ensure proper practices. Such regulations already exist in many occupational settings and could be more effectively implemented. The underlying safety problems may be more effectively addressed by a broadly-based systems-oriented focus than simply by reliance upon random tort actions.

Not all loss will be transferred through legal redress. Tort liability is not a system of universal insurance: it identifies certain categories of loss as being within its purview and excludes others. In particular, it excludes those losses which are produced by factors outside human agency, such as acts of God (earthquakes, lightning strikes, etc.). Similarly excluded are those losses which result from natural processes, such as disease or decay. These are the inescapable misfortunes of life which the victim is expected to bear.

Tort liability requires that an act which causes harm should satisfy certain criteria of wrongfulness. In western jurisprudence this has traditionally been defined as *fault*. Liability depends on the fact that the defendant was at fault in acting as he or she did. The legal definition of fault is clearly crucial. Does it mean *moral* fault, or is it fault in a non-moral sense?[7] If we examine the development of the law of torts in modern times, it will be seen that a strong moral element has rooted itself in the civil concept of fault. The exposition of the law of civil liability undertaken by the natural lawyers of the seventeenth century injected a strong overtone of moral wrongdoing into the concept of *culpa* embodied in the received Roman law then applying in western Europe. *Culpa* in earlier times may have had some moral significance, in that it was applied in situations where there may well have been moral fault, but the moral nature of the duty to compensate had not previously been made explicit. To a considerable extent, English common law developed in isolation from continental legal theory, but it too gradually moved from strict liability to notions of liability based on moral wrongdoing. In strict liability all that had been required was that the defendant should have caused the damage. The more modern view required that the conduct of the defendant demonstrate wrongfulness in the moral sense – in particular, a failure to show sufficient care. In this way, moral considerations came to permeate the very fabric of the law of negligence and the language used to express the duty of care. The essential philosophical foundation of this branch of the law of torts was that the right to damages depended on showing that the defendant *deserved* to pay for the damage that he had caused. This was expressed in the concept of negligence: the negligent actor should make good the damage he has caused because it was his fault (in the moral sense) that the damage had occurred. This is in accord with basic ideas of fairness in human transactions. By the end of the nineteenth century, fault was established as the basis of negligence liability, with the criterion of fault being a failure to meet the requisite standard of care. This standard was defined as that degree of care which was *reasonable* in the circumstances.

The role played by moral considerations in liability for negligence is subtle and uncertain. It is clear that the obligation to compensate is based on a moral conviction, namely, the idea that a person who causes harm to another ought to compensate the victim.[8] This is not incompatible with strict liability, in which the duty to compensate flows from the mere fact

---

[7] Whether blameworthiness (in the moral sense) should play a role in the law of torts is a matter of persistent debate. Useful contributions include D. G. Owen, 'The fault pit' (1992) 26 *Georgia Law Review* 703–23 Coleman, *Risks and Wrongs*.

[8] This is essentially the notion of corrective justice, which many tort law theorists see as the basis of tort liability. For discussion, see E. J. Weinrib, *The Idea of Private Law* (Cambridge, Mass., Harvard University Press, 1995).

of causing the loss. However, considerations of justice led to a refinement of the law and to the replacing of strict liability in many areas of the law of torts with liability based on moral fault.[9] At a later stage – most markedly in the second half of the twentieth century – the pendulum began to swing in the opposite direction, at least in respect of products liability and certain other forms of injury, and strict liability notions began to displace fault-based negligence.[10] For many personal injuries matters, however, liability has continued to be based on negligence, even if strict liability has made marked inroads in the area of product-related injuries.

The development of negligence was propelled by notions of fault in the moral sense, and this entailed imposing liability only for those acts which would normally be regarded as morally wrongful. The typical example of this would be a case where there was a failure to show proper care not to harm others – usually a matter of moral failing. However, the inquiry was not directed to the state of mind of the actual defendant but *to his actions*. The question was not whether the individual defendant had manifested any morally culpable state of mind such as indifference to the interests of others. All that was required was that he should have acted in a way which would *normally* be indicative of a morally blameworthy attitude. The moral judgement, then, had become focused on the externals of the action, with the question being asked: is the conduct in question of such a type as would *normally* be morally reprehensible, at least to the extent that a failure to take appropriate care to avoid harming another is morally reprehensible? It is important to note that, in spite of the objective nature of this standard, the terms used to describe liability continued to be redolent of subjective moral wrongdoing: *fault*, for example, suggests actual subjective culpability and *negligence* similarly implies morally culpable failure. In fact, as we have seen, a conclusion of objective liability says nothing about moral culpability of the actual defendant. It may be that he was morally culpable – in that his attitude was one of culpable carelessness or disregard for safety – but this is not necessarily so. This distinction has led to considerable confusion, and judges occasionally find

[9] G. E. White, *Tort Law in America: An Intellectual History* (New York, Oxford University Press, 1980).

[10] The embracing of strict liability in the United States is discussed in G. Schwartz, 'The beginning and possible end of the rise of modern American tort law' (1992) 26 *Georgia Law Review* 601–702.

it necessary to stress that, when they talk about negligence or fault on the part of the defendant, they are not necessarily implying moral culpability. Indeed, the very name of the entire branch of law has been detached from moral connotations; in the landmark case of *Overseas Tankship* v. *Morts Dock*,[11] an Australian appeal to the Privy Council, the court observed: 'The words "tort" and "tortious" have, perhaps, a somewhat sinister sound but, particularly when the tort is not deliberate but is an act of negligence, it does not seem that there is any more moral obloquy in it than a perhaps deliberate breach of contract.'

The proposition that negligence liability is quite distinct from moral culpability is supportable, but only to a degree. In fact, the bringing of a claim based on negligence amounts to an allegation of failure on the part of the defendant. For strictly legal purposes, this failure can be seen to have no moral overtones, in that it is merely a failure to meet what may be recognised by lawyers as an arbitrary standard of care. However, such an action is almost always viewed, both by the public and by the defendant, as an allegation of culpable conduct. For practical purposes, all the objectives listed above are served: the defendant feels that he is put on trial and if the case goes against him he will feel that he is the object of a punitive process. Lawyers who argue that the civil justice process should not be seen in this light – that it should be seen as doing no more than adjusting loss – ignore persuasive evidence of the effect of such litigation on a defendant, particularly when the latter is an individual rather than an organisation. There is evidence of a considerable impact on doctors and other health professionals of malpractice actions.[12] This should be taken into account in any assessment of the tort system: the efficacy of the system in achieving compensation for the injured person is one factor in the equation (and here the data reveal a picture of inefficiency in the medical context); other factors must include the system's impact on medical personnel and on the way in which medicine is practised.

---

[11] [1967] 1 AC 617.

[12] M. J. White, 'The value of liability in medical malpractice' (1994) 13 *Health Affairs* 75–87; J. Wiley, 'The impact of judicial decisions on professional conduct: an empirical study' (1982) 55 *Southern California Law Review* 345–96; B. A. Liang, 'Assessing medical malpractice jury verdicts: a case study of an anesthesiology department' (1997) 7 *Cornell Journal of Law and Public Policy* 121–64.

An example

The case of Dr Yogasakaran will be remembered from chapter 1. In chapters 2 and 3 we reviewed the specific problem of drug administration error in medicine and saw that these events are often slips or lapses, a form of skill-based error inevitably made by everyone at some time. We saw that distraction is a key precipitating factor for these errors, and reviewed the evidence that the vast majority of anaesthetists have given the wrong drug at some time in their careers. To reiterate the key features of Dr Yogasakaran's case: at the end of an anaesthetic an emergency developed for which Dr Yogasakaran wished to administer intravenously a drug called dopram. Unbeknown to him, a second person had incorrectly substituted dopamine for dopram in the appropriate section of the drug drawer. Under the distracting influence of the emergency and under acute pressure to react, Dr Yogaskaran drew up and administered the incorrect drug. This ultimately resulted in the patient's death. No suggestion was made that any other aspect of Dr Yogasakaran's management of the case was deficient. Dr Yogasakaran did not even know that he had given the wrong drug until he himself discovered the empty ampoule some time later. In chapter 3 we showed the difficulties involved in classifying the act of giving the wrong drug in this case. We also referred to doubts as to whether or not, in the actual case, he looked at the label on the ampoule. In our analysis below, we shall consider these events from the point of view of allocating blame, and suggest solutions based on whether his actions can be considered to represent an error or a violation in the strict sense in which we have defined these terms in chapters 3 and 4. We identify three possibilities, the first two involving second-level blame, and the third involving blame at the third level:

(a) The label is read incorrectly
For the reasons given under (b), it is entirely plausible that this would represent a problem of 'mindset', by which Dr Yogasakaran interpreted the label as saying what he expected it to say. This would be a variety of slip, a skill-based error and would involve no choice on his part. The culpability of this is discussed below.

(b) There is an unintentional failure to read the label
Given the pressure of time and the distracting nature of the emergency, the possibility of a lapse by which Dr Yogasakaran unintentionally failed

to read the label is plausible. The empirical evidence presented in chapter 4 makes it clear that this does happen to anaesthetists from time to time and expert evidence to this effect should have been readily forthcoming. It is hard to see how Dr Yogasakaran could have avoided a lapse of this type, particularly taking into account that he did not even know that he had made an error until later.

Blame in (a) and (b)

The interpretation of the facts in both (a) and (b) opens Dr Yogasakaran's action to second-level blame only. The failures in these two instances are both skill-based errors, and we consider them morally indistinguishable, but, as we shall see below, quite distinct from (c). Under the current test of liability the outcome would be uncertain, but nevertheless it is likely that a finding of negligence would be made. Whether such a finding is defensible depends on one's view of the purposes of tort law. If the goal is compensation irrespective of culpability, then this finding is acceptable. However, is this really any more than strict liability?

From the perspective of our understanding of the nature of human cognition and error, we have already noted that this type of error is unintended. In addition, although it is foreseeable in a general sense that such errors will be made from time to time, it would have to be said that this type of error is essentially unavoidable. Furthermore, it would seem inescapable that competent practitioners would make errors which, on the basis of the cognitive processes involved, are identical. The outcome of the error would depend more on chance than on any other factor, and is not relevant to our assessment of the standard of care, although it is obviously very important in other respects.

It is therefore very hard to see how any moral culpability can be attributed to Dr Yogasakaran for this error. If there is culpability, it is possibly better located in the decision to place a relatively inexperienced doctor in circumstances where he might be required to undertake anaesthesia for a high-risk case without the supervision that he might have needed. The central argument concerns the error itself and any antecedent issues in this case are unrelated to the actual error and probably not of Dr Yogasakaran's making. In particular, he had conducted an otherwise adequate and attentive anaesthetic, he was present in the operating theatre at the time of the crisis and no criticism has been made concerning any other aspect of his management of the problem when it arose.

This last point raises an important issue. Many theories of culpability – and this is notably true of legal theories – focus on human acts in isolation from those acts preceding and following them. We have already alluded to the wider issue of a doctor's performance over many years. In this case the judge made the point that Dr Yogasakaran's honesty, on discovering his mistake, in drawing the attention of all concerned to the true nature of the patient's problem was irrelevant to the question of guilt. This view makes perfect sense in the context of most criminal offences, and will strike the criminal lawyer as unexceptional. Yet there are powerful reasons why it should be considered a very dysfunctional approach in the context of medical errors. We have seen that errors are endemic in medicine. It is commonly taught that one important aspect of such errors is to identify them and then take all reasonable steps to limit or correct their consequences. This ethos pervades good medical practice and is very much in the interest of patients.

It could be argued that the error and the subsequent response by the maker of the error are two separate issues, each of which needs to be dealt with in isolation. Each act – the making of the error and the reaction to it – is to be assessed on its own merits. Thus, if there was culpability at the stage of making the error and no culpability associated with the response, even exemplary behaviour at a later stage – let alone the absence of culpability at that point – does nothing to alleviate the culpability attached to the first stage. An example from the criminal law might be where one person steals property from another, but then discovers that the property was of great sentimental value. He immediately returns it and does his best to make up for his wrongdoing. He is guilty of theft in the same way as if the property had not been returned, although his action in returning it would no doubt be taken into account in assessing the measure of punishment. This seems straightforward, and in most cases there is no alternative but for the criminal law to take this view of human conduct. However, when applied to more complex issues of culpability, the weakness of this approach becomes apparent. A particular objection to this way of regarding human action focuses on the fact that assessments of culpability are contextual. We make such judgements *with a purpose in mind*, and this purpose may determine the way in which we choose how to draw the boundaries of action.

A well-known Australian case demonstrates this. In *Ryan* v. *The*

Queen,[13] Ryan had decided to commit armed robbery. In the course of the robbery he told his victim to stand with his hands behind his back, in such a position that he could be tied up. Unfortunately, while the rifle was pointed at him, the victim made a sudden move. This caused Ryan's finger to squeeze the trigger in what he claimed was a reflex movement. It is a clear rule in criminal law that reflex actions do not 'count' as actions in respect of which there can be criminal liability. Ryan therefore argued that the act of killing the proprietor was an involuntary act for which he could not be held liable.

The court took a contextual view of the reflex action, pointing out that events cannot be 'sliced up' in this way. There was an overall act – the act of robbing the filling station – and this was overwhelmingly voluntary, even if there was a single, momentary act within the sequence which could be described as involuntary. Culpability lay in the voluntary nature of the overall sequence of action – the bigger act, so to speak – and it is this which had to be judged. Ryan's appeal against conviction was therefore rejected.

The problem of complex sequences of actions is one which has attracted the attention of philosophers of action, who talk of the *individuation of events*. Such analyses stress the importance of act description, which allows us to identify the boundaries of an act by choosing a broader or narrower act-describer, according to what seems to be most suitable for the purpose in hand. This technique has been aptly described by the legal philosopher Joel Feinberg as the 'accordion effect'.[14] The term used to describe an act may be 'extended' to embrace a whole series of events and actions. Thus *winning the war*, which is described here as one action, involves perhaps twenty individual battles (twenty actions), each of which involves possibly twenty individual conflicts, and so on down the action tree. These ideas are consistent with processes of human cognition in general, which we outlined in chapter 2.

The typical process of assessing conduct for the purposes of establishing negligence takes a highly individuating approach. This involves looking at each component of a cognitively integrated sequence of actions as if it had been performed in isolation. In terms of cognitive psychology, we have seen how quite complex sequences of actions can be understood

---

[13] (1967) 121 CLR, 205.

[14] J. Feinberg, *Doing and Deserving: Essays in the Theory of Responsibility* (Princeton University Press, 1970).

as an integrated whole: tying one's shoelaces or driving to work are examples. The intention of each individual component is subsumed under the overall intention of the larger identifiable cognitive unit. It is difficult to justify singling out one act within that unit for separate evaluation unless it can be shown that a separately cognised intent applied to that act. Thus, in the case of errors which are by definition unintentional, it is difficult to see logic in an approach which judges them as if they were separate or individuated intentional events. By contrast, violations in which the deviation from the normal procedure is actually intended can be separately delineated, and there is therefore at least some logical foundation for the position which requires such violations to be judged on their own merits. Even in this type of situation, however, acts immediately before and after the violation are relevant and cannot be discounted altogether.

In situations (a) and (b) above, it is hard to see a rational basis for treating an action which we have characterised as an unintentional error as if it warranted status as a self-standing morally significant act. This is particularly true in the context of the circumstances in which it took place and the exemplary behaviour immediately following it, by which every effort was made to deal with the consequences of the error. We shall deal below with the third possible interpretation, in which there is greater foundation for individuating the act. Even then, at least some cognisance should be taken of the context and of the response.

This shows that the assessment of negligence is strongly dependent upon where the boundaries of an act are set. Traditionally this has been done in a somewhat arbitrary manner, allowing for a conclusion of negligence which challenges our intuition as to the overall moral quality of the conduct involved. A powerful indication of this is our sense of the appropriateness of language. If it seems counter-intuitive to describe a painstaking and highly competent person as *negligent* simply on the basis of a momentary lapse, to which we can all relate on the basis of our own fallibility, it is precisely because of our inherent sense that assessment ought to be a contextual matter.

The taking of a contextual view of action, which should incorporate our knowledge of cognitive psychology, does not preclude focusing on highly individualised segments of conduct where appropriate. What it does is to increase the precision with which we can appropriately define the boundaries of the segments which need to be evaluated. The effect will by no means always be to excuse behaviour: the court's decision in *Ryan* shows how the appropriate drawing of act boundaries may lead to inculpation rather than exculpation. Indeed, in the majority of instances in which this is done in criminal law, precisely this result is achieved.

We accept, of course, that a highly atomistic analysis of events may be necessary to identify causes in the non-moral or scientific sense. Even here, as we have seen in chapter 2, a range of antecedent influences, including those of other actors, may be more important than the final identified human failure which led to a particular outcome.

Dr Yogasakaran's conduct as interpreted in (a) and (b) should be classified as blameworthy at the second level. It does not appear to involve moral culpability; whether it should be considered negligence for civil liability purposes depends on how the standard of care is set. This will be discussed in chapter 6.

Third-level blaming

The case of Dr Yogasakaran is subject to a third interpretation:

(c) The label is intentionally not read

Expert evidence led by the defence confirmed that some attempt should always be made to identify any drug before it is administered, even in an emergency. If we were to accept that Dr Yogasakaran *chose* not to read the label, then this was not an accident. Because the making of a choice would have been involved, it follows that an alternative, safer option would actually have been available to him. This allows us to attribute at least some degree of moral culpability to his failure. It should be noted that we would not accept that this was an error of judgement, in which his decision was an understandable choice to save time. This is because no expert evidence was advanced to support such a position. It would, of course, not be necessary for all experts to agree with this interpretation, but, at the minimum, at least a responsible body of such opinion would have to take this view (the *Bolam* test).

This view of the facts would place Dr Yogasakaran's action – a violation – into the sphere of our third level of blaming. At this level, there would be a strong case for a finding of negligence and consequent liability. (The actual context of this case was a prosecution for manslaughter, under the simple negligence test then applied in New Zealand. We are not concerned with the manslaughter issue here, except to state that we would not accept a simple negligence test as appropriate for criminal conviction.)

In this interpretation we are assuming that Dr Yogasakaran considered that the non-reading of the label was acceptable in the circumstances. This, however, does not reduce his blameworthiness below this third level of blame. Had he deliberately omitted to read the label in full knowledge that the risks involved were unacceptable, then his blameworthiness would have been higher, and he would have qualified for the fourth level of blame (discussed below). The fact that one does not appreciate the wrongful implications of an action is not of itself sufficient to excuse a conscious decision to carry out the prohibited action; the test is whether other reasonable doctors would have appreciated the wrongfulness of the course of action. As we have seen, the expert evidence in his case was clear: doctors should read the label of a drug, even in an emergency.

Level four blaming

There was never any suggestion that Dr Yogasakaran knew of an unacceptable risk and nevertheless chose to take it. Such conduct would amount to recklessness, which has been defined as acting with the knowledge that one's action involves a risk. This risk is usually, although not always, a risk of harm to another. It is also important to make a distinction between subjective and objective recklessness. Subjective recklessness requires that the risk-taker should be aware of the existence of the risk; objective recklessness may be inferred where the risk-taker acts in circumstances in which a reasonable person would have been aware of the existence of the risk. There has been an animated debate in the criminal law as to which form of recklessness is more appropriate. English courts have adopted subjective recklessness for the purposes of some crimes, but in respect of others they have been prepared to convict on the basis of objective recklessness.[15] A greater attachment to notions of subjective guilt has been evident in the practice of the Canadian courts.[16] Whichever form of

[15] A. Ashworth, *Principles of Criminal Law* (2nd edn, Oxford, Clarendon Press, 1995).

[16] For discussion of the subjectivist/objectivist positions in Canadian criminal law, see B. Rolfes, 'The golden thread of criminal law: moral culpability and sexual assault' (1998) 61 *Saskatchewan Law Review* 87–126; D. Stuart, *Charter Justice in Canadian Criminal Law* (Scarborough, Ont., Carswell, 1991).

recklessness is preferred for legal purposes, for purposes of the attribution of moral culpability, subjective appreciation of risk is essential.

An extraordinary degree of confusion appears to dog the distinction between recklessness and negligence.[17] This is understandable when an objective test of recklessness is used. In level three blame, the only distinction between negligence and objective recklessness appears to be the degree of risk. If a high degree of risk is entailed in negligent behaviour, the tendency has been to characterise it as reckless (in the objective sense), because in this way the riskiness is stressed. This reflects ordinary linguistic usage but it blurs the important distinction between the two concepts and deprives the concept of recklessness of its strong moral connotations. We must have a term for the deliberate taking of dangerous risks. Recklessness serves to do this work, provided we retain the subjective element.

An example might help to illustrate the distinction. There are frequently reports of boating incidents in which people fail to carry life-jackets in the boat. In many of these instances, this failure occurs in the presence of full awareness of the risk involved. Such conduct is unquestionably reckless. On occasions, however, particularly when the boat journey is made by persons with little experience or knowledge, such people may genuinely believe that the omission to carry life-jackets involves no significant risk. It could be argued that they *ought* to appreciate the degree of risk, and if the term 'objective recklessness' were to be used, this is a situation in which it might be applied. We would suggest that the concept of gross negligence would be more appropriate, because it retains the key distinction between negligence and recklessness, namely, awareness of risk.

Neither negligence nor recklessness is a monolithic concept. In reality, there is a spectrum of behaviour that runs from correct or acceptable behaviour at one end to intentional harm-doing at the other. Within this spectrum there are bands. The traditional bands are: blameless behaviour, negligence, recklessness and intentionally wrongful conduct. Our description of five levels of blame is an attempt to clarify and refine the last three of these. It seems better to qualify negligence and recklessness in terms of degree – for example, gross negligence – than to blur the distinctions

---

[17] For discussion of the distinction, see J. B. Brady, 'Conscious negligence' (1996) 33 *American Philosophical Quarterly* 325–35.

between the bands. For this reason, unless otherwise stated, our use of the term 'recklessness' corresponds to subjective recklessness.

Risk-taking: a medical example

In the case of the Bristol cardiac surgeons,[18] the key element for our purposes is that at least one of the surgeons concerned continued to carry out complicated heart operations in the face of repeated warnings that it would be unwise to do so. To say that one does not know of a risk after one has been warned by an appropriate person that the risk exists does not allow one to disclaim responsibility for the materialisation of the risk. Risk-taking may in some circumstances amount to recklessness. This will be the case if the risk is sufficiently major and the actor knows of the existence of the risk. It would be acceptable to set aside such advice only if one could show that a suitable review of the risk had been undertaken and the conclusion reached that the advice was unfounded. The conduct of the surgeon in continuing to operate in circumstances where the mortality rate was unconscionably high, even if well-intentional, was considered unacceptable.

Recklessness and culpability

The moral culpability of recklessness is not located in a *desire* to cause harm. It resides in the proximity of the reckless state of mind to the state of mind present when there is an intention to cause harm. The intention in reckless conduct is focused on the action, not the possible outcomes of the action. Nevertheless, there is a clear appreciation that harm of some type may well ensue from the action. There is, in other words, a disregard for the possible consequences. The consequences entailed in the risk may not be *wanted*, and indeed the actor may hope that they do not occur, but this hope nevertheless fails to inhibit the taking of the risk. As we saw in chapter 4, certain types of violation, called optimising violations, may be motivated by thrill-seeking. These are clearly reckless.

The culpability of recklessness lies in the moral offensiveness of the attitude of relative indifference to consequence. This links the actor to the consequence; he pursues a gain at the cost of another, implicitly

---

[18] See chapter 1.

valuing that gain above the interests of the person who stands to be harmed.

Level five blaming

This is appropriate to cases where there is a deliberate attempt to do harm. The culpability of this conduct is apparent; the only possible debate here is about the meaning of harm. It is beyond the scope of our enquiry to consider the defensibility of rules relating to, say, euthanasia or abortion.

Accidents and the levels of blame

In chapter 1 we proposed a strict definition of the word 'accident' which would preserve the exculpatory connotation of the term. To qualify as an accident, an event had to meet the following conditions: (i) that it was unintended; *and either* (ii) that it was reasonably unforeseeable *or* (iii) that it was foreseeable (in a general sense at least) but could not realistically have been prevented. Incidents associated with blame at levels one and two meet these criteria. At level three, because there is an element of choice associated with violation, an incident could be said to be foreseeable and preventable, and therefore not an accident. The boundaries between each of the levels described (including levels two and three) will of course be blurred – in reality we are dealing with a continuum.

Conclusion

This analysis has been concerned with clarifying culpability. We have set out to identify the various ways in which the language of blame is used. As we have seen, this useage is often loose, both in the popular arena and in the more specialised context of the law. It is notoriously difficult to tie language down. In some cases, this will matter little: we shall never agree on the precise meaning of a whole range of terms in our daily discourse, but the consequences here often do not extend beyond minor misunderstandings. However, when it comes to serious issues of culpability, in both the legal and the moral sense, terminological confusion is highly undesirable because the terms themselves exert considerable influence on the process of attributing liability. The term 'blame' is a prime example, but there are others, including 'negligence' and 'recklessness'. The use of one of these terms implies a judgement as to the quality of the conduct to which it is being applied. This judgement should be based on careful evaluation rather than on a superficial assessment based on the *external features* of action. In many cases, the allocation of an act to a particular category of blameworthy behaviour, such as negligence or recklessness, is fairly straightforward. Problems arise at the boundaries between categories and with actions in which the link to culpability is relatively subtle. Increasing the depth of the enquiry may not remove the need for judgement at these boundaries, but it will increase the precision with which these difficult cases can be allocated to their appropriate level of blame.

Where does negligence fit into this scheme of blame? Negligence, as understood by the courts, is conduct which fails to meet the required standard of care, defined as the standard of care of the reasonable person. Some instances of negligence, as determined by the courts, will involve morally blameworthy conduct, but some will not. There may therefore be a finding of negligence even where there is no moral culpability, as in a case where a defendant makes an error which the court considers a reasonable person should not have made, but which, as we have shown, might easily have been made by any reasonable person. Other instances of conduct currently regarded as negligent for civil liability purposes may indeed be blameworthy, in that they involve a violation, as in a case where there is deliberate and unjustifiable disregard of a rule or principle. There will also be cases where conduct found to be negligent is in fact really recklessness; here the defendant will have acted in the face of a risk of harm which he or she knows to be unreasonable.

Our interim conclusion, then, is that negligence, as it currently operates in tort law, does not always follow the contours of blame. In chapters 7 and 8 it will become increasingly clear that the problem lies not so much in the way the law is stated but rather in the way in which it is applied.

6

The standard of care

How are we to decide when an act is negligent? As is often the case with complex questions, the answer to the question may depend on the reason for asking it in the first place. If the question is asked when one is seeking to determine liability in tort, then the definition of negligence will be framed in such a way as to grasp those situations where it is thought that loss should be shifted from plaintiff to defendant. If the question is framed in the context of criminal punishment, or as part of an inquiry into moral blame, negligence may be given a very different definition. In this chapter we shall be concerned solely with civil liability and with the way in which negligence should be defined for those purposes.

A central question in tort theory in recent decades has been that of how we are to identify a satisfactory justification for transferring loss through the medium of civil liability. A prominent trend in this analysis has been the championing of economic theories which have sought to establish a broadly utilitarian theory for the attribution of liability.[1] In these theories, the aim of the law of torts is to shift loss where to do so will satisfy the economic interests of society. This was most famously stated in 1947 by Judge Learned Hand in *United States* v. *Carroll Towing Co.*,[2] in which he proposed that conduct will be deemed to be unreasonable (and therefore negligent) where

$$P \times L > B$$

where P is the probability of injury, L is the magnitude of the injury, and

---

[1] G. Calabresi, 'Some thoughts on risk distribution and the law of torts' (1961) 70 *Yale Law Journal* 499–553; W. M. Landes and R. A. Posner, *The Economic Structure of Tort Law* (Cambridge, Mass., Harvard University Press, 1987); G. P. Fletcher, 'Fairness and utility in tort theory' (1972) 85 *Harvard Law Review* 537–73.

[2] 159 F 2d 169 (1947).

B is the benefit to be expected from the conduct in question. Later theorists have attempted to abandon what they see as the crude utilitarianism of the economic theory of tort liability, preferring to invoke an ostensibly Kantian view in which the interests of others must be treated as of equal value to one's own – a position which gives rise to an obligation to ensure that one does not take risks which will threaten those interests. The duty to take care, then, is a moral duty which springs from respect for those who might be affected by one's acts. Reasonableness, in this analysis, need not be based on utilitarian considerations of the maximisation of benefit but on the equality of interests, and it is the objective of corrective justice to address imbalances resulting from a failure to give adequate attention to the interests of others. In one view, the apparent contrast between the utilitarian and deontological approaches to tort law may be reduced. Coleman, for example, defends a 'mixed theory' in which corrective justice is based on both economic and moral considerations. The moral justification of the duty to annul the harm one has caused is based on an idea of wrongfulness – the actor has caused harm by offending a community norm. This is because he has taken a risk which the norm defines as unacceptable, or, in the absence of deliberate risk-taking, his actions fail to meet an expected safety standard. In each of these cases, the negligent actor's conduct fails to meet a standard of care set out for the sort of behaviour in which he was engaged.

Where is the morality in this? In the case of deliberate risk-taking, the moral wrongfulness of the conduct is principally located in the attitude of disregard which the actor has for the welfare of the person who is placed at risk by his conduct: if I pursue my interests even at the cost of potential injury to you, then, in the absence of any justification for doing so, I fail to treat you as my moral equal. But if I do not deliberately place you at risk, my defective conduct is not necessarily indicative of moral wrong-doing. There *may* be moral wrongdoing on my part – in that I may fail to exert myself sufficiently to avoid harm to others – but subjective wrong-doing will be absent where I think that I have taken all the necessary precautions (and have not), or where I try, but fail, to conduct myself to a sufficiently high standard.

In a system of completely objective liability, the standard by which conduct would be measured could be set by purely utilitarian criteria. The question of liability would be determined by reference to what conduct promoted disutility, causing harm which, in the circumstances, could reasonably have been avoided. The setting of this standard need have nothing to do with the subjective capacity of the actor. Indeed, it could be achieved with reference to checklists of the most mechanical sort. One might say, for example, that if circumstances x prevail, then precautions a, b and c need to be taken; any failure to do a, b and c will amount to a departure from the necessary standard of care. The fact that the actor was unaware of the need to do c would be no excuse; nor would it be an excuse for him to say that he tried to do c but failed because of some incapacity on his part.

The law has never been this mechanistic. Not only would such a system seem unjustifiably arbitrary, but it would also fail to capture the essential morality underlying the obligation to compensate for harm caused. The standard of conduct expected is expressed in terms which provide *in themselves* a purported moral justification for the founding of the obligation. The law eschews, then, a purely arbitrary standard, and expresses the failure to meet the standard in terms of fault. You are liable for the consequences of your harmful act because you acted in a way which was *faulty*. Inevitably, this notion of faulty conduct carries with it a suggestion of culpable failure, a phenomenon which, as we have already pointed out, was already present in the notions of *culpa* developed by the natural lawyers of the seventeenth century.

Because of the moral element implicit in the standard of care, this standard should, in theory, be one which the actor whose conduct is being evaluated could have achieved had he been conscientious. If the standard is pitched at too high a level, then it becomes unattainable and it loses its flavour of fault. Liability, under these circumstances, is to all intents and purposes strict. The law seeks to prevent this result by employing the notion of the reasonable. We have a duty to take steps so as to avoid causing harm to those who might reasonably be foreseen as being at risk from our actions. This is the language of the classic tort case, *Donoghue* v. *Stevenson*,[3] in which the court expresses the essence of liability in negligence, using language which is clearly moral in tone. Not only is the notion of what is reasonable a moral one but foreseeability itself has moral overtones in that it is the justification for requiring a precaution. By declaring that a consequence is foreseeable, the court is

---

[3] [1932] AC 562.

effectively making a judgement as to the defendant's capacity to avert the occurrence of that consequence.

The standard of care, then, is best seen as an adjustable criterion by which the law infers liability. The moral backdrop against which it is defined dictates that the standard should be couched in terms of what can reasonably be expected of people. In so far as one cannot be blamed for a failure to achieve the impossible, the standard is couched in the language of culpable failure. In its application, however, questions of moral culpability may be overshadowed by utilitarian considerations, the effect of which is to impose an objective enquiry. In the end, the question before the court is not: *was the state of mind of this particular defendant a careless one?* but, rather: *was the behaviour of this defendant below the standard which can be expected by the plaintiff in the circumstances in question?* Ultimately, then, the law imposes civil liability in those cases where the defendant has risked harm, whether or not he intended to place others at risk, and whether or not he was actually capable of acting to a higher standard. This appears to be a form of objective liability, but, significantly, the objective standard is not plucked out of the air without reference to what is humanly possible. The courts do not set out to impose an insupportable burden in respect of the taking of precautions; their aim is, as they have repeatedly stated, to set the standard at such a level that most people might reasonably meet it. The standard, then, is pegged to a sense of the possible and, furthermore, the reasonable.

In this chapter, we ask whether the standard of care, as it is applied in common-law systems of tort law, is pitched at an acceptable level, or whether it has been raised excessively. If the latter is true, then the effect will be twofold. First, the extent of civil liability will be expanded, in much the same way as the extent of liability is expanded when a duty of care is imposed in circumstances where previously no duty of care was deemed to exist. Secondly – and this is a consideration which has been given scant attention – the raising of the standard of care may impose on individuals a burden of anxiety which may, in the end result, have a deleterious effect on safety standards. We have suggested elsewhere that the protection of the public is not necessarily achieved by the encouraging of a punitive culture. Yet the effect of applying an unrealistic standard of care may be to do just that, in that the connection between subjective culpability and blame is lost, and liability is imposed on those who could not reasonably have avoided it.

Occurrences of subjective fault in the traditional definitions of the standard of care

A truly objective system of civil liability would require no more than the externals of action on the part of the defendant. In fact, more than this is required: in the absence of a minimum mental element in the action in question, the defendant may escape liability, a fact which is suggestive of a moral fault requirement. An example of this is provided by the case of *Mansfield* v. *Weetabix Ltd.*[4] In this case a driver suffering – without knowing it – from malignant insuloma lapsed into a state of hypogly-caemia while driving his vehicle. As a result of the impairment of his consciousness, he drove into a shop front, causing the death of one of the occupants of the building. In the subsequent civil action, the defendants (the driver's employers) argued against liability on the grounds of absence of fault. This argument was upheld by the court of first instance, where the judge stated the law in the following terms:

> The position is . . . that if the driver suffers a sudden, unexpected, onset of some condition which then and there affects his ability to drive, and because of that sudden onset he has an accident which he is unable to prevent by the exercise of all reasonable care and skill, there is no liability, because it is that sudden disabling event that causes the accident in question.

This view was endorsed in the Court of Appeal, where it was accepted that, in the absence of fault on the part of the driver, there could be no liability. There is an interesting contrast here with cases in which a driver has gone to sleep at the wheel. In these cases, the courts have tended to hold that there is liability – civil and criminal – on the grounds that the driver must have received some warning, through drowsiness, of the fact that he was about to go to sleep. (In fact, sleep experts say that this may not always be so: a tired person may not be aware of his or her state and sleep can overcome a person without any warning.) A point of similarity, however, is the emphasis on fault: if there were no warning of the onset of sleep, by inference there should be no liability.

A similar result has been reached in cases where a defendant is suffering from mental disorder. In the past, the common law provided for strict liability in respect of damage caused by the insane; a more recent line of

---

[4] [1998] 1 WLR 1263.

authority recognises mental disorder as a defence to liability. In the case of *Canada (Attorney General)* v. *Connolly*,[5] the defendant, who suffered from severe bi-polar disorder, caused serious injury to a police officer by driving his car while the latter's arm was trapped in the window. The court held that he was not liable in negligence on the grounds that his illness prevented him from being able to foresee the consequences of his action. The court admitted that this was a departure from the objective test usually applied in negligence, but said that 'the foreseeability of the reasonable person is normally the measure of liability in an action for negligence', continuing: 'negligence, perhaps more than most other torts, is about fault and mental state'.

The mental disorder cases give a role to subjective fault. The mentally disordered defendant may not be held to the same standard of care as the normal defendant, but are there other instances in which the courts are prepared to take into account individual characteristics of a defendant which will have the effect of moderating the standard of care? There are two categories of case in which this issue becomes a live one: the liability of children and the liability of novices. In each of these the law is faced with a defendant who might claim, with some justification, that it would be inappropriate to judge him by the normal standard of care. In the case of children, one of the most influential decisions is *McHale* v. *Watson*,[6] in which the High Court of Australia considered the question of the liability for personal injury damages of a boy of twelve. The defendant had been throwing a piece of sharpened welding rod at a target but hit a nine-year-old girl in the eye instead. The court was faced with a dearth of modern authority on the liability of children. It accepted that, in general, the standard of care by which a defendant's conduct would be measured was an objective one which would not afford a defence in respect of his being 'abnormally slow-witted, quick-tempered, absent-minded or inexperienced'. It did not follow, however, that this would exclude the taking into account of a limitation in capacity relating to foresight and prudence which was not personal to the defendant but which was, in the language of the court, a 'characteristic of humanity at his stage of development and in that sense normal'.

---

[5] (1989) 64 DLR 4 d 84.
[6] [1966] ALR 513.

By bringing such limitations into account, the court went on, '[the defendant]

> appeals to a standard of ordinariness, to an objective and not a subjective standard. In regard to the things which pertain to foresight and prudence – experience, understanding of causes and effects, balance of judgement, thoughtfulness – it is absurd, indeed it is a misuse of language, to speak of normality in relation to persons of all ages taken together. In those things normality is, for children, something very different from what normality is for adults.

The standard of care for children, then, is subjective in the sense that it takes into account the *capacity* of typical defendants of that age; it is objective in that the extent to which that particular defendant deviates from the norm for his age group is not taken into account. In Canadian law, a further twist has been added to the matter by those decisions which have imposed on children liability in those circumstances where they engage in activities of an 'adult' nature (such as driving a snowmobile).

Inexperience is obviously one of the reasons why a lower standard of care should be applied to children, and yet the fact that the defendant is a novice is not in general taken into account in determining the standard of care. Here the objective principle is firmly applied, as the court made clear in *Nettleship* v. *Weston*,[7] one of the leading decisions on the matter. In this case a learner driver caused personal injury to the person who was teaching her to drive. The defendant's driving fell below the standard to be expected of a competent driver, but it was claimed on her behalf that she should be assessed by the standards of the reasonable learner driver rather than by those of the reasonable licensed driver. The court rejected this argument, pointing out that it would be an impossible task for a court in every case to assess the level of competence to be expected of an individual driver. It suggested, too, that to apply such a variable standard in the context of driving would lead to demands to apply it to other activities, asking – rhetorically – whether an inexperienced surgeon would be held to a lower standard of care than an experienced one.

The refusal of the court in *Nettleship* v. *Weston* to lower the standard of care in order to take inexperience into account has been widely accepted in common-law countries, with only one major court venturing a con-

---

[7] [1971] 3 All ER 581.

trary view, and that in a case in which very special factors were operating.[8] In the medical context, the issue arose in the case of *Wilsher* v. *Essex Area Health Authority*,[9] in which injury was caused to a patient being treated by a team of several persons of differing medical rank. The case is principally of interest in respect of what it says about causation, but the court observed that the standard of care to be applied in such cases was determined by the post which the defendant occupied rather than by the defendant's rank. This is consistent with the argument that a major reason for not departing from an objective test is the public's entitlement to rely on a certain level of competence from those engaged in potentially hazardous activities. We are entitled to expect a certain level of care from the drivers, pilots, lifeguards or doctors whom we encounter, not the least because our own affairs are planned on the basis that such a level will be met.

This is another important factor in the philosophical underpinning of tort law. Increasingly, in cases concerned with the scope of the duty of care (the issue which determines the *boundaries* rather than the *level* of liability), courts have acknowledged that one of the main grounds for the attribution of liability will be considerations of justice and equity. This test, which has most notably been articulated by the House of Lords in cases such as *Caparo* v. *Dickman Industries*[10] and *Marc Rich*,[11] asks whether it would seem *just* to transfer the loss from the defendant to the plaintiff. The debate in the duty of care cases has usually taken place around the notion of economic loss, which admittedly is different from cases involving personal injury, but the frank recognition by the courts in *Caparo* and in other cases of the role of considerations of justice involved in determining these issues might be extrapolated to the whole range of tort liability. One factor in this process of equitable balancing is the notion of reliance, a concept which has played a very important role in founding liability in duty of care cases. The fact that one person has relied on another may be grounds for constructing a legally recognised duty of care between them, but it may also be relevant in determining the

---

[8] The Australian High Court's decision in *Cook* v. *Cook* [(1986) 162 CLR 376] applied a lower standard of care in a case where a totally inexperienced driver injured the person who had persuaded her to attempt to drive. The court was likely to have been influenced by the fact that the plaintiff brought her own misfortune upon herself.

[9] [1988] 1 All ER 871 (HL).

[10] [1990] 2 AC 605.

[11] [1995] 3 WLR 227.

standard of care expected. If *A* relies on *B* to perform to a particular level, then *A*'s expectation may go some way towards defining the level which the law will regard as the appropriate standard of care. This is a matter of entitlement flowing from the relations between the parties, although the reliance which *A* places on *B* must be deemed to be reasonable (*B*, for example, must be aware that *A* is relying on him).

Patterns of reliance within society will therefore have some bearing on the development of legally recognised standards of care. The standard of care is not defined purely in terms of what the court, as detached arbiter, thinks will be appropriate; the standard will reflect general social expectations and the general social sense of what is equitable. This general expectation is that, in relation to hazardous or specialised activities, a minimal level of competence will be required as people cannot investigate in every case what is the actual level of competence of the person with whom they come into contact. But social expectations may play another, more subtle role. If it becomes widely believed in society that we are entitled to expect the highest possible standards, and if this expectation is expressed in terms of reliance, the courts will in due course interpret the standard of care in such a way as to reflect that reliance. The effect of this may be to drive up the standard of care from that which is reasonably attainable to that which is expected of a flawlessly functioning system. If social expectations are unrealistic – and we have argued in chapters 2 and 3 that this is indeed the case in respect of many mishaps – there is a risk that the legal standard will in due course reflect these expectations and become unrealistic too.

Setting the standard

Our enquiry so far has revealed that the law of negligence applies what is, for the most part, an objective standard even if it is a standard which relies for its legitimacy on expression in terms redolent of fault and culpability. But how is this standard actually articulated? A distinction must be made here between the formal test and what the formal test means in practice. In what follows, this gap between theory and practice will be explored at greater length and the conclusion reached that the standard of care as applied by the courts has departed to a significant extent from what might reasonably be expected of a conscientious and competent person of only average ability.

There is no shortage in common-law systems of judicial explanations of the standard of care expected of a defendant. A classic, and frequently cited, exposition of this is to be found in *Glasgow Corporation* v. *Muir*,[12] in which Lord Macmillan begins his account of the standard of care by stating that legal liability 'is limited to those consequences of our acts which a reasonable man of ordinary intelligence and experience so acting would have in contemplation'. This is the foresight test, which defines the standard in terms of a failure to avoid *foreseeable harm*. This restricts liability to a certain identifiable category of risks and excludes liability for the materialisation of other risks. It should be remembered that the test is not what the defendant actually foresaw, but what was *foreseeable* in the circumstances, which is effectively what he ought to have foreseen.

Some judicial definitions of the reasonable person are more complete. In the Canadian case of *Arland* v. *Taylor*,[13] for example, the judge observed that the reasonable person

> is not an extraordinary or unusual creature; he is not superhuman; he is not required to display the highest skill of which anyone is capable; he is not a genius who can perform uncommon feats, nor is he possessed of unusual powers of foresight. He is a person of normal intelligence who makes prudence a guide for his conduct. He acts in accord with general and approved practice.

To foresight, then, is added a certain degree of skill and a willingness to adhere to recommended practices, both of which can be explained in terms of risk. The unskilled operator poses a risk to others, even if he is not aware of the fact; the person who departs from the approved way of doing things may also create a risk, in his case a risk which could exceed the acceptable level of risk tolerated in the 'normal' or recommended way of doing things.

The writer A. P. Herbert, whose parodies of legal obfuscation are still capable of striking a chord, described the reasonable man as an 'odious individual'. Priggish he may seem, but there are other reasons for challenging the concept. Prominent amongst these is the fact that the argument that the reasonable person test is no more than a cipher: the real decision is based on the judge or jury's perception of acceptable risk. In this view, the reasonable person is no more than a justification for a

---

[12] [1943] 2 All ER 44.
[13] [1955] OR 131 at 152.

decision that is taken on other grounds. In an attempt to find out how people determined negligence, Green distributed a set of 'facts' to a wide sample of research subjects, asking them to assess negligence in relation to a hypothetical swimming-pool accident.[14] The results disclose that factors which play a part in this process include suggestion from judicial instructions and the magnitude of injury risked. The inclusion of a reasonable person test in the jury instruction did not appear to influence the outcome to any great extent.

We have seen how central to the notion of the reasonable person is the role of foresight. If the reasonable person would have foreseen a risk of harm, then it becomes negligent not to have done so. Yet how are we to tell whether the reasonable person could have foreseen that risk? The person making such a decision – whether it be a judge or a jury-member – must surely imagine himself in the position of the defendant, even if he is consciously attempting to imagine how the hypothetical reasonable person would have viewed the situation in which the defendant found himself. The difficulty with this exercise, of course, is that it is an after-the-event process, and the person who makes the appraisal is in possession of facts which the defendant would not have been in possession of at the time when he was actually faced with the circumstances in question. It is easy to say, today, that the *Challenger* space shuttle should not have been launched when it was, but this is because we know what happened when the O-rings failed. We know that crucial information about the state of the seals was available prior to the launch and we are therefore inclined to say that the decision to go ahead with it should not have been taken. This is the wisdom of hindsight, a wisdom which often leads us to conclude that we would have foreseen disaster even if those who acted did not themselves foresee it.

The hindsight factor has been extensively studied by psychologists. The first major study of the distorting role played by hindsight was that undertaken by Fischhoff, who argued that people frequently exaggerate the extent to which outcomes could have been anticipated once they know what the actual outcome was.[15] Fischhoff tested his supposition

---

[14] E. Green, 'The reasonable man – legal fiction or psychosocial reality?' (1968) 2 *Law and Society Review* 241–57.

[15] B. Fischhoff, 'Hindsight [≠] foresight: the effect of outcome knowledge on judgement under uncertainty' (1975) 1 *Journal of Experimental Psychology: Human Perception and Performance* 288–99. See also S. A. Hawkins and R. Hastie, 'Hindsight: biased judgments of past events after the outcomes are known' (1990) 107 *Psychological Bulletin* 311–27.

about hindsight bias on a group of student subjects, giving them an account of an obscure nineteenth-century British colonial war. Some subjects were informed of the actual outcome; others remained in ignorance of it. When asked to rate the probability of each of four possible outcomes occurring, those who knew what the actual outcome was tended to rate the probability of its occurring much more highly than those who were ignorant of it. Since the carrying out of this study, numerous subsequent studies have tested the effect, using a range of different situations.[16] Fischhoff's conclusions have been consistently supported: once we know what happened, we are much readier to state that such an outcome was predictable.

Various explanations have been suggested for the existence of hindsight bias. One of the more promising of these involves what Fischhoff termed 'creeping determinism', whereby people tend to attribute a narrative pattern to past events in order to make sense of them.[17] We all have a desire to see the world as coherent rather than as unpredictable and uncertain. If we feel that we can interpret the world correctly, then it is a less threatening place. So we impose order on events that might actually be beyond our capacity to interpret correctly. Closely connected with this tendency is a tendency to attribute blame. The attribution of blame fulfils an explanatory role: if we can identify somebody to carry the blame, then the uncertainty of an event is removed. The random nature of the outcome, which is potentially threatening, is 'domesticated' by our being able to lay the event at another's door. A bad outcome is not a question of fate – of hazard – but the responsibility of an identified individual.

Blaming brings into focus another form of bias which, like hindsight, has been the subject of psychological enquiry. *Outcome* bias causes us to attribute blame more readily when the nature of the outcome is serious than we would do when the outcome is comparatively minor. This must be distinguished from a mere failure to enquire as to responsibility: where damage is slight, it seems reasonable not to bother to ascertain who caused it. What is the point, one might ask, in making the enquiry in such a case? By contrast, where the damage is substantial, then we feel more

---

[16] Examples include: D. C. Pennington, 'The British firemen's strike of 1977/78: an investigation of judgements in foresight and hindsight' (1981) 20 *British Journal of Social Psychology* 89–96; N. E. Synodinos, 'Hindsight distortion: "I knew-it-all along and I was sure about it." ' (1986) 16 *Journal of Applied Social Psychology* 107–17.

[17] Hawkins and Hastie, 'Hindsight'.

inclined to identify the person responsible because there are pragmatic reasons to do so: the identification of the person responsible may help to prevent such a thing from happening again. But blaming is more than a mere pragmatic exercise in the prevention of future harm: it satisfies a psychological need to find an object of punishment. By punishing another we feel that we annul the wrong; we lessen the hurt.

The significance of outcome bias is that if the harm or suffered loss is great, then the desire to find somebody to blame may mean that we may find wrongdoing or negligence in those circumstances in which, were we to examine the situation dispassionately, there is none. It may also obscure the fact that responsibility for an outcome is, in fact, multi-factorial. Thus a search for a single wrongdoer who can be blamed may mean that we pay insufficient attention to the role played by other actors in the event and by system factors. The possibility that harm is accidental may also be obscured. We may accept a minor injury, for example, as being an inevitable concomitant of the operation of a complex system. 'Something is inevitably going to go wrong,' we may say when the loss is slight, but when it is considerable we are much more likely to say: 'Somebody must be to blame for this death: people don't just die for no reason at all.'

Is the standard of care excessively high?

We have seen that the courts have set out to define the standard of care in terms which suggest that it is well within the reach of the 'average' person. If this is how the standard is applied in the courts, then it is probably not too high. Yet there are grounds for arguing that in some areas of activity the standard has risen to a point where levels of litigation are counter-productive, distorting the relationship between providers and recipients of services and, in some cases, preventing providers from discharging their duties in a way which they consider ethical. So-called 'malpractice crises' in medicine are examples of this distorting effect. If these crises exist, then the social purpose of the law of torts is not being served. The same argument may apply in other areas such as product liability: if the prospect of liability deters innovation in the development of products, then the public suffers. It is a matter of getting the balance right.

But why would the courts allow the standard of care to be raised above an appropriate level? One way in which this may happen is through the operation of pro-plaintiff views on the part of jurors. This is always a possibility in systems in which civil juries determine liability, although the evidence for perverse verdicts of this sort is uneven. The raising of the standard of care is also, however, a feature of systems in which judges, rather than juries, make decisions as to liability – pro-plaintiff prejudice is therefore not always going to be an explanation of the phenomenon. To understand why the standard of care has a tendency to impose unduly on the defendant, we might examine how it operates in the context of medical negligence. In what circumstances will a doctor be adjudged to have failed to achieve the necessary standard of care?

The general standard of care is that of the reasonable person. This suffices for many activities, but the exercise of a special skill calls for something more – the standard of skill of the person performing those professional or skilled functions. The surgeon, therefore, is judged not by the standards of the reasonable amateur trying his hand at surgery but by the standards expected of a surgeon. This is trite law, but the issue becomes more complicated as we enquire further into the question of how this special standard is to be determined.

In English law, the classic case on this point, even if beleaguered by academic criticism, is *Bolam* v. *Friern Hospital Management Committee*,[18] a case which continues to be applied by the courts over forty years after its hearing. The plaintiff in this case had suffered a fractured hip after electro-convulsive therapy had been administered to him without his having been given a relaxant drug and without having his convulsive movements restrained. The defendant argued that he had acted in accordance with good practice, and that there was therefore no negligence. This was accepted, the judge ruling that there could be no finding of negligence if a doctor acted in accordance with 'a practice accepted as proper by a responsible body of medical men skilled in that particular art'. Negligence would not be inferred merely because there was a body of medical opinion that took a contrary view.

The judge in *Bolam* was echoing a test which had articulated a slightly earlier Scottish medical negligence case, *Hunter* v. *Hanley*,[19] where the judge observed:

In the realm of diagnosis and treatment there is ample scope for genuine

---

[18] [1957] 2 All ER 118.
[19] 1955 SLT 213.

difference of opinion, and one man clearly is not negligent merely because his conclusion differs from that of other professional men, nor because he has displayed less skill or knowledge than others would have shown. The true test for establishing negligence in diagnosis or treatment on the part of a doctor is whether he has been proved to be guilty of such a failure as no doctor of ordinary skill would be guilty of if acting with ordinary care.

The *Bolam* test, as it has come to be known, has been criticised on the grounds that it will allow the defendant to escape a charge of negligence if he can show that what he did was in accordance with an established and professionally approved practice within the medical profession. This, it has been argued, is to allow the medical profession to set its own standards irrespective of whether the practices adopted by the profession provide an adequate level of protection for patients.

Bolam is an instance of what has become known in the law as the 'custom test' of negligence. Its status in the law of torts is well established, although there are now chinks in its armour. Under the custom test, expert evidence establishes what the reasonably skilled and prudent person in a particular profession or trade would do in the circumstances, and the defendant's conduct is then measured against this. In the medical context, a robust (and, by the standards of today, somewhat unsophisticated) defence of the test can be seen in the judgement in *Marshall* v. *Lindsey County Council*.[20] In this case the judge said:

> An act cannot, in my opinion, be held to be due to a want of reasonable care if it is in accordance with the general practices of mankind. What is reasonable in a world not wholly composed of wise men and women must depend on what people presumed to be reasonable constantly do. Many illustrations might be given and I will take one from the evidence given in this action. A jury could not, in my opinion, properly hold it to be negligent in a doctor or a midwife to perform his or her duties in a confinement without mask and gloves, even though some experts gave evidence in their opinion that was a wise precaution. Such an omission may become negligent if, and only if, at some future date it becomes the general custom to take such a precaution among skilled practitioners.

The recognition of the legitimising force of custom, supported in *Bolam*, was to be further entrenched in *Maynard* v. *West Midlands*

---

[20] [1935] 1 KB 516.

Regional Health Authority.[21] This was a decision of the House of Lords in a case in which there was a difference of expert opinion as to the reasonableness of conducting a diagnostic operation on a patient who suffered vocal chord paralysis as a result of this procedure. According to expert medical evidence adduced for the plaintiff, the carrying out of this operation was inappropriate, a view which was ultimately preferred by the trial judge. On appeal, it was held that the judge was not entitled to prefer one view to another: on the basis of *Bolam*, if what the defendant did was in accordance with an accepted body of medical opinion – which it was – then he could not be held to be negligent simply because another body of opinion held otherwise.

The privilege accorded to customary practice has not gone unchallenged in the courts and there are cases in which judges have asserted that the ultimate arbiter of whether a professional practice is acceptable will be the courts themselves, rather than expert witnesses from the professions. The customary conveyancing practice of Hong Kong solicitors was rejected by the court in *Edward Wong Finance Co. Ltd* v. *Johnson, Stokes and Master.*[22] The court said that the fact that what the defendant did was in accordance with what was normal amongst her professional colleagues was not conclusive evidence that it was prudent, and the fact that other solicitors did the same did not make the risk 'less apparent or unreal'.

A number of courts have directly challenged customs of the medical profession. The Supreme Court of South Australia considered the matter in *F.* v. *R.*,[23] an action for damages brought by a patient who had undergone sterilisation by tubal ligation and who claimed that she had not been warned of the possibility of subsequent failure of this method to prevent conception. The court accepted that there will be many cases where evidence of professional practice will be decisive, but cautioned that 'professions may adopt unreasonable practices. Practices may develop in professions, particularly as to disclosure, not because they serve the interest of the clients, but because they protect the interests or convenience of members of the profession. The court has an obligation to scrutinise professional practices to ensure that they accord with the standard of reasonableness imposed by the law.' The ultimate question, the court said, was not whether the defendant's conduct conformed with

---

[21] [1985] 1 All ER 635.
[22] [1984] AC 296.
[23] (1983) 33 SASR 189.

the practices of the profession but whether it conformed with the law's standards of reasonableness. A similar willingness to reserve to the court the question of whether a customary practice is reasonable emerged in the decision of the High Court of Australia in *Rogers* v. *Whittaker*,[24] another case of failure to disclose a risk to the patient. The adoption of a 'patient-oriented test' in the face of evidence of medical custom was greeted with enthusiasm by opponents of the custom test. But the English courts were still bound by *Bolam* – until the decision in *Bolitho* v. *City & Hackney Health Authority*[25] appeared to question at the highest level the particular authority accorded professional custom.

The litigation in *Bolitho* followed a hospital doctor's failure to intubate the trachea of a child who was experiencing respiratory distress. Expert evidence was given to the court to the effect that a reasonably competent doctor would have intubated in the circumstances, but there was also evidence from the defendant's expert that not intubating the trachea was a clinically justifiable course of action. The issue of *Bolam* arose: if a practice was in accordance with a responsible body of medical opinion, then there should be no liability – or so *Bolam* suggested. However, in *Bolitho* the judge qualifies this by saying:

> In particular, in cases involving, as they so often do, the weighing of risks against benefits, the judge before accepting a body of opinion as being responsible, reasonable or respectable, will need to be satisfied that, in forming their views, the experts have directed their minds to the question of comparative risks and benefits and have reached a defensible conclusion on the matter.

This would appear significantly to restrict the effect of *Bolam*. However, there is a caveat: the court in *Bolitho* was clearly of the view that any challenge to professional custom would be rare. As the judge said:

> In the vast majority of cases the fact that distinguished experts in the field are of a particular opinion will demonstrate the reasonableness of that opinion. But if, in a rare case, it can be demonstrated that the professional opinion is not capable of withstanding logical analysis, the judge is entitled to hold that the body of opinion is not reasonable or responsible . . . I emphasise that, in my view, it will very seldom be right for a judge to reach the conclusion that views genuinely held by a competent medical expert are unreasonable.

[24] (1992) 67 ALJR 47.
[25] [1997] 4 All ER 771 (HL).

Even if the decision in *Bolitho* is interpreted conservatively, it demonstrates a position for which there is a consistent line of authority over the years, a position which, moreover, is attuned to recent decisions in Australia and Canada. In view of public sensitivities over the exercise of professional power, the likelihood of the courts endorsing purely professional setting of standards is slight. However, there are inherent difficulties with this approach, particularly when one asks whether a defendant can reasonably be expected to meet a purely court-determined standard when he or she is operating within the context of a profession which *expects* its members to comply with what it identifies as the appropriate standard.

Imagine that *A* is a doctor who is trained to carry out a medical procedure in a specified way. The reason for following the recommended course of action may be one of patient safety, but it may also relate to resources considerations. In the latter case, it may be that resources simply do not permit the carrying out of a particular diagnostic test; an expensive test may be thought to be unjustified in that it will deprive other services of funds. Every health service must make such choices unless it operates within the context of patient payment for the full cost of treatment. If *A* carries out the procedure in accordance with the practice recommended by the profession itself, he cannot be negligent under a *Bolam*-type test. He will also be aware – or should be aware – of what is required of him. By contrast, if his conduct is to be assessed by another, external standard, how will he be able to assess whether his conduct satisfies the expected standard of care? It is surely exceptionally difficult for a person engaged in a technically complex activity to imagine how his conduct will be viewed by a future court. Inevitably the question: *how should I do this?* is answered by imagining how professional colleagues – and, in particular, those who give professional training – would do it. This is the basis of much medical training; the neophyte learns by working with and observing others. It is impossible to develop medical skills on the basis of first principles alone. Experience must be gained and procedures learned from assisting or being supervised by more senior colleagues. If the law fails to recognise this, then it misses an essential feature of medical practice.

A move from the *Bolam*-type *reasonable doctor* test to a *Rogers and Whittaker*-type *reasonable patient* test will present particular difficulty for defendants in cases involving informed consent. The traditional approach of some doctors who may have thought it adequate to tell a patient only what they thought the patient *ought* to be told was unacceptably paternalistic. Under the *Rogers* v. *Whittaker* approach, the doctor must disclose to a patient those risks which a *reasonable patient in the position of that patient* might wish to know. On the face of it this is perfectly acceptable, but there are some practical difficulties created by expressing the test in this way. How is the doctor to know what information an individual patient would wish to have? The problem is compounded by the fact that a patient cannot necessarily be expected to know what questions he or she should ask. It has been shown that patients' assessment of the appropriateness of the information provided to them changes in the light of knowledge subsequently gained. Once the patient knows in detail about a risk, he or she is likely to think this information should have been imparted before the procedure.[26] A patient who suffers a particular complication is likely to become very well informed concerning that complication. After the event, that patient may understandably feel that inadequate disclosure took place in respect of the harm which actually occurred. What, however, of all the other possible complications which did not in fact occur and concerning which the patient does not possess the same level of information? For the doctor to provide enough detail about a complication which does occur to ensure that a patient is satisfied *after the event* with the adequacy of the disclosure would imply giving equal quantities of information about all the possible risks of a procedure. In some cases, before a procedure, the risk of possible adverse events may be very long indeed, although the chances of any one of these occurring may be very low. There is a real risk that the conscientious doctor will overload the patient with information and actually create a situation in which the patient's decision is rendered unnecessarily difficult. Ultimately, the doctor will assess his own conduct in terms of what a hypothetical conscientious doctor in his position would do. This standard, of course, is quite capable of taking into account the expressed or implicit desire of a particular patient to know certain information, but there is no escaping the fact that the doctor must use his or her judgement to work out what this is. There is no doubt that the doctor should try to see the

---

[26] A. L. Garden, A. F. Merry, R. L. Holland and K. J. Petrie, 'Anaesthesia information – what patients want to know' (1996) 24 *Anaesthesia and Intensive Care* 594–8.

situation from the patient's point of view, but the professional standard is quite capable of allowing for this and of embracing the evolution of patient expectations as society changes. The fundamental problem with the decision in *Rogers* v. *Whittaker* lies not in the implication that doctors should perhaps tell patients more than they have done in the past – a perfectly acceptable proposition; the problem lies in the uncertainty that it creates. Under this test the doctor cannot rely on his understanding of what a reasonable *doctor* in his or her position would think the patient would wish to know. It disregards the principle of peer guidance. It is hard to see on whose advice or evidence the court is going to come to an informed decision as to what a reasonable patient would wish to have known in the circumstances. Under *Bolam* it is open to both the plaintiff and the defendant to call experts, and the court may have to decide which expert evidence it prefers. Under *Rogers* v. *Whittaker*, presumably the court will have to decide this matter on the basis of its own assessment of materiality of risk, and will view such expert advice as irrelevant. Apart from any other objection, the court's view will inevitably be highly subject to the influence of outcome bias.

This objection to attacks on the *Bolam* standard, of course, is based on the perspective of the defendant rather than the plaintiff. The latter might be expected to respond by pointing out that he is entitled to the protection of a system which allows for external review – by the courts – of standards developed by the profession. The issue appears, then, to be one of conflicting claims or interests. The plaintiff has an interest in protection; the defendant has an interest in not being put into a position where he is uncertain as to what is the right thing to do. Which side of this conflict of interests is to be preferred depends on one's view of the role of the law of torts. This must be to achieve some sort of balance. We do not accept strict liability in this context, and it is therefore legitimate to balance the plaintiff's interest in compensation with the requirement that the defendant should not have an impossible burden placed on him. It could be argued that a movement away from the custom test could place some defendants in a position of unacceptable uncertainty. Furthermore, to impose liability when a person has conscientiously followed recommended practices strikes at the fairness which, as we have seen, remains a goal of the law of torts.

Room for human error?

In chapter 3 we examined the role which human error played in many mishaps. The argument we advanced then was that a degree of human error is inevitable, and that much of this error does not involve culpability. We now turn to the issue of whether the standard of care allows adequately for human error.

Mistakes are inevitable, and even the most careful person can be expected to make mistakes. The reasonable person can therefore be expected to make mistakes, although the reasonable person may be expected to commit violations less frequently than the unreasonable person, who, by definition, cannot be relied upon to take adequate precautions. How far does the standard of care, as it is applied under the reasonable person test, allow for the making of errors? The standard of care is not portrayed as being a standard of perfection, as is apparent in the definitions of the reasonable person we cite above. In his judgement in *Whitehouse* v. *Jordan*,[27] an obstetric negligence case, Lord Denning observed that an error of judgement in a professional context did not amount to negligence. To test this, he said, 'one might ask the average competent and careful practitioner: "Is this the sort of mistake that you yourself might have made?" If he says: "Yes, even doing the best I could, it might have happened to me", then it is not negligent.' At the House of Lords, however, this passage was 'corrected'; Lord Fraser courteously suggested that what Lord Denning had *meant* to say was that an error of judgement was not *necessarily* negligent. Lord Fraser said:

> The true position is that an error of judgment may, or may not, be negligent; it depends on the nature of the error. If it is one that would not have been made by a reasonably competent professional man professing to have the standard and type of skill that the defendant held himself out as having, and acting with ordinary care, then it is negligent. If, on the other hand, it is an error that a man, acting with ordinary care, might have made, then it is not negligence.

What Lord Denning probably meant to stress is that there are some errors which are inevitable, and that a perfectly competent practitioner is likely, at some stage, to make them. The occurrence of such errors is arbitrary and does not necessarily reflect on the level of competence of the

---

[27] [1980] 1 All ER 650.

person who makes them. Indeed, increased expertise may predispose to certain types of error.[28] This is surely correct; Lord Fraser, however, was right to refine the proposition, pointing out that whether or not an error of judgement will or will not be negligent depends on whether it *demonstrates a lack of care* on the part of the person making it. If the error is one which is compatible with the taking of due care, then it will not be negligent.

In theory, then, some mistakes will be permissible. In practice, though, most errors will be viewed as incompatible with the exercise of due care because due care, at the time, would have prevented them. The point is that a reasonably competent person will, *over a period of time*, manifest a lack of care for short spells, simply because it is humanly impossible to satisfy a requirement of full care all the time. But the assessment of such a person will not be based on their record over time but will look at a particular moment. In the examples that we have considered there seems to have been some variability in the way in which this is actually done in different cases. It is therefore misleading to talk about the reasonably competent person being the yardstick, because the way in which reasonableness is defined is neither clear nor consistent. All too often the yardstick is taken to be the person who is capable of meeting a high standard of competence, awareness, care, etc. *all the time.* Such a person is unlikely to be human.

One response to the difficulties posed by this essentially normative approach is to resort to an empirical definition of reasonableness and to suggest that the yardstick should be the *average* person. This would permit the courts to take account of inevitable human errors, but in fact confuses two issues. One of these issues is that individuals vary considerably in their level of skill, knowledge and ability. It is an obvious but easily overlooked fact that half of those performing a particular task will be below average in its performance. The other issue is that all people are subject to error, and that certain types of error are made more likely by increased levels of skill. Thus the best practitioners may suffer slips or lapses.

The truth is that a simplistic empirical approach is also unsatisfactory. We know that the required standard for any activity is not that which is attainable by half the people by whom it is undertaken. Rather it is a

---

[28] See the section on skill-based errors in chapter 3, pp. 75–83.

standard that produces an acceptable result with acceptable safety. In general, most individuals who are trained should be able to achieve this standard. For example, the vast majority of people can learn to drive with adequate levels of skill. It is possible to define a minimal level of accomplishment that is acceptable, and in reality it is this standard that we all expect of one another. In other words, we have returned to a normative definition, but one that takes for its reference the task under consideration and the minimal level of knowledge, skill and care that is generally considered reasonable by society. To take an example, consider the situation in which a child runs into the road unexpectedly in front of a car. There will be some circumstances in which the distance between the child and the oncoming car is such that no driver would be able to stop in time to avoid impact. In such circumstances, no blame could be attached to a failure to avoid hitting the child. How do we determine the distance which is reasonably required before blame should be attributed to the driver who fails to stop in time? Some drivers will be able to stop more quickly than others. A highly expert driver with the fast reactions of comparative youth may be able to stop within a shorter distance than a less skilled and perhaps older driver. It would be at least theoretically possible to determine the distance which would be required by the average driver: in other words, the distance in which half of all drivers would be able to stop. However, to set the standard at that point, that is, at the average level, would be to set a standard that 50 per cent of drivers would fail to achieve. Clearly this would not be reasonable. If 50 per cent is too high, as it obviously is, then is 10 per cent a better figure? We would certainly be more comfortable at this level because we should not be surprised to learn that one in ten drivers fell below a standard that we would endorse. In fact, it is impossible to express this standard in terms of the precise percentage of the population in question who can be expected to meet it. The best we can say is that the standard should be one which most people, with the exercise of care, could meet.

In addition, however, this standard must make allowance for occasional human errors. In a sense this approach is still normative, but in a sense it is also empiric. We know empirically that such errors are inevitable, and it would therefore be unrealistic to set an expected (or normative) standard that we knew to be unattainable. Also, to a degree, the level of skill which we would define as acceptable on normative grounds (for the purposes of granting a licence, for example) would be strongly influenced by our empirical experience of the attainable. To some extent, defining a minimal acceptable standard also addresses the question of whether any distinction should be made between the learner driver or trainee surgeon and the fully qualified person. The answer is that the required standard, being a minimum, must be met by all who undertake the activity, and that appropriate supervision or assistance must be available when necessary to ensure that it is met.

We have seen that judicial direction plays an important role in determining the outcome of a jury's deliberations. It is likely that the precise phrasing used in explaining the concept of reasonableness is very important. There is a key difference between asking whether an event (such as an error) represented a reasonable standard of practice and asking whether it was something that could have happened to the reasonable and conscientious person. The latter is much more likely to facilitate a judgement which is in accordance with the facts of real life and normal human cognition.

In this chapter we have argued that the standard of care is not as consistently and clearly defined as it should be. Often it seems to have been defined without reference to what is practically possible or, on the other hand, statistically inevitable. Because of this, there is often a tendency to set the standard at too high a level. In this way the balance of interests between plaintiff and defendant may be tipped too far in the direction of the plaintiff.

The issues discussed in this chapter relate to the theoretical concepts underpinning the standard of care. In practice, there are many features of the tort system which may confound the outcome. We are of course aware of the difficulties that plaintiffs may experience in seeking compensation for injury. These difficulties, including those related to establishing causation, have been widely acknowledged in tort scholarship. At times, problems related to the practical conduct of the case may disadvantage the defendant. In the next chapter we shall examine some of these influences. In particular, we shall consider the importance of expert witnesses in placing flesh on the conceptual bones of the standard of care.

7

Assessing the standard – the role of the expert witness

The central thesis of this book is that many incidents currently defined as negligent – in both a criminal and a civil context – do not, on close analysis, reflect significant blameworthiness. Our discussion of the standard of care concluded that this standard will tend to be driven up by the way in which it is applied in negligence litigation. The expert witness plays an important role in this process.

The court is the trier of fact in any legal action. In jury-based systems, it will be the jury that performs this role; in non-jury systems, it will be the judge. Whichever system is favoured, the task will be the same – that of deciding whether a particular fact existed. To do this, courts will listen to the evidence of those who witnessed or participated in the events under dispute. The law of evidence is designed to ensure that the court considers only that evidence that will enable it to reach a reliable conclusion. Opinion evidence – evidence about what people *thought* about a matter is usually excluded,[1] as is evidence of knowledge that is indirectly obtained (*the hearsay rule*).[2] Opinion evidence, however, may be allowed where the opinion is necessary to enable the trier of facts to understand the facts in question. So, for example, a witness may be asked whether, in his opinion, a person was intoxicated at the time of his observation, or whether he was in a state of distress. Another form of opinion evidence which is admissible is expert evidence, and it is here that one finds the most significant exception to the general inadmissibility of statements of opinion.[3]

There are several important requirements which expert evidence must

[1] A. A. S. Zuckerman, 'Relevance in legal proceedings', in W. Twining (ed.), *Facts in Law* (Wiesbaden, Steiner Verlag, 1983), 145–55.
[2] *R. v. Sharp*, [1988] 1 WLR 7.
[3] T. Hodgkinson, *Expert Evidence: Law and Practice* (London, Sweet and Maxwell, 1990).

satisfy if it is to be admissible in court. The first, and most important, of these is that it must be necessary to hear expert evidence. This means that the expert's evidence must address a matter which the trier of fact (the judge, or a member of the jury in a jury trial) cannot determine for himself or herself. The test here is whether the evidence relates to matters which are outside the knowledge and experience of the lay person. In many cases, there will be little doubt about whether evidence falls into this category: scientific questions will normally be assumed not to be within the court's knowledge, and therefore it will be necessary to hear expert evidence where there is, for example, a medical or engineering issue to be settled. A matter of, say, the stress-bearing capability of a construction material will need to be explained by an expert in civil engineering as a judge or a jury cannot be expected to be able to pronounce on such a matter. Expert evidence will often be concerned with issues of cause and effect. Is a particular injury, for example, capable of being caused by a particular chemical agent? This is the day-to-day activity of expert witnesses involved in toxic tort cases where plaintiffs have been exposed to allegedly harmful substances. The determination of such questions may be far from simple, particularly where a condition may be multifactorial in its aetiology, and experts may be called upon to commit themselves to causal judgements of considerable subtlety.[4]

In cases where the science involved is highly specialised, and perhaps even esoteric, there may be little disputing the central role of the expert witness. There are areas, however, where the issue is less clear-cut, and where there may be some dispute as to the admissibility of the expert opinion. Human psychology is one such area, and in this context there has been considerable tension between the courts, jealous to guard their role as the triers of fact, and psychologists, who claim professional insights denied the lay person.[5] In general, courts have tended to hold that matters of normal psychology – how the average person reacts to situations – are

[4] The question of what scientific evidence will be acceptable has been the subject of considerable debate. In the United States, the Supreme Court addressed this controversial issue in its decision in *Daubert* v. *Merrell Dow Pharmaceuticals*, 113, Sup. Ct. , 2786 (1993). For background and discussion, see L. Loevinger, 'Science as evidence' (1995) 35 *Jurimetrics* 153–90.

[5] R. D. Mackay, and A. M. Colman, 'Equivocal rulings on expert psychological and psychiatric evidence: turning a muddle into a nonsense' (1996) *Criminal Law Review* 88–95 (discussing, inter alia, the decisions in *R.* v. *Turner* [1975] QB 834 and *R.* v. *Graham* (1982) 74 Cr. App. Rep. 235).

questions for the judge or jury to decide, based on common sense and their ordinary experience of life, whereas matters of abnormal psychology may be commented upon by forensic psychologists.[6] This debate is relevant to our current theme, in that matters of error, in relation to which psychologists profess expert knowledge, may be viewed by the court as a matter of ordinary knowledge, and thus within the trier of fact's competence to determine. The reality is in fact quite different. There is a substantial body of specialist knowledge relevant to the analysis of the cognitive processes which underlie unsafe acts. A number of concepts must be understood, and some of these are actually counter-intuitive. It should be obvious from the material presented in chapters 2, 3 and 4 that this is, without doubt, a field in which the courts should seek expert evidence.

The other requirements for the admissibility of expert evidence are that the expert must speak within a recognised field of expertise, that the evidence must be based on reliable principles, and that the expert must be qualified in that discipline.[7] Of these requirements, the one that is of greatest interest for our current discussion is the reliable principles requirement, because it is against the background of this need for a principled basis to the expert opinion that expert pronouncements on the standard of care may be assessed. It is this basis of principle which gives expert evidence its authority and promotes an opinion into a normative conclusion. But how far does an expert pronouncement on a standard of care issue actually have scientific weight behind it? In other words, if an expert witness says that it is not reasonable to do *x*, is this statement based on *knowledge as to the practice of the hypothetical reasonable practitioner* (who is, as we saw in chapter 5, the yardstick against which conduct is measured), or is it based on what the expert himself or herself would do? If it is the former, then does the statement satisfy the requirement normally made of expert evidence that it is based on a body of theory which is susceptible to testing and indeed has been subjected to testing? If it is based – as we shall argue below to be the case – on the actual practice of an appropriate doctor from a comparable background, then obviously, in the case of a reputable expert, it will satisfy these criteria and will have

---

[6] D. Sheldon and M. D. MacLeod, 'From normative to positive data: expert psychological evidence re-examined' (1991) *Criminal Law Review* 811–20.

[7] See Hodgkinson, *Expert Evidence*.

been subjected to the objective scrutiny provided by peer review and publication. But this, we suggest, is not necessarily always the case.

The selection of expert witnesses

Before expert evidence can be led it is necessary to establish the qualifications of the expert witness. Counsel for the other side may challenge these qualifications, especially if the opinion given is thought likely to be unhelpful to that side's case. Furthermore, such unhelpful opinion is likely to be countered by contrary expert evidence, and one of the factors influencing the weight given by the jury or judge to two conflicting expert opinions will be the relative standing of the experts involved. A prominent international authority on a subject may well be thought more reliable than a junior consultant from the defendant doctor's own department, for example. In reality, however, the latter may have a much better idea of the prevailing standard of care in relation to the issue in question.

Bona fide expert witnesses are therefore likely to be selected in the first instance on account of their eminence in general. Such eminence is usually achieved by extensive research and numerous publications. Often they will hold a senior academic position and perhaps a senior administrative position as well. It is also unlikely that individuals of this standing will be of average or below average age in relation to all specialists in their field.

The second factor leading to the selection of genuine experts is their standing in relation to the specific issue in question. For example, if the case is about a central venous catheter (CVC) insertion, a specialist who has not only performed many such procedures but has also written and lectured on the specific issue of the use of CVCs is likely to be seen as more credible than a practitioner whose practice involves only an occasional CVC insertion, even if the latter's experience is much closer to that of the defendant.

The third factor in the selection of experts relates to their ability to communicate and to think rapidly under pressure. The expert is there not only to inform but, from counsel's point of view, also to persuade. There is furthermore little value in an expert who can easily be discredited by aggressive cross-examination.

There is much to be said in favour of this approach to selecting an expert. Assuming the person selected is honest (and we shall consider the alternative possibility in due course), a well-informed, articulate and confident person of some standing is likely to provide high-quality evidence and unlikely to be easily influenced by either side into modifying his or her genuine opinion to suit a particular point of view. Whether such a person has much in common with the majority of practitioners who carry out most of the day-to-day clinical work within the particular speciality is another matter altogether. More importantly, some such super-specialists may have relatively little sympathy for the difficulties faced by the journeyman who must turn his or her hand to a range of procedures, who may undertake some of these only occasionally, and who may be familiar only with the basic literature on any given procedure, and in some cases only with rather out-of-date literature at that. Obviously it would be better if all practitioners who undertake procedures or care for patients with a given condition are as well informed and current in their understanding as the super-specialist just described. Unfortunately, the majority are not. Much medicine is of necessity carried out by individuals who are broadly trained and able to cope with a wide range of situations. Inevitably their knowledge and skill in relation to any given situation will be adequate rather than outstanding.

This, after all, is the assumption on which medical examinations are based, even at the specialist level. The knowledge of the new medical graduate must encompass the whole of medicine, but only in broad terms. The specialist orthopaedic surgeon, for example, is able to forget most of his or her basic obstetrical knowledge but must still cover the whole range of acute and elective orthopaedic surgery. The expert who has gone on to spend ten or more additional years working in the sub-speciality of (let us say) elective spinal surgery has been able to forget about hip replacements, acute fractured femurs, and shoulder repairs. This type of sub-specialist may even have refined his or her knowledge in one or two specific aspects of spinal surgery to the point where he or she has achieved recognition as an international authority. The general orthopaedic practitioner, who may have to undertake some spinal surgery, will be expected to have sufficient knowledge and skill to undertake such surgery adequately and safely, as well as the core procedures in hip surgery, knee surgery, shoulder surgery, hand surgery and so on. Notwithstanding the fact that specialist examinations are very rigorous indeed, the expectations of training and examination are of general all-round competence rather than focused brilliance.

This too is the stated expectation of the courts in reference to the standard of care. We repeat the comments from the Canadian case of *Arland* v. *Taylor*,[8] quoted in chapter 6. The judge said that the reasonable person

> is not an extraordinary or unusual creature; he is not superhuman; he is not required to display the highest skill of which anyone is capable; he is not a genius who can perform uncommon feats, nor is he possessed of unusual powers of foresight. He is a person of normal intelligence who makes prudence a guide for his conduct . . . He acts in accord with general and approved practice.

It seems, however, that the expert retained to assist in determining the standard of care is often possessed of something very like the characteristics which this judge discounts.

The gap between the knowledge of the expert (in court, after the fact) and the practitioner faced with his or her next patient in routine practice is even greater than the above facts would lead one to expect. Having been selected, the expert is not likely to offer an opinion without first revising his or her knowledge of the topic in question to ensure that this is indeed completely up to date and properly founded in the medical literature. The more conscientious and cautious experts may supplement this process by discussion with colleagues of the issues at stake, although the courts do not necessarily encourage this very useful precaution. Such revision and discussion will probably be undertaken after a review of the specific facts of the case, and it will therefore be possible for the expert to focus on those aspects of the topic that are relevant and spend less effort on those that are not. This is a very different situation from that facing the practitioner treating a particular patient. Such a person will need a very broadly based knowledge which covers all aspects of the management of the patient and all possible eventualities, some of which will be rare. Thus this person may know only enough about any complication that may arise during a procedure to identify it and undertake the basic preliminary steps of management if it occurs. The risk of certain rare complications of a procedure and the incidence of certain unusual medical conditions may be so low that the average practitioner is unlikely ever to be confronted with such a problem. After the event, an expert selected because he or she has made a special study of the particular rare complication or malady is

[8] [1955] OR 131 at 152.

then able, at leisure, to refresh his or her knowledge of this very narrow subject. This, then, is the 'peer' who will comment on the standard of care to be expected from the clinician who, having had the misfortune of actually meeting this complication, was perhaps required to respond to it immediately, with no opportunity for consultation or reference to the literature.

We have seen in chapter 6 that a trainee who undertakes a procedure is likely to be expected to meet the standards of any competent practitioner undertaking that procedure. Equally, the qualified specialist will be expected to undertake any given procedure or care for a patient with any given condition in the so-called 'correct' way. The sub-specialist is certainly likely to know more about this than the generalist, but is the standard of the sub-specialist really the standard one should expect of all practitioners in the field? We recognise that the question which would be put to the expert would be: 'What could be expected of the ordinarily competent practitioner practising in that particular speciality at the level he or she professes to practise?' However, it is entirely understandable that the expert, in answering this question, is liable to describe what *ought* to be done rather than necessarily what *is* commonly done. Even if he or she makes reference to differences between common practice and pre-ferred practice, some bias towards high standards rather than minimally acceptable standards is likely. The same sub-specialist conducting a seminar for generalists would teach the correct approach, and would encourage aspirations to perfection. That is appropriate. Every effort should be made to promote the best possible standard of practice. Whether this role can be separated form the role of the expert in describing the true current standard of the ordinarily competent practi-tioner is less certain. Counsel for the plaintiff is not likely to phrase questions in such a way as to encourage such an emphasis. Even if the expert acknowledges such differences, or even if concessions are subse-quently obtained in cross-examination, it is very likely that the court will at least hear a description of a standard of care which is very high indeed, presented as the 'right way' of managing the case.

An example may help to illustrate this. A specialist anaesthetist working in a small centre was asked by a surgical colleague to insert a CVC into a patient who needed ongoing intravenous feeding. He used a CVC which had been given to his department as a free sample. He had therefore not used this type of CVC before. In a position such as his, an anaesthetist might be required to insert a CVC a few times a year. In training, he might have inserted a number of CVCs under supervision, but the exact number varies from person to person, and this particular specialist had been fully qualified for more than ten years.

The CVC in question turned out to be longer than the recommended size for insertion into the internal jugular vein via the neck – the route used by this specialist. It was in fact 30 cm long, whereas the usual length is not more than 20 cm, and ideally only 15 cm. This was because the CVC was primarily designed for insertion by a different route. Typically, a CVC placed via the internal jugular vein should be inserted to a depth of about 13 cm, although this varies a little from patient to patient. The anaesthetist failed to recognise that his CVC was too long for the purpose and inserted it to its full length of 30 cm. This resulted in a malposition of the CVC and subsequent complication. There were other points of practice which were subject to criticism as well: notably, a chest radiograph to check the position of the CVC tip was not obtained within a reasonable period of time, as it should have been.

The expert called to give evidence in the disciplinary proceedings that followed was a cardiac anaesthetist.[9] In this capacity he inserted several CVCs per week – sometimes two or more in one day. It would have been immediately obvious to him that a 30 cm catheter was far longer than the CVCs he normally used. In his hospital the process of obtaining chest radiographs after the insertion of a CVC was routine. Before appearing before the tribunal, this expert took great care to refresh his knowledge of the recommendations concerning the depth to which a CVC should be inserted, as well as various other related matters including details of the use of radiographs to confirm the placement of CVCs.

The expert was very conscious of the differences between his practice and that of the anaesthetist concerned. Obviously the baseline expertise of a practitioner whose practice includes inserting several CVCs a week would usually exceed that of a more typical practitioner who inserted only a few CVCs each year. In addition, the recently refreshed knowledge which he brought to his role as an expert actually exceeded his normal level of knowledge. Had he been approached without warning, he would have been far less certain of all his facts than he was when appearing

---

[9] The details of this case are directly known to one of the authors (Merry), who assisted with the proceedings.

before the disciplinary tribunal. It is also likely that the generalist in a situation such as this will have a broadly based knowledge which would exceed that of the expert in many other areas of practice.[10] The expert was very well aware of all this. However, he was obliged to outline his view of the correct procedures in relation to CVC insertion. In dealing with details of the management of CVCs, this witness could hardly fail to convey a picture of competence and knowledge that would contrast strongly with the picture conveyed by the details of what the defendant had actually done. Inevitably, the latter would tend to look incompetent, although in truth he was probably at least as competent as most of his peers in relation to the insertion of CVCs, and quite possibly as competent (or perhaps even more competent) overall than the expert. An attempt to present the tribunal with a perspective that placed the defendant's failure into this sort of perspective would probably have less impact than the description of what ought ideally to have been done.

The case is of even greater interest because of a subsequent study[11] published in the medical literature from which two facts emerged. First, about half the anaesthetists in a cardiac surgical unit were found to be in the habit of inserting CVCs somewhat deeper than the depth recommended by the expert on the basis of the published literature at the time – although still nowhere near as far as 30 cm. In other words, many highly experienced practitioners were breaking the rules in this regard. The main implication of this would probably be that these practitioners were not convinced of the importance of the rule in their practice – an issue we discussed in relation to violations in chapter 5. Yet this was the very rule that had been evoked in evidence against the defendant. Secondly, this new study showed that the conventionally accepted method by which a chest radiograph was used to determine the depth to which a CVC had been inserted was in reality unreliable, and proposed new and better landmarks for this purpose. In other words, some of the information conveyed by the expert, although accepted at the time, was actually wrong. Yet the defendant who had failed to use this unreliable method could not have failed to look incompetent on account of this failure.

---

[10] The court, of course, is interested only in the particular incident – not in the overall standard of practice of the defendant.

[11] J. S. Rutherford, A. F. Merry and C. J. Occleshaw, 'Depth of central venous catheterization: an audit of practice in a cardiac surgical unit' (1994) 22 *Anaesthesia and Intensive Care* 267–71.

This leads us to the question of the source of an expert's knowledge, and of its reliability.

The source and reliability of an expert witness's knowledge

Expertise is developed over years. In chapter 2 we discussed the importance of the development of rule-based and skill-based behaviour in this process, and made the point that expertise also involves the possession of a substantial base of knowledge. This knowledge is derived from teachers, text-books, refereed journal articles, the guidelines and other documents of the medical colleges, from colleagues and from personal experience. Goldman has shown that the level of agreement between physicians asked to review quality of care may be very low.[12] There are a number of possible reasons for this, but one reason relates to the mass of often conflicting information from all these sources that must be synthesised into a coherent whole. Data not only have to be learned, they need to be interpreted. A hierarchy of evidence is recognised, in which personal experience stands rather low and the well-designed, prospective, randomised, double-blind clinical trial much higher.[13] This should be helpful, but in chapter 2 we discussed the issue of bounded rationality in human cognition. One manifestation of this is the tendency to give undue weight to personal experience, particularly experience which is recent and which has made a powerful impression on the individual. However, even clinical trials which are prospective, randomised and double-blind may be badly flawed, or may be wrong on the basis of chance alone. It is not surprising that there are different views on many issues in medicine.

In recent years this has led to the emergence of so-called evidence-based medicine, and to the development of clinical practice guidelines which are alleged to reflect the evidence. The starting point of this approach is a recognition that much that is contained in textbooks, taught in medical schools and used as a basis for medical practice has very little scientific basis, and at times is actually in conflict with the best evidence. The main tool of evidence-based medicine is the structured review. Traditional or narrative reviews have long been used as a means

[12] R. L. Goldman, 'The reliability of peer assessments of quality of care' (1992) 267 *Journal of the American Medical Association* 958–60.
[13] For a discussion of this issue see: A. F. Merry, J. M. Davies and J. R. Maltby, 'Editorial III: Qualitative research in health care' (2000) 84 *British Journal of Anaesthesia* 552–5.

for producing coherent recommendations from the conflicting mass of information on a topic. Structured reviews bring a systematic and repeatable procedural approach to this task and when relevant use the statistical method of meta-analysis to synthesise the data of the various studies on a given topic. A group called the Cochrane Collaboration has established standards for the conduct of such reviews and has established a web site to make these Cochrane reviews readily accessible.[14] This approach should improve the quality of the information available for expert witnesses, but it is important to understand the limitations of systematic reviews and of the guidelines which may be derived from them (and other sources of information). The principal advantage of a systematic review is its repeatability and its formalised approach to dealing with the possibility of bias in a narrative review. There is likely to be a greater consistency between two systematic reviews than between two narrative reviews. For example, two narrative reviews published within months of each other in the journal *Pain* on the same subject (the efficacy of epidural steroids in low back pain and sciatica) came to rather different conclusions.[15] While this would still be possible with systematic reviews, the reasons for any differences would be clearer and more easily evaluated. However, it does not follow that systematic reviews will always give the right answer, or that narrative reviews will necessarily be unreliable. Any review can only be as good as the studies on which it is based, and as good as the interpretative acumen of the reviewer. In particular, negative findings may simply mean that no benefit has been shown, which is different from saying that no benefit exists.

All of this may be summarised by saying that medicine continues to be an art as well as a science. Attempts to formulate firm guidelines and protocols do find fertile ground in a number of areas but are defeated by the complexity and diversity of information and opinion in many others.

A review of any type, or a chapter in a book (which often amounts to a type of review), amounts to a document describing evidence from research, the author's interpretation of this evidence, and the author's recommendation of what he or she thinks ought to be done in a given

---

[14] *http://www. cochrane. org/*

[15] E. R. Kepes and D. Duncalf, 'Treatment of backache with spinal injections of local anesthetics, spinal and systemic steroids. A review' (1985) 22 *Pain* 33–47; H. T. Benzon, 'Epidural steroid injections for low back pain and lumbosacral radiculopathy' (1986) 24 *Pain* 277–95.

situation. Even if the message conveyed is correct, very few book chapters or reviews contain a description of what actually *is* done. When surveys are undertaken to establish the answer to this question, the results are disconcerting. The consistent message is a widespread failure to meet the standard of practice as defined on the basis of what ought to be done. As we have already noted, practitioners give the wrong drugs, insert CVCs further than the accepted guidelines dictate, work considerably longer hours than is sensible, fail to wash their hands between examining different patients in intensive care rooms, construct records that are unreliable, and make numerous errors and mistakes in every field of medical practice. We have examined some of the reasons for this in chapters 2, 3 and 4.

Consider the implications of this for expert evidence. We have seen that the expert may be unusually knowledgeable and highly skilled in relation to the issue on which he or she has been called. In addition to this, it should by now be apparent that this knowledge may be substantially derived from sources which are theoretical, based on ideas of what should be done rather than what actually is done, and at times even unreliable.[16] Given that some experts may, on account of their senior positions, spend more time on research and administration than in actual clinical practice, this gap between the theoretical and the actual may at times be very great indeed. In some cases the expert will have actually written the relevant review or textbook chapter. It is relatively unusual for such chapters to dwell on the sad failure of practitioners to achieve perfection. That is not the purpose of such communications. As with teaching, textbooks, guidelines and reviews are intended, quite rightly, to set high standards and to encourage the best possible practices.

Amongst the various documents available to the expert, formal guidelines are unusual in that they are directly concerned with describing appropriate clinical practice in defined situations. They are therefore an attractive source of evidence as to whether or not there has been a departure from acceptable practice. There is a real possibility that they will be accepted on face value as the norm to be followed in all cases.

[16] L. Rowe, D. C. Galletly and R. S. Henderson, 'Accuracy of text entries within a manually compiled anaesthetic record' (1992) 68 *British Journal of Anaesthesia* 381–7; A. F. Merry and D. J. Peck, 'Anaesthetists, errors in drug administration and the law' (1995) 108 *New Zealand Medical Journal* 185–7; Rutherford et al., 'Depth of control venous catheterization'.

This will not be problematic in cases where the guideline is widely accepted, based on firm knowledge, and does indeed embody what might be described as universal practice. However, this is not always so, and as guidelines proliferate, increasingly they will deal with situations where there is not necessarily an established consensus and where the information underpinning the guidelines is equivocal. The quality of guidelines will vary. Some may be local in their effect and may represent no more than the preferences of a particular department or even individual. Others will be formulated with great care and wide consultation and will certainly reflect at least a section of authoritative opinion. Yet even such well-supported guidelines may fail to indicate the existence of alternative opinion. When they are used to support expert opinion, the impression may easily be created that they represent the only proper approach to a given situation. The insertion of a standard or general disclaimer may not adequately offset this effect.

Guidelines emanating from learned institutions such as the medical colleges will have considerable authority, but they will naturally tend to represent a particular section of medical opinion – that precise section which is likely to be put forward in court. There will be considerable overlap between expert witnesses and people who write this type of guideline. Guidelines are a powerful force in the promotion of advances in practice, and it has been shown that they may have a beneficial effect on patient care.[17] Indeed, they are at times used deliberately to support innovations – the introduction of pulse oximetry being an example. Guidelines from the Australian and New Zealand College of Anaesthetists were very helpful in persuading hospitals throughout the region to meet the cost of introducing this technology. Pulse oximetry is widely held to have made an important contribution to increased safety in anaesthesia and has been almost universally adopted in the western world. The use of pulse oximetry in anaesthesia is now accepted as the standard of care. This is a good example of the way in which medical practice evolves. This is at the heart of the rationale for guidelines. They are designed to

---

[17] J. E. Pelly, L. Newby, F. Tito, S. Redman and A. M. Adrian, 'Clinical practice guidelines before the law: sword or shield?' (1998) 169 *Medical Journal of Australia* 330–3. For discussion of the potential impact of such guidelines on medical malpractice actions in the United States, see A. J. Rosoff, 'The role of clinical practice guidelines in health care reform' (1995) 5 *Health Matrix* 369–96.

improve the standard of medical practice; they are not written with an eye to assisting the courts in setting the standard of care.

We have seen that experts tend to be selected from amongst those doctors who may be at the forefront of medical research and therefore probably working in leading institutions. A problem may arise where an expert has strong views that are ahead of those of many other medical practitioners. Innovations are not implemented overnight, and conservative practitioners may be slow to adopt new approaches to practice. Future developments may vindicate either position, but if an expert is persuaded of the merits of his particular view and has the moral support of a guideline (which he may well have written, or at least contributed to) there is a risk that the standard presented to the court will be unrealistically high, or at least may differ from that accepted by a substantial group of practitioners. It is exactly this point that the *Bolam* test implicitly recognises.[18] A move away from *Bolam* could result in the courts preferring the apparent authority of guidelines to alternative but nonetheless supportable approaches.

Of course, a defendant whose practice has conformed to a guideline will find the guideline very helpful in justifying his or her actions. One who has deliberately chosen to deviate from a guideline, for sound clinical reasons related to some unusual feature of a particular situation, should be able to defend such a departure. This will be easier if the reasons have been documented and even more so if it has been possible to obtain endorsement for the decision by a colleague beforehand. More difficulty will be encountered if the practitioner simply was unaware that the guideline existed. As more and more guidelines are promulgated from an increasing variety of sources, this possibility is becoming inevitable. In the same way that it is already quite impossible for any practitioner to keep up with all publications related to a particular speciality, the number of guidelines will soon defy even the most conscientious efforts to remain abreast of them.

The gap between practice and preaching

Thus far we have considered the possibility that the standards advanced by an expert witness may be higher than those prevailing in general, and

---

[18] For further details on the *Bolam* test, see p. 165 above.

we have advanced a number of reasons to support this contention. There is an additional possibility – namely that the standard described by the expert might at times exceed that actually practised even by the expert him or herself.

We have seen that experts are likely to be unusually well informed on the specific matter before the courts. There is a flattering aspect to being called as an expert witness. Even the name 'expert' conveys a certain sense of pre-eminence, although the term is of course simply a technical one in law. Having described how practice ought to be conducted, some experts may not be entirely comfortable about admitting the ways in which their own practice actually falls short of this. Even more worryingly, some may have restricted clinical workloads, which are furthermore not strictly comparable with that of the defendant. Not only may some become quite out of touch with the standards in their own departments, they may also practise in very narrow fields and very circumscribed circumstances. Some may even be retired, or come from different specialities of medicine.

An example of this involved an anaesthetic case in which the post-operative management of the patient's electrolyte balance was in question. The patient had suffered complications attributable to having developed a low sodium concentration in the blood – the condition of hyponatraemia. The expert called by the plaintiff was not a currently practising anaesthetist at all – he was an intensive care specialist. As such he was very well qualified to talk about the condition of hyponatraemia in general terms and in relation to the management of such patients in an intensive care unit. In advancing an opinion on what tests the anaesthetist should have done to avoid the development of the problem, he certainly could not have been describing his own practice, simply because the care of routine post-operative patients was not a part of this practice. This is not to say that an authority from one field may not make a useful contribution to the evidence in a case concerning a defendant from another field. It is important, however, that the standard of care is not defined in a court by such a person's idea of what *should* be done rather than by evidence describing what usually *is* done by competent practitioners in the defendant's position, and what could therefore reasonably be expected to have been done.

The changing nature of professional knowledge and practices

As in any area of modern scientific endeavour, the boundaries of medical knowledge have been expanded in modern times at a much faster rate than at any point in the past. This has had two main effects. The sheer amount of knowledge in any given area has increased to the point where it will be impossible for any one person to master more than a portion of it, and, even when knowledge has been mastered, it may quickly become outdated as further developments take place in the field. The resulting challenge for the person engaged in any professional activity – but particularly for those engaged in medicine – is one of keeping abreast of a rapidly changing, complex body of knowledge if professional competence is to be maintained. This challenge is further compounded by the fact that continuing professional education must be undertaken at precisely the time when other pressures have made the discharge of day-to-day professional responsibilities increasingly arduous.

The reasonable practitioner standard undoubtedly requires of the doctor that he should not be out of date. This seems simple enough, but obviously a great deal depends here on what is meant by not being out of date. It will be impossible for any specialist to be aware of every development in his or her field. The volume of publications generated in every area of medicine today would make it humanly impossible for any person to read, or even to skim through, every report of every piece of research published in his field. Many practitioners may manage to keep up with two or three journals in their speciality and therefore to be familiar, at some level at least, with the matters reported in the columns of those journals. However, the mere reading of articles may be of limited use. What is really required is thoughtful evaluation of their contents and of their implications for practice. Given the level of research activity within all specialities today, this task will make major demands on the increasingly limited time of the practitioner.

There are other ways by which one may attempt to keep up with developments. Most doctors would be expected to attend a certain number of meetings or courses at which new developments are discussed. In many countries there are now formal requirements for continuing professional education which need to be fulfilled to maintain licensing. But even this level of activity may not be enough to ensure that practitioners are comprehensively aware of *everything* that is happening in their speciality, and there will almost certainly be matters which the expert witness may be aware of which may have passed the ordinary practitioner by or which may not yet have attracted his attention. Will such ignorance amount to a failure to meet the standard of care? If the expert witness concludes that a particular procedure could have been used at the time, but that the defendant did not know of the existence of this option, does this mean that the defendant was not a reasonably competent practitioner?

It is clear that the courts accept the changing nature of the corpus of medical knowledge and have also recognised the difficulty of dissemination of this knowledge. A decision of the Supreme Court of Canada illustrates this. In *ter Neuzen* v. *Korn*,[19] the appellant had participated in an artificial insemination programme run by the defendant, an obstetrician and gynaecologist. The period during which this treatment was provided ran from 1981 until January 1985. On the last of these procedures, she became infected with HIV, the risk of which she had not been informed of by the defendant. In the resulting litigation, the question before the court was whether the defendant's failure himself to be aware of this risk, together with his failure to screen his donors in such a way as to reduce the level of risk, amounted to negligence. The appellant argued that he could have been expected to know of the risk, even if the majority of medical practitioners might not have been aware of it at the time.

Reports of heterosexual transmission of HIV were first published early in 1983. It was not until October 1983, however, that the first mention was made in the medical literature of the possibility of transmitting sexually transmitted diseases through the medium of artificial insemination. This came in the form of a letter published in the influential – and widely circulated – journal, the *New England Journal of Medicine*. However, this journal, in spite of its general pre-eminence, was not widely read by obstetricians and gynaecologists. In September 1985 a medical journal published a report of a case in which HIV had been transmitted through artificial insemination. This was not mentioned in obstetric literature, and it was not until 1986 that an article appeared in which a complete list of known risks of artificial insemination was published.

At this stage of the HIV pandemic, information was sketchy and there were significant regional differences in respect of what was known about the virus. The issue of transmission through artificial insemination had

---

[19] [1995] 3 SCR 674.

been a matter of some discussion in Australia, where, in 1984, it had been established that a number of babies had become HIV-positive as a result of blood transfusion. The discussion in Australia, it appeared, was not widely reported in North America, and it was not until later in 1985 that it became generally known amongst doctors in North America that these events had occurred in Australia. Finally, in September 1985 an article appeared in *The Lancet* reporting cases in which Australian women were found to have contracted HIV through artificial insemination. It was at this point that the defendant halted his artificial insemination programme and recommended to his patients that they be tested for the virus.

It is clear that the defendant *could* have been aware of the risk in question when he administered the final insemination in January 1985. It also became apparent on the basis of evidence put before the court that the defendant's practice in relation to artificial insemination was in line with such practices in Canada at the time. In holding that the defendant was not negligent, the court recognised that, in spite of the theoretical availability of this knowledge, in actual fact the defendant could not reasonably be expected to have discovered it. This suggests an acceptance of reasonable limitations on the extent to which a practitioner, even in a fairly specialised area of activity such as artificial insemination, may be expected to follow international developments. The use of electronic dissemination of medical information may change the precise nature of the problems associated with keeping up to date, but it is unlikely to eliminate them.

In this case not only were the difficulties of keeping up with medical developments acknowledged, but the court also heeded Lord Denning's advice in *Roe* v. *Ministry of Health*[20] that 'we must not look at the 1947 accident with 1954 spectacles'. As a general rule the courts will try to ensure that judgements are made according to the knowledge and practices prevailing at the time of the incident. This is not always easy to do as changes in knowledge and practice may sometimes occur gradually over a period of time. In this sort of situation individual practitioners do not all change abruptly at the same moment. For example, attitudes to internal or other intimate examinations have changed markedly over the last twenty years. The training of doctors who qualified at the beginning of this period usually placed great emphasis on the importance of

---

[20] [1954] 2 All ER 131 (CA).

conducting such examinations in any circumstances in which there was the remotest possibility that they could be helpful. It is still considered just as important as ever that the clinical information elicited from such examinations be obtained. However, several factors have contributed to a change in approach. New technology has allowed doctors to obtain images of the internal organs in a way not previously possible. There is now also a more ready availability of specialists who could be expected to conduct internal examinations more skilfully than their generalist colleagues. Some of the latter would therefore see less point in subjecting a patient to an uncomfortable and embarrassing examination which they knew would need to be repeated later by someone else. Most significantly, there has been a striking change in awareness of the sensitivities of patients, and in the importance placed on these. Obviously, patients still need to have internal examinations carried out, and at times it will be quite appropriate for this to be done by a general practitioner. Indeed, it would often be negligent to omit such an examination. However, a practitioner who continued to follow the previous practice in this regard, even on patients for whom the examination could be justified only on the grounds of completeness, might well be open to criticism of sexual impropriety in a way that would not have been likely when he first qualified. In New Zealand an otorhinolaryngologist was subject to prolonged disciplinary proceedings precisely in this context, in relation to the examination of lymph nodes in the groins and axillae of female patients whose complaint related to the throat or nose.[21] Another example of change of this sort is provided by the highly publicised inquiry into practices at the National Women's Hospital in Auckland in the 1980s. During this inquiry it emerged that a common practice in this major teaching hospital involved the permitting of medical students to conduct vaginal examinations on patients who were undergoing gynaecological procedures under anaesthetic. The lack of consent in regard to this training exercise was the central point of criticism. However, one of the outcomes of the affair was the implementataion of clinical surrogates. These are women who are paid to undergo vaginal examinations in a teaching context in order to satisfy the requirements of training without necessarily having to seek the participation of patients. Once again, there is a substantial change between the earlier and later approaches. Many of

---

[21] '"No need" to touch genitalia', *New Zealand Herald* (28 November 1995).

the doctors involved in the inquiry argued that their practices were standard and ethically acceptable. The presiding judge left no doubt that she considered them unacceptable, not only at the time of the inquiry, but for a considerable period prior to it.[22]

The argument here is not about the need for change. What we want to illustrate is how, when practices change over a period of time, some practitioners may unwittingly find themselves out of kilter with the new consensus. It may be very difficult to distinguish inappropriate activity from insensitivity, and insensitivity from conscientious compliance with rules emphasised as extremely important during a doctor's training but now no longer always (or perhaps ever) applicable.

It may be even more difficult to establish the appropriate standard at the time if events of this sort are brought before the courts many years after they occurred. It is not suggested here that failure to adjust to more enlightened practices should be condoned. We simply draw attention to the difficulty a court might have in determining whether a given incident would have been acceptable at the time it occurred. This is particularly so when the change involves human considerations rather than scientific or technological developments. The assessment of past practices in relation to informed consent provides a particularly pertinent example of this difficulty. This is an area which has undergone progressive evolution over the last decades, and in which it is difficult to establish a precise chronology of change. Not only has the norm changed, but, as discussed in chapter 5, concepts of what is legally acceptable have changed as well.

Outcome bias – looking beyond the individual accident

In chapter 5 we mentioned the work of Fischoff, which showed that knowing what did in fact happen makes people much more likely to state that such an outcome was predictable. Caplan, Posner and Cheney have shown that knowledge of outcome has, in a similar way, an important confounding influence on physician's judgements of appropriateness of care. One hundred and twelve practising 'anesthesiologists'[23] were asked

---

[22] Committee of inquiry into allegations concerning the treatment of cervical cancer at National Women's Hospital and into other related matters, *The Report of the Cervical Cancer Inquiry* (Auckland, Government Printing Office, 1988).

[23] In the USA, an 'anesthesiologist' is medically qualified and distinguished from a nurse 'anesthetist'. In British practice nurse anaesthetists are very unusual, and the term 'anaesthetist' is equivalent to the American term 'anesthesiologist'.

to judge the appropriateness of care in twenty-one cases involving adverse anaesthetic outcomes. For each case two outcomes were provided, one involving temporary harm and one involving permanent harm. A significant inverse relationship was observed between the severity of the outcome and the judgement of appropriateness of care in 71 per cent of the matched pairs of cases.[24] Being informed that permanent harm occurred made it much more likely that the reviewer would be critical of the appropriateness of care than being told that the harm was only temporary – although the facts were identical in each case. In a situation such as that involving Dr Hugel (discussed in chapter 1), in which an essentially healthy child undergoing a relatively minor procedure died, this influence is very powerful. The tragedy of the outcome demands a response. Reviewing such a case, even the most conscientiously objective expert witness could not but feel deeply moved by the loss of a young and promising life. Emotionally, the sense that such a disaster simply should not have occurred would be almost overwhelming. The truth is that disasters of this type do occur, not only in medicine; it is by no means always the case that they are avoidable, or that someone is to blame, but it may be very difficult to remain dispassionate. Simply framing the question in such a way that it focuses on the care provided rather than the outcome which resulted – as the courts would do – is not enough to prevent outcome bias; that is the precise message of Caplan et al.'s study.

It may be useful to consider once again the example of drug error discussed in chapter 2. Clearly, the defendant in a case where a wrongly administered drug has caused harm to a patient may have been no more negligent than the majority of his or her colleagues, who will themselves have made very similar, but harmless, errors at some time. Thus the defendant is to some degree the victim of two influences beyond his or her control. The first relates to outcome bias. The second, well recognised within the law, is often referred to as *moral luck*;[25] had no harm occurred, it is almost certain that no case would have been brought. It has not escaped us that the patient is also a victim of this lottery and has in all likelihood paid an even higher price for this misfortune. In judging the degree of negligence involved, however, it is instructive to compare the

---

[24] R. A. Caplan, K. L. Posner and F. W. Cheney, 'Effect of outcome on physician judgments of appropriateness of care' (1991) 265 *Journal of the American Medical Association* 1957–60.

[25] Alternatively, the phrase 'outcome lottery' is sometimes used in this context.

difference between the opinions which might be expressed in this situation and in the situation in which exactly the same slip or lapse produced no harm. In the latter case, most practitioners would probably be inclined to accept the error as inevitable, and worthy only of minor comment or discussion. In the former, harsher criticism would be likely. We think neither position is entirely correct. The former tends to place undue responsibility for a systems problem onto an individual practitioner; the latter discounts the importance of the problem. In our opinion incidents which are hazardous but which do not cause harm should be taken very seriously indeed. Every effort should be made to identify the factors which predispose to them, and to find ways to make their occurrence less likely. This type of approach has been gaining greater acceptance in medicine in recent years,[26] but, as we discussed in chapters 2 and 3, there is still room for improvement. For the purposes of the assessment of the standard of care, it is important to distinguish between two different issues. The fact that serious harm may result from errors is one issue, and implies that errors are important whether that harm occurs or not. It also implies that the standard of care *required* is high. The fact that there is a risk of serious harm must place a considerable onus on practitioners, *and on institutions*, to ensure that considerable care is taken. This principle is well established in the law of negligence, where the courts have frequently stressed that the more serious the possible harm that can be caused, then the higher will be the standard of care expected. The classic statement of this proposition in English law is to be found in the case of *Paris* v. *Stepney Borough Council*[27] in which a workman to whom the council owed a duty of care had only one eye. It was held that the seriousness of any eye injury to such a plaintiff meant that a much higher degree of care than normal was required. The second issue is the level of care actually *observed*. The fact that harm actually has occurred in a particular case does not necessarily imply that the high level of care *required* was not actually *observed*. The distinction could be expressed as follows. The possibility of a harmful outcome may raise the standard of care required; the actual occurrence of a bad outcome says nothing about whether the appropriate degree of care was or was not taken.

---

[26] D. Blumenthal, 'Making medical errors into "medical treasures"' (1994) 272 *Journal of the American Medical Association* 1867–8; L. L. Leape, 'Error in Medicine' (1994) 272 *Journal of the American Medical Association* 1851–7.

[27] [1951] AC 367.

In assessing the standard of care it may sometimes be more relevant for the expert to examine the contribution of general or systemic factors to the prevailing standard of practice within an institution rather than to focus on the individual. In a case of a drug administration error, for example, the individual will probably have been practising at the same standard as his or her colleagues in the same institution. The contribution of rostering systems to fatigue is an obvious example of an institutional factor which might be relevant to the generation of an error – and there are many others.

Unfortunately, liability depends (amongst other things) on proof of causation. It is usually easier to prove that a certain doctor administered an identified drug which harmed a patient than to show that general aspects of an institution's organisation were important in the generation of the error. Once again, it is apparent that the standard which comes to be expected of the individual practitioner may at times be rather higher than that which prevails in practice.

Statistical approaches to assessing acceptable standards of technical performance

In chapter 3 we noted that the case of the Bristol cardiac surgeons raises the question of defining acceptability in relation to performance in a technical sense. Typically this arises in the context of measurable outcomes such as mortality, post-operative infection rates or rates of perioperative myocardial infarction after coronary surgery.

This is a complex subject and numerous methods have been developed to assist the audit of practice standards. Often these involve comparing the results of an individual with those of a group – all the cardiac surgeons in Britain, for example. This may be done on an ongoing basis, using cumulative outcome plots, and might make use of certain percentiles (such as the 10th percentile) to set limits which reflect the practice of the group as a whole. Variations in patient risk factors ('case mix') must be taken into account, and random variation must also be allowed for.[28] The appropriate use of these methods is not simple, and as yet they have not been widely adopted into medical practice. Typically the approach is

---

[28] J. Poloniecki, O. Valencia and P. Littlejohns, 'Cumulative risk adjusted mortality chart for detecting changes in death rate: observational study of heart surgery' (1998) 316 *British Medical Journal* 1697–700.

normative: performance is considered acceptable provided it is better than that of a certain percentage of the group. Being in the top two-thirds might be considered reassuring, for example, and being the worst member of a department might be cause for concern – but is this valid? A moment's reflection will show that it is a matter of statistical inevitability that, in any group, someone will be the best and someone the worst. The worst can only improve his or her ranking at the expense of others, but improvement on the part of the worst individual is not evidence of deterioration on the part of those he or she has passed. Surely the important question relates to whether all or any of the group are good enough. However, the alternative of defining acceptable limits from first principles raises the issue of what is achievable, and in the end this can only be determined from results obtained in actual practice. One factor may nevertheless assist: for most procedures it may well be that the distribution of results is skewed, with the majority of competent surgeons achieving relatively similar results, and a small number of less competent operators performing at a markedly different level. Thus it may be possible to establish a national standard for a procedure, with the expectation that such results will be achievable by any competent and well-trained practitioner.

The larger the group, the more reliable normative approaches will be. Comparing across a country will be more robust than comparing across a unit. Even then, allowance will be needed for differences in the mixtures of cases. It must also be realised that the numbers needed to show statistical differences are often very large. For example, two deaths out of twenty cases may seem very high – a mortality rate of 10 per cent. In fact the 95 per cent confidence limits for this rate are 1.2 per cent, 31.7 per cent (i.e. there is a 95 per cent chance that this result reflects a true performance within these limits). This result (two deaths out of twenty) is in fact not significantly different from a result of two deaths out of 100 (Fisher's exact test: $P = 0.13$).[29] This may be important if a review is carried out on a relatively small sample of a practitioner's cases. Inquiries may (quite reasonably) be precipitated by a short run of deaths in close succession. Often the approach is to focus on just those cases in which the patient died or had major complications. It would be much more

---

[29] G. E. Dallal, 'PC-Size: Consultant – a program for sample size determinations' (1990) 44 *The American Statistician* 243.

appropriate to review a large body of work – five years' worth, for example, but this may be more difficult and more expensive. A further problem arises from the interpretation of any criticism. An audit or review may identify problems without the reviewers necessarily intending to imply a degree of negligence. In exactly the same way as expert witnesses, those conducting audit are likely to focus on any areas where improvement might be possible. There is a grave risk that such constructive criticism will precipitate legal or disciplinary proceedings in which the chance of a balanced view of the statistical significance of an isolated problem is even less likely.

When used appropriately and with proper allowance for the complexities of different situations, statistical methods can be very helpful in monitoring performance and identifying substandard care. However, these methods are no more than tools, and their use requires considerable expertise and judgement.

The unethical expert

Up to this point we have confined our discussion to ethical, well-motivated experts who are genuinely trying to give fair and balanced opinions. We have argued that even highly qualified, honest and sympathetic experts may at times provide an opinion which describes a standard that is unrealistically high.

Not all expert witnesses are completely ethical. We have discussed the variability which may occur between experts in their honest assessment of the care given to a patient. In practice it is often necessary to approach only three, or perhaps four, individuals in order to find one whose opinions are genuinely helpful to a particular point of view. However, if the stakes are high, experts may be found who are willing to express a certain view even if such a view is essentially untenable. There are individuals who have made a career out of this sort of activity, and there may be those who are particularly skilled in developing certain fundamentally dishonest lines of evidence.[30] While it is hard to assess how wide-

---

[30] This problem has been most acutely felt in the United States, where concern over the standards of highly partisan expert evidence has led to demands for professional disciplining of unscrupulous medical witnesses: C. Terhune, 'Beset by suits, doctors target enemy within', *Wall Street Journal* (29 April 1998), commenting on the attempt by the Florida Medical Association to subject testimony to peer review and to resort to

spread this type of behaviour actually is, it does not seem that such unethical witnesses are often a major problem, although they may occasionally be the direct cause of a profound injustice, equally for a plaintiff or a defendant.

The subtle nuances of complex evidence

The evaluation of complex issues in medicine and other technical activities is very demanding. It is probably beyond the ability of many members of an average jury to undertake this task adequately. A particular risk is that juries will be more swayed by an expert who is a skilled and arresting speaker with a clear, one-sided and well-presented message than one who is conscientiously determined to present a balanced viewpoint. Again, this problem may be thought to apply equally to defendant and plaintiff, but in reality the emotional aspects of a case tend to be on the plaintiff's side, and it is these that lend themselves to dramatic presentation. The argument that because there has been injury there must have been negligence is easily run from the starting point of a manifestly bad outcome for the patient. It is more often the defendant's expert who has the task of conveying facts which may be both difficult to grasp and perhaps somewhat uninteresting.

The importance of appropriate expert evidence

The medical profession is grappling with a rapid transition. The emerging emphasis on evidence-based medicine is challenging many traditional views of what constitutes good medicine, and the skilled use of sophisticated statistical and scientific techniques which has been integral to medical research for several decades is applying, increasingly, to everyday practice as well. Many doctors are struggling with the demands for increased rigour in their decision making, and it is not always easy to make sense of different views of the same information. However, the fact is that much progress has been made by the medical profession in understanding how to reach a valid conclusion about a complicated issue. It is important that the courts take cognisance of these advances in the

professional sanctions against unethical conduct by expert witnesses. See, however, page 222 for discussion of reforms in the system of expert evidence in England and Wales.

approach to sorting out conflicting or inconclusive evidence. To some extent this is happening. The retention of an expert by the court rather than, or in addition to, one side of a dispute or the other, and the expectation that experts called by the plaintiff and the defendant should confer and together identify points of agreement and disagreement are sensible innovations which deserve to be more widely used. It is highly ironic and totally unacceptable that inquiries (or other proceedings) into alleged failures on the part of an individual or institution to meet an appropriate standard should themselves fall short of an appropriate standard of process – and yet it is clear that this does occur from time to time.[31] In addition to insisting on proper legal process, it seems reasonable to expect courts, disciplinary bodies and those who run inquiries to embrace, if not the sort of scientific rigour that would be expected of modern medical research, at least the basic messages of statistics, cognitive psychology, and the empirical data concerning the nature of expert evidence. Appropriate expert advice is needed not only on the facts of a case, but also in relation to the structure and conduct of the proceedings. We have discussed the sources of an expert's knowledge; in our view, the presentation of opinion in court frequently places too little emphasis on those sources. We have presented the concept of a hierarchy of evidence;[32] in this hierarchy anecdote and personal opinion rank relatively low. It does seem unsatisfactory, therefore, for a viewpoint to be accepted as expert evidence on the basis that the witness begins a statement with a phrase such as 'In my opinion' without thorough justification. In a medical forum, explicit reference to research and clinical experience would be required before much credence was placed on an individual's opinion. Certainly, reference to sources and authorities are permitted in court, but there may be a case for arguing that they should be *required*. This would be very helpful for evaluating the quality of each of two conflicting opinions, and would provide at least some assurance that claimed expertise was based in fact.

A key message of this book relates to the importance of expert evidence in evaluating adverse events in medicine, particularly evidence concerning the cognitive and systemic factors which underlie errors and violations. In this chapter we have discussed some of the difficulties related to expert

---

[31] R. Smith, 'Editorial: inquiring into inquiries' (2000) 321 *British Medical Journal* 715–16.
[32] See n. 13 above.

evidence in general. This is not to diminish the value of expert evidence. On the contrary, we would emphasise the importance of ensuring that the required evidence is obtained, that it is of a high standard and that it relates not only to the theoretical ideals of the textbook but also to the realities faced by normal human beings (albeit highly trained and often very able human beings), working with limited resources, in real hospitals or in real communities, to treat real people who, at times, are very ill indeed.

8

Beyond blame: responding to the needs of the injured

Our concern in this book has been to assess how we respond to accidents – with a focus on accidents in medicine. We have indicated that many events which are judged to constitute instances of medical negligence are, in fact, the inevitable concomitant of human limitations in the face of demanding situations. We have argued for a re-examination of the process of the allocation of blame in such cases and suggested that an excessive focus on fault may be unjust and counter-productive to the improvement of safety. Such claims, though, may easily be misinterpreted. It might be thought that to argue against an undue emphasis on blame is to favour the doctor and pay inadequate attention to the plight of the injured patient. After all, this is not merely a matter of academic interest but concerns real people who have suffered injury.

One might recall at this stage the studies (reviewed in chapter 2) which show just how extensive the harm from error and negligence in medicine may be. As we have pointed out, estimates as to incidence vary, but the central conclusion is clear: too many patients are being harmed in this way, often quite seriously. Behind these statistics there exists substantial suffering, not only in the shape of the pain and discomfort of physical injury but also in financial terms, with loss of earnings and costs associated with disability. In general, however blameless the doctor, the patient is even less to blame for the injury. Furthermore, it is perhaps asking too much to expect the majority of injured patients to weigh the concepts outlined in this book and concur with our conclusion that certain types of error (a slip or a lapse when a doctor is trying to deal with several matters at once, or a deliberative error in a crisis, for example) are not necessarily culpable. Even those who accept the point that these are errors of the type made by everyone and that they are, in a statistical sense, inevitable may understandably feel less than comforted by this insight. It is worth remembering that the objective of medical treatment is usually to cure or alleviate a patient's illness. It is hardly surprising, then, that a patient who, instead of being helped, has been made worse might feel aggrieved. It is even less surprising that the publication of the statistics reviewed in chapter 2 has led to much adverse comment. For many, the question might seem to be, not why so many doctors face litigation, but why so few. A balanced response to the problem of medical injury must include consideration of the claim of its individual victims to compensation for misfortune for which they regard the medical system as being responsible. It must also take into account the pressing need to improve safety within the healthcare system as a whole. There can be no doubt that these are primary and central concerns. However, there are other considerations which also need to be taken into account but which have often been ignored. It has been argued in this book that tort-based compensation is an unreliable and inefficient means of compensating injured patients, may often produce unjust results, has placed undue and unproductive pressure on doctors, and has not turned out to be particularly effective in improving safety. In the wider sense we have attributed at least some of these drawbacks to the climate of blame which pervades modern society. But a critique of current approaches should also address the issue of alternatives.

If there were no viable alternative to a fault-based tort system, then it could be argued that these negative consequences should be accepted as inevitable. In such a view, any human activity, and especially any high-risk area of activity such as medicine, will involve pressure and conflict; this being the case, the distress implicit in the issue of compensation simply cannot be wished out of existence. Ultimately it is better, in this view, for as many people as possible to be compensated, even if the result is an increased burden on providers of services. At present, the proportion of those who suffer medical injury who actually receive compensation is small; indeed, that is one of our criticisms of the tort-based system. To reduce this number further, by making the burden of bringing a personal injury action greater, would be an altogether socially undesirable consequence of relieving some of the burden on providers. Not only would this be economically unjust – at least from the viewpoint of social risk-sharing – but it would also lead to a sense on the part of many victims that they had been badly treated by both the medical and the legal systems.

Against the background of these considerations, the question that needs to be addressed is whether there is any reasonable alternative that is compatible with the major goal of this book, which is that there should be a fundamental re-evaluation of the way in which we think about accidents and blame. There are alternatives to the current system of fault-based compensation which would not only deal with the human costs which flow from excessive readiness to infer fault but which would also prove much more cost-effective in securing compensation. Economic and practical problems do present a formidable barrier to the establishment of a satisfactory system, but these difficulties may be overstated. The real barrier may be cultural, and lie in an excessive readiness to respond to misfortune by blaming others, combined with the lack of will on the part of substantial segments of society to pay for a socially adequate and equitable approach to compensating injury. So long as the focus is on finding some individual to blame every time things go wrong, and making that person pay, it is unlikely that much progress towards a safer and more equitable system will be made. That does not mean that nothing can be done. Reforms are possible within the framework of tort law which could remove some of the adverse effects of the current system. Indeed, in some jurisdictions, examples of such reform are already in place. In addition, there are more radical possibilities, such as the approaches adopted in Finland and New Zealand.

The merits of tort law

Tort lawyers are accustomed to suggestions for radical reform. Broadside attacks on tort-based compensation were common in the second half of the twentieth century, either focused on particular areas of the problem – such as motor accident compensation – or concerned with compensation for all forms of personal injury. Such criticisms have met with a broad measure of support, but just as often the conclusion has been reached that tort, for all its faults, works and that schemes for its replacement in the area of personal injury are unjustified.[1] This was the conclusion of the Pearson Commission, which considered possible reform in the law of England and Wales and recommended against fundamental change in the

---

[1]   See, for example, the conclusions of the Tito Report in Australia: Law Reform Committee of Victoria, *Legal Liability of Health Service Providers, Final Report* (Melbourne, Parliament of Victoria, 1997).

way in which such injury was compensated.[2] Even when recommendations have been made for the replacing of tort with a system of no-fault
compensation – as was the conclusion of the Woodhouse Report in New
South Wales, Australia – these have tended not to be implemented. New
Zealand was one exception, with the central recommendations of a Royal
Commission, chaired by the same Sir Owen Woodhouse, being introduced as one of the few comprehensive no-fault systems of compensating
injury in the world. Overall, however, tort law appears tenacious, and in
most countries has survived a continuing barrage of academic and
political criticism.[3] One explanation for this survival is that the cost of
radical reform is just too great to be attractive to governments; another
possibility is that, for all its faults, the current system of tort-based
compensation has merits which justify its retention. As a result, recent
efforts at reform have tended to confine themselves to speeding up the
process of compensation and to removing some of the most glaring
deficiencies. This was the approach adopted in the wide-ranging review of
civil justice in England and Wales undertaken by Lord Woolf, who had
identified medical negligence claims as being the area where civil justice
was 'failing most conspicuously'.[4] It was also the approach adopted by the
Law Reform Commission of Victoria in its investigation of the issue.

Justifications of tort-based compensation may be made on both
theoretical and pragmatic grounds. The theoretical justification of the tort
system is that considerations of justice require fault-based compensation
to be sought from the person who is causally responsible for a loss or
injury. In this view, the denial to an injured party of the right to bring a
legal action amounts to a condonation of a wrong. The process of suing a
defendant is more than a mere attempt to recover a loss or to seek
monetary compensation for pain and suffering: it may represent the
desire to seek an explanation of what happened and, indeed, may also be
an attempt to secure some form of retribution.[5] To remove this oppor-

---

[2] *Report of the Royal Commission on Civil Liability and Compensation for Personal Injury*
(London, HMSO, Cmnd 7054, 1974).

[3] For a general review, see P. Cane (ed.), *Atiyah's Accidents, Compensation and the Law* (6th
edn, London, Butterworths, 1999). Medical calls for no-fault liability include: British
Medical Association, *Report of the BMA No Fault Compensation Working Party* (London,
BMA, 1987).

[4] Lord Woolf, *Access to Justice: Final Report to the Lord Chancellor on the Civil Justice System
in England and Wales* (London, HMSO, 1996), 15. 2.

[5] See F. A. Sloan, K. Whetten-Goldstein, S. S. Entman, E. D. Kulas and E. M. Stout, 'The road

tunity to have the nature and circumstances of a wrong aired in open court is likely to cause resentment and frustration. In addition, this may also face objection on constitutional or human rights grounds.

There may also be defendant-oriented justifications for the retention of the tort system. A system of automatic compensation, which makes an award to the injured party, irrespective of whether the defendant was at fault in causing a harm, may well be objected to by the person who is implicitly blamed for what went wrong. A defendant may wish to protect his or her reputation from a suggestion of incompetence or negligence, and this is one reason why insurers at times refuse to settle certain claims. Again, the assertion of a right to defend oneself against an imputation of negligence is entirely understandable, and denial of this right is equally likely to give rise to a feeling of resentment. The tort system, for all its imperfections, at least allows a defendant to mount a vigorous defence with a view to establishing that an injury is not due to incompetence but instead reflects no more than an inevitable concomitant of an inherently risky procedure.

Arguments against tort

The importance of caring for patients

One of the consequences of the tort system is that those who are unable to establish that their injury was caused by the fault of another are expected to accept that some risk of injury is an inevitable part of life, and that they must therefore be prepared to bear the cost of their injury themselves. Other than in special circumstances, such as workplace injuries, very few societies have embraced the contrary position and enshrined the right of a person to be compensated on the sole basis that an injury has occurred, regardless of the cause of that injury. On an analogous basis, most societies place the primary burden of an *illness* on the individual affected, and at best provide support only for those who are unable to meet that burden. In general, there is no one to blame for the contraction of an illness. Even when it is clear that a patient has contracted an illness from an identifiable second person, it is unusual to hold that person accoun-

from medical injury to claims resolution: how no-fault and tort differ' (1997) 60 *Law and Contemporary Problems* 35–70.

table.[6] The risk of contracting an illness is held to be part of the background risk of life. Similarly, many injuries are considered to be part of that background risk. In general it is only the identification of fault on the part of another which justifies the transfer of loss from the injured person to the person who caused the injury. In the absence of fault it is usual to leave the loss where it lies. Thus the doctor who has been the direct cause of a patient's injury but who can mount a defence that he or she was nevertheless not at fault can argue that it is perfectly reasonable to leave the entire burden of the injury to be borne by the patient. Obviously this result may be seen as very unsatisfactory by the patient or the wider public, who may have strong expectations of a more sympathetic approach. It is a result which sits poorly with the notion of medicine as a caring and responsible profession.

A particular reason for sympathising with the viewpoint of patients in this regard is that their injuries have taken place in the context of the special relationship which exists between doctor and patient. The purpose of healthcare is to help patients, specifically in relation to their personal health and well-being. In this respect healthcare differs from many other activities in which people may be injured. Doctors in particular tend to have a very direct relationship with individual patients. This is in contrast to those situations such as the accidental injury of a pedestrian by a motorist in which no such relationship exists. It is inappropriate when medical treatment goes wrong for the patient to be deserted, simply on the grounds of a moral argument that no fault was involved. The health system should not abandon the ill, and there is certainly no justification for abandoning those who are injured by medical treatment. To do so diminishes the role of the doctor and of the hospital. The needs of patients injured in accidents associated with little or no blame are no less than those of patients injured negligently. It is in the interests of the patient, the doctor, the healthcare organisation and society to find a way of providing for the needs of all those who are injured during healthcare, whatever the cause.

Accepting the proposition that a patient should be compensated even for injuries in which no fault can be established does not necessarily imply

---

[6] In particular, doctors who become infected by patients are generally expected to accept this as a risk of their profession. On the other hand, patients who become infected by a doctor may at times hold the doctor responsible and argue that some response is required. There are other exceptions, such as in relation to liability for the sexual transmission of disease.

that the process of compensation, with its attendant element of blame, should be focused on the doctor, even if the real financial burden is borne by insurers. This raises the question of a role for the state, and of whether it is justifiable to identify medical injuries as a special case deserving special treatment.

There are a number of situations where the claims of a specific category of injured persons are given particular consideration irrespective of fault. Workman's compensation schemes are one example; the victims of road traffic injuries and product liability cases are others. In all of these categories society has decided that compensation is appropriate whether fault is involved or not, because there are reasons to underwrite the risk. For example, the social consequences of leaving workplace injuries uncompensated have been deemed unacceptable. Admittedly, this is to privilege such victims over those, for example, whose injuries do not fall into one of these special categories: such victims may say that there is no justice in singling out certain categories of injury and that what really matters is the need of the victim rather than the source of the accident. In a typically thought-provoking contribution to the debate, Harris has argued that there is a fundamental unfairness in paying awards to the victims of medical injury even when fault can be established, given that there are other pressing demands being made on the same funds.[7] He suggests that, although victims of negligence may have a claim, this claim should not have priority over the needs of those whose claim is for treatment for a medical condition. This idea has attracted little support,[8] but it serves as a vivid reminder of the fact that compensation claims are, in fact, competing for scarce resources, and are given priority in the process (because they are, after all, legally enforceable as opposed to moral claims). The point applies equally to no-fault systems of compensation such as that which operates in New Zealand. If social need is to be the criterion of allocation of resources in the public sector, there is a case for arguing that the claim of one who has been injured through negligence is not necessarily morally stronger than the claim of one in urgent need of an organ transplant (for example). The argument advanced by Harris is stronger when applied to cases in which no negligence can be established. The issue of fairness becomes particularly acute when alternative re-

---

[7] J. Harris, 'The injustice of compensation for victims of medical accidents' (1997) 314 *British Medical Journal* 1821–3.

[8] For discussion, see Letters (1998) 316 *British Medical Journal* 73–4.

sources are inadequate for those whose injuries (or illnesses) do not qualify for compensation. A system seems unsatisfactory if it provides inadequate funds for potentially life-saving coronary artery surgery while at the same time providing relatively generous access to operations for the repair of tissue damage in shoulders simply because the latter arose during accidents, yet this seems to be the case in New Zealand.[9]

Some societies are in fact prepared to provide a high level of social support for all who need it, but in others economic arguments result in more stringent limits on resources and in greater pressure to identify those needs which can be recognised. This matter is often discussed within the framework of rationing or even of triage. In fact, there are limits to the available resources in every society, and no society is able to ignore these considerations completely. In addition, there are those commentators who point to perceived disadvantages of excessive welfare support and argue that there are merits in promoting at least some degree of self-reliance. In the extreme form of this view it is no business of the state to compensate the victims of accidents; such claims are left to the individual to pursue as best possible, using the courts if appropriate.

In reality few, if any, countries will be prepared to provide for the needs of all. This will mean that some process of selection will be necessary. This being the case, is it reasonable to privilege some claims, or would it be better to follow the more equitable argument and leave the same requirement to establish fault on all who have been injured? This fundamental question has already been answered by most societies, in that, as we have seen, they already recognise categories such as workman's compensation as special cases. This is because the pragmatic consequences of not compensating in such cases would be too disruptive or divisive for society. As we have argued above, a strong case can be made for treating medical injuries as another special category, justifying compensation even in the absence of fault. The challenge in those cases associated with little, if any, fault is to provide compensation without invoking for the doctor the adverse consequences associated with inappropriate blame.

---

[9] J. Neutze and D. Haydock. 'Prioritisation and cardiac events while waiting for coronary bypass surgery in New Zealand' (2000) 113 *New Zealand Medical Journal* 69–70; during the period considered in this editorial, which discussed the inadequacies of publicly funded coronary surgery in New Zealand, public funding was readily available from a separate stream for the compensation of accidents such as disabling but not life-threatening shoulder injuries.

Compensatory inefficiency

One of the most powerful criticisms of the tort system is that it is strikingly inefficient in delivering compensation to an injured person. This operates at various levels. In the first place, the difficulties of establishing causation and negligence may make it hard to make a successful claim. In the Harvard Medical Practice Study, for example, only a small proportion of negligently injured patients received compensation through successful litigation. Then, even if a causally significant breach of the standard of care is established, the slow and expensive nature of the legal process absorbs a great deal of the total cost of the system, resulting in the injured party's receiving in damages only a small part of the overall cost.

This criticism is made from the point of view of the patient; a similar criticism may be made from the point of view of overall social efficiency. Compensation for medical injury may come from a variety of sources. In a system of state-financed medical care, it is ultimately the state that will pay for such compensation, even if individual hospital authorities place the risk with private insurers; the state pays the insurance premiums. In a system of private medicine, the cost of legally compensated medical injury will be borne by the insurers of doctors and hospitals, the costs of the premiums being passed on to patients. In either model, the public ultimately pays, although in the private system the cost is more narrowly focused: the non-user of private medicine, for example, will not contribute to the insurance cost. In the United Kingdom, until 1995, health authorities and, later, National Health Service Trusts shared the costs of awards with doctors' insurers, employees' premiums being paid for by the trusts. After that date, all claims in respect of treatment by the NHS were met from its general funds. The cost of such awards, therefore, is covered by the money that has been allocated for treatment. If damages become payable, then that means that there is a correspondingly reduced amount available for the maintenance of wards and equipment, the purchase of drugs, or the provision of treatment. A medium-sized award, therefore, may be crudely translated into ten fewer hip replacement operations.

Whichever system pertains, the cost of managing medical accidents is an integral part of the overall cost of healthcare, and in the end is borne by the public. Therefore the case for efficiency is very strong.

The limitations of tort liability as a deterrent

The formal justice argument in favour of tort law holds that it is a legitimate function of civil liability to encourage people to take care in their dealings with others. According to this argument, the possibility of legal action acts as a deterrent against lack of care. This claim is difficult to assess but it remains unproven that the level of care adopted by people engaged in hazardous activities will necessarily be affected by the likelihood or otherwise of a personal injury action. Dewees and Trebilcock, for example, have pointed out that doctors in the United States are five times more likely to be sued for malpractice than their Canadian equivalents, yet there is no reason to believe that Canadian doctors are less careful than their professional colleagues in the United States.[10] On the other hand, there may be some connection between careful driving and levels of concern over being sued for damages in respect of road injury. In one Australian study, it was found that after the introduction of a no-fault system of compensation for injuries sustained in road accidents, the level of fatal accidents on the road increased by 16 per cent.[11] Similarly, successful actions for failure to obtain adequately informed consent have been associated with the spending by doctors of increased time in communicating with their patients. In a study of the influence of a seminal informed consent case on the practice of Canadian physicians, Robertson found that, even if there was not widespread medical understanding of the precise legal implications of the judgement, the court's decision was still understood as having a symbolic function in underlining the importance of effective communication between doctor and patient.[12] This suggests that the medical response may be a very generalised one; the precise features of the law may not be what prompts a change in medical behaviour so much as an understanding that there is a 'medico-legal threat'.

We showed in chapters 3 and 4 that deterrence is unlikely to be effective in preventing errors, but may produce worthwhile changes in behaviour in the case of violations. In this regard there may be particular

[10] D. Dewees and M. Trebilcock, 'The efficacy of the tort system and its alternatives: a review of empirical evidence' (1992) 30 *Osgoode Hall Law Journal* 57–138.

[11] I. McEwin, 'No-fault and road accidents: some Australasian evidence' (1989) 9 *International Review of Law and Economics* 13–24.

[12] G. Robertson, 'Informed consent ten years later: the impact of *Reibl* v. *Hughes*' (1991) 70 *Canadian Bar Review* 423–47.

value in actions against organisations or the management of organisations. Civil actions against employers in respect of harm caused by employees who have been required or permitted to work excessive hours are a case in point.[13] Recently, in a non-medical criminal case, two directors of a transport company were convicted of manslaughter after ignoring the excessive working hours of one of their drivers, who caused a fatal crash after falling asleep at the wheel.[14] If hospitals were held accountable for errors made by junior doctors after they had worked even longer hours than the 60 per week attributed to this driver, the likelihood of change would be considerable. It is neither just, however, nor likely to produce change, to punish the doctor forced by the system to work while tired. Similarly, it is pointless to focus on junior doctors who make mistakes when they are unsupervised, without at least considering the responsibilities of the absent supervisors and of the hospital for failing to implement policies to ensure that adequate supervision is the norm. Obviously, there will be times when the junior doctor is to blame, but if the objective is to deter unsafe practices it is very important to include within the scope of that deterrence those who actually have the authority to change those practices.

In chapter 1 we alluded to work which argues convincingly that there is no foundation in the principles of any school of psychological thought to support the belief that tort law will be effective in promoting greater care by individuals – even in the case of most violations.[15] The point here is that remote but serious consequences are less effective in this regard than sanctions which are less serious but more likely to occur. For example, the thought of the remote possibility of a terrible death is less effective in promoting the use of seatbelts than a well-enforced policy of fines. Proactive measures to promote and enforce high standards on a day-to-day basis are much more likely to improve safety and quality than the threat of litigation. Furthermore, the effect on behaviour of threats perceived as very serious may often be perverse, leading for example to the practice of defensive medicine.

---

[13] *Faverty v. McDonald's Restaurants of Oregon*, 892 P 2d 703 (1995).

[14] A. Leathley, 'Firm's directors convicted over fatal crash', *The Times* (20 November 1999).

[15] D. Shuman, 'The psychology of compensation in tort law' (1994) 43 *Kansas Law Review* 39–77.

The association of tort liability with the practice of defensive medicine

The connection between high levels of personal injury litigation and the practice of defensive medicine continues to play a major role in the debate over tort law reform. In one view, a fear of being sued encourages doctors to practise defensive medicine, in which inappropriate investigations are carried out to exclude every possibility, however unlikely. Defensive medicine, it is argued, subjects the patient to unnecessary expense, inconvenience and sometimes risk, and distorts the doctor's exercise of clinical judgement.

Attempts to verify whether defensive medicine does, in fact, result from a fear of litigation have tended to confirm anecdotal accounts that this is indeed happening. An important collection of empirical data on the effect of liability on medical practice is that which was gathered in Canada by the Review on Liability and Compensation Issues in Health Care (the Prichard Review). The Prichard studies were focused on anaesthesia and obstetrics and gynaecology, two areas of medicine which have been particularly associated with a high level of legal claims. The studies looked at the way in which doctors working within the specialities in question viewed and responded to legal threats. It is irrelevant that the real risk of litigation might have been misunderstood by some doctors; what mattered was how a *perceived* threat affected clinical practice. A wide range of responses was obtained, but a substantial proportion of those doctors canvassed indicated that their practice had changed as a direct result of their understanding of the medico-legal situation. In some cases, areas of practice had been abandoned out of concern over a heightened medico-legal risk; general practitioners, for example, reported a reduced offering of obstetric and anaesthetic services. There was also evidence of increased use of tests. Thirty per cent of responding practitioners in obstetrics and gynaecology stated that concern over litigation made them feel obliged to order patient-requested tests.[16] Although the overall picture was one of increased concern over and responsiveness to what was seen as a high level of medical litigation, caution should be exercised in attributing changes in practice solely to medico-legal factors. It was also apparent that improved record-keeping and resort to further investiga-

---

[16] Submission of the Working Group on Obstetrics and Gynaecology, 9–10, quoted by B. Dickens, 'The effects of legal liability on physicians' services' (1991) 41 *University of Toronto Law Journal* 168–233, at 186.

tions was prompted, in part, by a desire to respond to developments in diagnostic tools. By the same token, greater care to communicate risk may be a result of a growing awareness of the general moral claims of patients to be informed of medical procedures rather than a fear of being sued should there be a failure to impart adequate information.

One of the difficulties in this argument relates to knowing the difference between defensive medicine and appropriately increased care. For example, it may be better for general practitioners to withdraw from anaesthesia or gynaecology provided an adequate number of more highly trained specialists is available. Obviously, litigation can have desirable effects on medical practice, but it is an uncertain and unpredictable means of achieving sensible and rational change.

The effect of litigation on the doctor

The Prichard Review in Canada considered in some depth the adverse consequences of litigation on the morale of doctors. Doctors gave evidence of the profound effects which being sued had on their psychological health and their ability to do their job. In his analysis of the Prichard findings, Dickens quotes the account of a Canadian doctor who describes his experience in the following vivid terms:

> First of all, I experienced 'denial' . . . A nasty part of the denial reaction was the way it scrambled up my memory of the events so that what I believed had happened did not actually happen . . . Worse still, it blinded me to the fact that I was blameless . . . The part which was very hard to take was that I felt very badly about myself and my fitness to act as a physician. I lost faith in my judgement.

Dickens comments on these feelings:

> This anecdotal narration of a legal suit inducing feelings of denial, confusion of events, self-blame, anger, unworthiness, hesitancy, and insecurity is graphic not simply in itself, but also because it is so closely identifiable with the grief reaction following bereavement. It appears that being sued may be like suffering a death in the family, the more stressful because the death may not be sensed to be of the defendant's self-image, self-esteem, and self-confidence.[17]

Just as the Prichard Review confirms that practice is affected by doctors'

[17] Ibid. at pp. 181–2.

understanding of the existence of a legal threat, so too do American studies reach the same conclusion.[18] Working under a threat of litigation creates a climate of fear, which cannot be conducive to the best use of human resources within the medical system. Moreover, the impact on a doctor, once a complaint has been made, is likely to be deleterious to his or her subsequent discharge of professional duties. The adverse effect of excessive stress on performance is well known, and a person experiencing the trauma of litigation is therefore likely to be a greater safety risk than one who is not under such personal pressure. Furthermore, in the same way as an injury to a patient has implications for that patient's family, friends and colleagues, the effects of a civil or disciplinary action will extend beyond the doctor concerned, to those who are closely associated with him or her. In both cases, the spouse and children are likely to be the most affected, but beyond that, it can be very demoralising to observe the impact of medico-legal proceedings against a close colleague, particularly if the colleague is respected and the proceedings are seen from a medical perspective as unjust.

It may be thought that many of these problems can be alleviated by timely out-of-court settlements. Such settlements might also be seen as solving the problem of the patient who has a serious injury but where no fault is involved. However, there are difficulties with this approach. The insurers argue that a reputation for readiness to settle will quickly result in a huge increase of unmeritorious claims. In addition, there are difficulties for the doctor, whose reputation will be damaged by the settlement. Many medical institutions (particularly in the USA), as part of employment screening, enquire into a candidate's history of settled claims, and might be almost as reluctant to employ a doctor with a track record of out-of-court settlements as one who has been successfully sued. Thus an element of punishment is present even though the terms of the settlement may expressly state that no fault is acknowledged.

Of course, everything that is said here about the doctor could equally be said about the injured patient, who in addition must contend with the direct physical consequences of injury. In serious cases these may be death, brain damage or paraplegia. We do not suggest that the adverse effects for the doctor usually equal those faced by the patient, although in

---

[18] D. P. Kessler and M. B. McClellan, 'The effects of malpractice pressure and liability reforms on physicians' perceptions of medical care' (1997) 60 *Law and Contemporary Problems* 81–106.

some cases they may well do. At a psychological level, the traumatic effects of unanticipated injury and the stress involved in making a claim and pursuing it through a tortuous legal process will also entail a considerable level of distress. Irrespective of outcome, both plaintiffs and defendants are affected, sometimes profoundly, by the adverse psychological consequences of litigation with its adversarial nature and its delays. For both parties, plaintiff and defendant, the whole experience is a highly fraught one. Reform directed solely at the alleviation of the defendant's position would be correctly subject to the criticism that it ignored the difficulties faced by the plaintiff and thereby worsened the position of disadvantage in which the victims of medical injury find themselves.

Such criticism would be justified, if the correction that was made in the system were to result in an *unfair advantage*. If it were merely designed to restore balance between the parties, then it could be defended against such criticism. This assumes, though, that a fair balance between parties to this particular form of litigation is achievable. In theory, the elements of a successful claim for damages – duty, breach and causation – adjudicated before an impartial tribunal would seem to satisfy criteria of fairness. In practice, one might argue that it is inherently unfair on plaintiffs that, for example, they should have to establish causation according to stringent legal criteria. Similarly, defendants could argue that an inherent unfairness of the system is that it may attribute enormously burdensome consequences in respect of a momentary lapse on their part and that account should be taken of an overall record of competent and conscientious practice. The current system of tort-based liability is overwhelmingly one-dimensional. It looks at a single decision or act and imposes, on that basis, consequences which may be quite out of proportion with the degree of wrongdoing. Thus a doctor who carries out one thousand complex procedures may make an error in respect of one of them; this single error may result in months or years of anxiety and stress and, at the end of the day, loss of professional reputation or self-esteem. The fairness of this, in terms of overall desert, might well be questioned.

Politically, any adjustment of the current system of compensation which made it more difficult for a successful negligence action to be brought against a doctor would be treated with suspicion. Current attitudes towards professional privilege are hostile: the notion, then, that the doctor's position in medical injury should be given special treatment in the legal system is likely to be taken exception to by patients' groups and advocates of easier access to civil justice. The difficulty is that there are actually three elements which need to be considered in the response to accidental injury: compensation, accountability (ensuring safer practice) and, where appropriate, punishment. Problems arise from attempts to achieve all three of these objectives by a single mechanism – that of the law of torts. As long as the compensation of injured patients is linked to the accountability and punishment of doctors, it is only to be expected that doctors will defend themselves on the latter two fronts, and little progress will be made towards alleviating the difficulties of the patient. Promotion of safety is no doubt the biggest challenge facing healthcare at present, but once an injury has occurred, high priority should be given to addressing the medical, rehabilitative and financial needs of the patient. It follows that the primary objective of reform should be the provision of speedier compensation for a larger proportion of claimants, but consideration should also be given to the need for a more discriminating evaluation of culpability and of the lessons to be learned from the event with a view to preventing recurrence.

Options for reform

Although the existing system of tort-based compensation has its defenders, the extent of dissatisfaction over its failings cannot be ignored. Broadly speaking, two options present themselves, one being the retention of tort, subject to the carrying out of various reforms, and the other being the introduction of a radically different system of no-fault compensation. Examples are to be found in New Zealand and Finland, and, in respect of birth injury, in Virginia and Florida.[19]

Adjusting the system: making tort more responsive

One of the main arguments for the reformist approach is that, since considerations of cost and political opposition to no-fault compensation seem to have prevented the introduction of such schemes in more than a handful of jurisdictions, then the most productive approach might be to retain the main features of the tort-based system but to improve it

---

[19] Virginia: Birth-Related Neurological Compensation Act (Virginia Code, s. 38. 2–5000–21); Florida: Birth-Related Neurological Injury Compensation Act (Florida Statutes Annotated 766).

through reforms which address its shortcomings. These measures have included the introduction of screening methods to ensure that only serious cases succeed in getting into the courts, the encouragement of mediation and alternative dispute resolution procedures, the development of case management techniques designed to ensure the speedy passage of cases through the courts, and the capping of damages. In each case, the reform must be tested according to the criteria which have been established by critics of the current system. Does it diminish the level of confrontation and help the meritorious plaintiff to overcome the hurdles of obtaining information and proving negligence? Does it provide reasonably quick compensation to the injured patient? Does it ensure rapid identification of those doctors whose degree of negligence or incompetence requires an uncompromising response? Does it discourage frivolous actions? Finally, but importantly, does it provide a less blame-oriented environment in medical practice?

Screening

Screening devices, which are designed to stop unmeritorious claims at an early stage, were introduced in a number of jurisdictions in the United States as a legislative response to what was widely seen as a 'malpractice crisis'. Under these arrangements, a person seeking to establish medical negligence is required to satisfy a sifting panel that there is a prima-facie case against the defendant. Failure to do this would not preclude further action in the courts, but obviously would act as a deterrent. Although there is obviously an advantage to the patient in obtaining early advice on the strength of the claim, there are critics of this approach. In the view of some, this sort of device merely serves to create a further hurdle in the way of the plaintiff. Constitutional challenges to these measures have usually been unsuccessful.[20]

Mediation and alternative dispute resolution

Many victims of medical injury claim that one of the main reasons why they pursue a claim in the courts is the desire to find out what happened. They report considerable difficulty in obtaining an explanation from the

---

[20] See, for example, *DiAntonio v. Northampton-Ammomack Memorial Hospital*, 628 F 2d 287 (1980).

doctor or hospital, and the decision to sue is then taken to reveal the truth as to the circumstances of the injury. Whether or not such stated motives represent the real reasons of those who profess them, it is probable that the desire to find out the truth does assume a very important role in the minds of many prospective litigants. Certainly, the possibility that frank communication, and an apology, may defuse an otherwise fraught situation is widely recognised, and any system which facilitates this might be expected to reduce the incidence of litigation and improve the satisfaction of patients. This is recognised in systems of risk management which recommend a courteous and communicative response to patient complaints as a means of reducing the level of litigation.[21]

Considerable attention has been paid to mediation in both the United Kingdom and the United States. In the UK, two National Health Service regions carried out a study between 1995 and 1999 of mediation procedures, comparing the outcomes to a cohort of cases in which conventional tort-based measures were used.[22] The sample examined was fairly small, owing to a low rate of uptake of mediation, but the patients who were involved in the process appeared to be satisfied by the results (which included financial settlements). Significantly, mediation was seen by patients as being a very satisfactory way of obtaining objectives which they regarded as very important, namely, an explanation and apology, as well as assurances to the effect that steps would be taken to ensure that such incidents would not happen again.[23] In New Zealand a positive development in this direction has been the establishment of the office of the Health and Disability Commissioner, with an emphasis on accessibility for patients and on mediation as a first step towards resolution of disputes. Some Australian states have similarly sought to encourage mediation, whether or not the parties agree to it: in Victoria and Queensland, for example, the court may order mediation at any point in the proceedings.

Reference to arbitration is becoming an increasingly popular way of ensuring the resolution of a dispute outside the framework of litigation. This has been little used in healthcare, but its attraction would be speed and financial efficiency, the costs of arbitration usually being considerably

[21] L. L. Wilson and M. Fulton, 'Risk management: how doctors, hospitals and MDOs can limit the costs of malpractice litigation' (2000) 172 *Medical Journal of Australia* 77–80.

[22] L. Mulcahy, *Mediating Medical Negligence Claims: An Option for the Future?* (London, HMSO, 1999).

[23] C. Dyer, 'Patients, but not doctors, like mediation for settling claims' (2000) 320 *British Medical Journal* 336.

lower than the costs of court-based litigation. A further advantage of arbitration and mediation is that they are both considerably less confrontational approaches to disputes, and they do not involve the same element of blame which formal litigation involves for the defendant who is found liable. We have referred above to the difficulty for the doctor whose record now includes a settled claim. This seems to be a genuine problem in the USA, where prospective employers ask about such settlements, but it appears to be less of an issue elsewhere, and if this type of mediation is to be facilitated it is important that a reasonably enlightened attitude is maintained in respect of those doctors who willingly take part in the process.

The case management approach

Reforms of this sort may seek to combine features of mediation with measures designed to ensure openness and adequate dispatch in the preparation and conduct of legal actions. Major reforms of this sort have been implemented in England and Wales following upon the report of Lord Woolf into access to civil justice.[24] This report acknowledged that civil proceedings were frequently slow and frustrating for the parties, and that this was particularly so in medical negligence actions. In this area, Lord Woolf was of the view that the civil justice system was failing badly, and that the need for reform was pressing. The resulting reforms, which have now been introduced, constitute a major remodelling of the way in which civil justice is administered, with a strong emphasis on the power of the court to ensure that actions proceed without undue delay. In the new system, parties are given major incentives to resort to mediation and to settle actions. They are also encouraged not to proceed to court without thorough preparation and agreement amongst themselves as to the issues which the court will be asked to determine. There are also major changes in the role played by expert witnesses: the new Civil Proceedings Rules stress the role of the expert not as a partisan witness but as one who has an overriding duty to the court to assist it to discover the truth. The effect of the Woolf reforms on medical litigation are proving to be significant: there will certainly be diversion away from litigation – which will undoubtedly benefit both sides to a dispute – but the system should also be less

---

[24] Lord Woolf, *Access to Justice*.

confrontational in respect of those cases that do get to court. However, the basic nature of the process, which will be the determination of negligence according to the same substantive rules of law, will remain in place.

Controlling damages

The capping of damages is designed to keep down the cost of medical malpractice insurance and thus to control medical costs in general. In principle, too, it may be prudent to exclude juries from the setting of damages and leave this task to judges. Control of the level of damages is also intended to reduce the difficulty of ensuring specialist cover in those areas of medicine where the risk of liability is sufficiently high to make insurance prohibitively expensive. Such an approach has been tried in a number of states in the United States, most notably in California, where the Medical Injury Compensation Reform Act of 1975 introduced a variety of measures including a cap on non-economic damages; a study by the American Academy of Actuaries in 1996 confirmed that the reforms had led to a substantial fall in medical malpractice costs in California. Furthermore, in their study 'Do doctors practise defensive medicine?', Kessler and McClellan found that reforms of this type result in a reduction of 5–9 per cent in the costs of treating cardiac disease, a reduction which was not accompanied by any significant effects on mortality or other medical complications.[25] It is important to note, though, that the reforms have not had a marked effect on the frequency of medical negligence claims. In general, such schemes address the financial implications of the growth of medical litigation, rather than changing in any substantial way the litigious climate.

No-fault compensation[26]

It is not our purpose to provide a detailed review of all (or any) existing approaches to the compensation of accidents in and out of the workplace.

---

[25] D. Kessler and M. McClellan, 'Do doctors practice defensive medicine?' (1996) 111 *Quarterly Journal of Economics* 353–90.

[26] I. B. Campbell, *Compensation for Personal Injury in New Zealand: Its Rise and Fall* (Auckland University Press, 1996); R. Harrison, *Matters of Life and Death: The Accident Rehabilitation and Compensation Insurance Act 1992 and Common Law Claims for Personal Injury* (Auckland, Legal Research Foundation, Publication 35, 1993); S. A. M. McLean (ed.), *Law Reform and Medical Injury Litigation* (Aldershot, Dartmouth, 1995).

There are aspects of the approaches used in Sweden, the Netherlands, Britain, Switzerland, several states in America and Canada, and no doubt many other countries, which could illustrate points we wish to make. However, the New Zealand and Finnish experiences are particularly relevant to our concerns. The New Zealand scheme is the only comprehensive system which has attempted to provide compensation for all forms of accidental injury on a no-fault basis, in which the common-law right to sue for compensation of negligently caused harm has been set aside. For this reason we shall discuss it in some detail. Notwithstanding several changes to the name of this scheme, it is known to most New Zealanders as 'the ACC', an abbreviation for the Accident Compensation Corporation, which emerged from the former Accident Compensation Commission in 1981. The ACC was the result of the 1967 Report of the Royal Commission of Inquiry for Personal Injury in New Zealand, chaired by Sir Owen Woodhouse. This report was a response to many of the deficiencies discussed above in the systems of tort and workman's compensation which preceded the ACC. The report identified five principles. These were:

1 community responsibility
2 comprehensive entitlement
3 complete rehabilitation
4 real compensation
5 administrative efficiency.

In other words, the community was to share the costs of providing realistic levels of compensation for all injuries (not just those occurring in the workplace) and rehabilitation of the injured (so far as possible) to their former position, in a way that was efficient in time and costs. On the face of it these principles would meet many of the objectives identified in our discussion so far.

Regrettably, there are many who believe that some or all of these principles have been lost from the scheme as it now operates. There has been much criticism of the ACC in recent years and it would be all too easy to dismiss the experience as having shown that comprehensive no-fault compensation is too expensive. In fact, it is not the process of compensation which is expensive, it is the cost of the injury itself and of the rehabilitation and support of injured people which is expensive. The New Zealand scheme has been subjected to an astonishing number of reviews since the Accident Compensation Act came into force on 1 April 1974 (five reviews in the six years leading to 1991, for example). There have been important changes in its direction and scope, and it is clear that political and organisational factors have had a major influence on the degree to which it has succeeded or failed to meet the needs of New Zealanders. The relationship of the scheme to medical injury has been a good example of such vacillation.

The introduction of ACC amounted to an implicit social contract by which people set aside their common-law right to sue for compensatory damages for negligently caused personal injury for the provisions of the scheme, which included lump sums for pain and suffering, and realistic levels of earnings-related compensation on an ongoing basis. The scheme covered all types of injury. Medical injuries were not differentiated in any way, and the right to sue doctors was lost along with the right to sue anyone else.

The last point was to become highly contentious. It was not long before commentators were alluding to the loss of tort as a means of ensuring accountability by the medical profession and other health professionals. Much of this commentary highlighted the loss of the right to sue doctors without necessarily acknowledging the general nature of the loss of the right to sue anybody on the grounds of personal injury. In particular, the critics often failed to acknowledge that a specific concomitant of losing the right to sue others in this context (be they doctors or not) was that those others had also lost the right to sue them. Thus if they, the critics, were accidentally or negligently to cause an injury, they would enjoy exactly the same level of immunity from a civil action as anyone else. This is a part of the 'contract' which is often overlooked and yet it is central to the discussion. Even if the ACC has failed to fulfil other aspects of its obligations, it has created in New Zealand a haven from tort law. The right to pursue exemplary damages remains, but only in very limited circumstances. Other exceptions to the prohibition on the right to sue have increased, but in effect it is very difficult to bring an action against another for personal injury in New Zealand and, notwithstanding a recent increase in attempts to do so, such actions remain extraordinarily uncommon. As a result, a whole legal industry around the hearing of civil cases has gone from New Zealand. The courts, the judges, the administrative staff and the tort lawyers which would have existed had the 1972 Act not been introduced are simply not there. Unfortunately, in their place is an army of administrators and case managers running the ACC, and at least some of the saved legal activity, perhaps most of it, has been taken up by appeals or actions arising from disputes between injured people and the ACC itself.

Amongst many reviews and minor changes, there have been several landmark reforms to the ACC. The Accident Compensation Act 1982 replaced the 1972 Act and came into force in 1983. This extended the definition of 'accident' to include heart attacks and strokes, set limits on lump-sum payments and reduced the first week's compensation for work accidents to 80 per cent of earnings. The inequity of compensating disability from accidents more generously than disability caused by illness has always been a criticism of the scheme, and the 1982 revisions made some small progress towards reducing this gap. In the 1989 government budget, plans were announced to take this further and extend ACC to all forms of incapacity. Unfortunately, the 1992 Accident and Rehabilitation and Compensation Insurance Act turned the scheme in the opposite direction. This act introduced the words 'insurance-based', a quite different emphasis from Woodhouse's concept of 'community responsibility'. It also used the phrase 'financially affordable', shifting the scheme's priority from Woodhouse's desire to provide 'real compensation' to that of limiting expenditure. New and narrower definitions of the term 'accident' were introduced, and lump sums were abolished. The scheme had become significantly more restrictive than on its introduction.

From the point of view of the present discussion, the most significant feature of the 1992 Act was the identification of medical injuries as different from all others. The term 'medical misadventure' was introduced. This was justified on the grounds that alternative means for calling medical practitioners to account for alleged negligence were considered inadequate in the absence of the right to sue. For reasons which have not been made clear, only health professionals were singled out.

To make matters worse, for accidents involving health professionals and health professionals only, the concept of fault was reintroduced. Thus in s. 5, 'medical misadventure' was defined as 'personal injury arising from medical error or medical mishap'. 'Medical mishap' is defined by the Accident Rehabilitation and Compensation Insurance Amendment Act (no. 2) 1993 as:

an adverse consequence of treatment by [or at the direction of] a registered health professional properly given if –

(a) The likelihood of the adverse consequence of treatment is rare; and

(b) The adverse consequence of the treatment is severe.

With some caveats, 'rare' is defined as something that would not occur in more than 1 per cent of cases, and 'severe' is dealt with in an equally arbitrary manner. Even more worryingly, the Act defines 'medical error' (again with caveats) as:

the failure of a registered health professional to observe the standard of care and skill reasonably to be expected in the circumstances.

The Act required committees to determine whether or not medical error had occurred and, where it was determined that it had, to refer the case to the appropriate authority, which usually meant the Medical Council, the Health and Disability Commissioner or the police. Health professionals were permitted to respond in writing to the allegations against them. However, the hearings of the Medical Misadventure Committees did not provide an opportunity for the defendant to appear or to be represented. In some cases doctors felt (with good reason) that they had been denied their rights to natural justice.

It appears that these provisions were intended to address the public perception that the loss of the right to sue had left a serious gap in medical accountability. Where medical error was found, discipline would now be considered as part of the process by which compensation was awarded. This reintroduced fault, but only for injuries involving health professionals.[27] Furthermore, patients who failed to qualify under the highly arbitrary definition of 'medical mishap', in circumstances which did not amount to negligence, were no longer covered. This single fact defeated the main attraction of the ACC as a response to the problems we have discussed above. Note, however, that this deficiency is specific to the 1992 provisions, which were quite contrary to the founding principles of ACC, and it does not follow that similar deficiencies would be a problem with no-fault schemes in general. An important lesson is to be learned from this experience, however: namely, that the removal of the right to sue must be accompanied by some acceptable alternative to ensure that reasonable complaints against doctors can be heard, and dealt with.

---

[27] There was also a plan to introduce a Medical Misadventure Account, funded by registered health professionals.

There is a further objection to the provisions related to medical misadventure. The definition of medical error within the Act is, in effect, a description of civil negligence. Not only does this definition fail to recognise the nature of human error and its distinction from violation, or to recognise the considerable body of science underpinning these concepts,[28] but it also sets a low threshold for possible disciplinary action. In effect, tort liability has been replaced by an increased potential for disciplinary sanctions. The acceptability of this is to some extent dependent on the way in which these provisions are implemented. Certainly there have been instances in New Zealand where mistakes or errors involving little if any moral culpability have resulted in findings of 'conduct unbecoming' – the lowest level available to the authorities. The implication would seem to be that the doctor is to accept that the opprobrium of such a finding is not unduly harsh. Whether a doctor would prefer a relatively high risk of such a disciplinary finding on his or her record to a similar risk of facing civil litigation is moot. Doctors' views on the matter may not be thought very important if the system succeeded in providing adequate and timely compensation to the patient. Unfortunately, many observers believe the levels of compensation provided by the ACC are now seriously inadequate. They are certainly much lower in most instances than those which a successful litigant might expect from the courts.

Matters changed again with further legislation in 1999 which opened ACC to competition from private insurance and made some changes to the above provisions. Very shortly after this a new government instituted an about-turn, with private insurers being removed from accident compensation almost before they had begun to take part in this activity. Other changes are likely and it is too soon to say to what degree the original principles enunciated by the Woodhouse Commission will be reinstated.

One of the criticisms often raised about schemes of this type is that they are too expensive. Unfortunately, few statistics are available to allow a useful comparison of the financial performance of ACC with the costs of compensating accidents elsewhere. It does seem that the government has at times felt under considerable pressure to contain costs. It is clear that at least part of the perceived problem of escalating costs relates to certain decisions by management. For example, policies

---

[28] See chapters 2 to 5.

introduced in 1982 to run down reserves and move to 'pay-as-you-go' financing were overdone.

Overall, it is obvious that the scheme has not been run as well as it might have been, that it has been subjected to excessive political interference, and that it has fallen short of the public's expectations. Nevertheless, it remains relatively popular, and there seems to be no strong desire on the part of the legal profession, the public or the politicians to replace it. There is certainly no enthusiasm for a return to tort law as an alternative.

The Finnish experience provides some interesting contrasts to that of New Zealand. The Patient Injury Act of 1986 placed on all healthcare providers a duty to insure against awards for medical injury. Given the high proportion of public health in Finland, the government would have been the main funder of this scheme, but a contribution was also expected from private providers. An injured patient applies directly to the insurer and will receive compensation on a no-fault basis provided the injury falls into one of the four main categories identified in the Act: treatment injuries, infection injuries, accident injuries and misdiagnosis injuries. Not all injuries qualify. For treatment-related injuries, it is necessary to show that the injury could have been avoided. There is some potential for distortion in this approach, but in practice it appears to work reasonably well. The Act does not exclude the use of alternatives, and there are other very well-developed provisions in Finland's social welfare system to support many of those who are not catered for by the Patient Injury Act. The right to sue is retained. However, its use in Finland was never very frequent and seems now to be even less so. Overall, the system appears to work well, with low levels of confrontation between doctors and patients.

Reporting and the need to promote safety

When considering possibilities for legal reform it is easy to lose sight of the fact that the real problem is the continuing occurrence of avoidable adverse events in medicine. Errors and violations will never be completely eliminated from any complex system of human endeavour, but there is room for improvement in healthcare. The fewer the patients who are harmed during treatment, the lower the cost of dealing with that harm. In a safe system the tensions between doctors and patients are minimised.

Ultimately, the overriding legal, regulatory and medical objective should be the reduction of the human cost of iatrogenic harm.

A great deal is already being done by health professionals to reduce error and improve the standard of care given to patients. Sight of this fact is all too readily lost in the glare of publicity associated with figures such as those reported by the Institute of Medicine.[29] The mortality rates of most major forms of surgery are steadily improving.[30] Voluntary incident-reporting is well established in the culture of anaesthesia, is gaining strength in other specialities, and has led to a number of important advances in safety.

Reporting is a fundamental requirement for the continuous improvement of quality and safety in any complex system. Much of the information in this book arises directly or indirectly from reports of one sort or another. There are various approaches to reporting. For example, in voluntary incident-reporting, as practised in anaesthesia, a practitioner (usually the anaesthetist, but occasionally a nurse or other person involved with patient care) fills in a form anonymously and forwards it to a central agency for inclusion in a large database. Usually, this is done in two stages. A departmental database forms the basis for local feedback and quality control. The information is then forwarded to a national or international centre for amalgamation with reports from other departments, in order to create a much larger database. An incident is defined, in effect, as any event which does or could reduce safety for a patient.[31] In some cases, harm will have occurred, and this is reported. In others, known as 'near misses', it is obvious that harm might have occurred. The information collected typically includes a description of the incident and an opinion on factors which predisposed to its occurrence, factors which facilitated its avoidance or the minimisation of the consequences of the incident, and other relevant details. An example of this type of reporting is the Australian Incident Monitoring Study (AIMS),[32] from which over

[29] L. T. Kohn, J. M. Corrigan and M. S. Donaldson (eds.), *To Err is Human: Building a Safer Health System* (Washington, D.C., National Academy Press, 2000), 1.

[30] T. A. Brennan, 'The Institute of Medicine report on medical errors – could it do harm?' (2000) 342 *New England Journal of Medicine* 1123–5.

[31] W. B. Runciman, A. Sellen, R. K. Webb, J. A. Williamson, M. Currie, C. Morgan and W. J. Russell, 'Errors, incidents and accidents in anaesthetic practice' (1993) 21 *Anaesthesia and Intensive Care* 506–19.

[32] R. Holland, 'Editorial: Symposium – the Australian Incident Monitoring Study' (1993) 21 *Anaesthesia and Intensive Care* 501.

five thousand reports have now been collected. Information from the AIMS database has resulted in numerous publications in medical journals, and has influenced practice in a number of important areas. For example, the introduction of pulse oximetry as a routine standard of monitoring in anaesthesia in Australasia by anaesthetists in the face of scepticism, if not outright opposition, from fundholders was greatly facilitated by reference to these data.

A different approach to reporting involves specific, prospective projects looking in detail at particular problems. Thus the practice of central venous cannulation has been the subject of a study at Green Lane Hospital in Auckland, which identified that, in a high proportion of catheters, tip placement was deeper than ideal.[33] In the event of a rupture of the catheter through the wall of the central vessel, or heart chamber, this sub-optimal placement increases the risk of death (by pericardial tamponade). This was addressed in several ways, including the simple systems-related measure of shortening the length of the central venous catheters for routine use. The study also raised awareness of the issue in the department, and promoted greater care. A subsequent study showed a much improved incidence of this problem.[34] This example illustrates the concept of 'closing the loop'. There is little point in reporting unless action is taken on the reported data. Furthermore, it is important to confirm the value (or otherwise) of any changes made. The 'loop' may be summarised as *data–action–data*.

In both the New Zealand and Australian examples, reporting is anonymous, participation is voluntary, and the identity of individuals is protected. This usually results in ready compliance, open and comprehensive communication, and worthwhile information. However, there are many who criticise the confidential nature of the exercise and suggest that any adverse events identified in such studies should be disclosed to the authorities and subject to formal inquiries and possible discipline or litigation. It is important to understand that confidential or privileged reporting does not in any way inhibit alternative means of identifying and

---

[33] J. S. Rutherford, A. F. Merry and C. J. Occleshaw, 'Depth of central venous catheterization: an audit of practice in a cardiac surgical unit' (1994) 22 *Anaesthesia and Intensive Care* 267–71.

[34] A. F. Merry, C. S. Webster, I. C. van Cotthem, R. L. Holland, J. S. Beca and N. G. Middleton, 'A prospective randomised clinical assessment of a new pigtail central venous catheter in comparison with standard alternatives' (1999) 27 *Anaesthesia and Intensive Care* 639–45.

responding to the same events. Thus, if a patient is injured, the information in the notes is available, the participants can be asked for reports, and all the normal mechanisms for investigating and dealing with the problem can be pursued. All that is protected is the information provided voluntarily and confidentially to the study or audit activity. It is reasonable to expect honest professionals to provide all the facts to any appropriate authority. However, as part of the adversarial nature of litigation and most disciplinary systems, individuals are not required to give an opinion which may be self-incriminatory.[35]

They are also entitled to seek legal counsel, and to adequate time for the preparation of their responses. The advantage of confidential, privileged voluntary reporting is that the same individual can with confidence provide a timely and frank account of what went wrong, including his or her opinion of the causes of the event, even if this opinion is damaging to any defence. Thus information is readily gathered which in some cases might never be elucidated by an adversarial system, or in others be discovered only after prolonged proceedings. In addition, it is collated into large and useful databases from which general conclusions can be drawn and recommendations made for safer practice in the future.

Provisions exist in many countries for the protection of information collected on a voluntary basis for the purposes of improving safety and quality, but they are not universal, and there are often exceptions which reduce the level of protection they provide. The Institute of Medicine has recommended that such protection be provided throughout the United States, and has endorsed the value of voluntary reporting systems. However, it has gone further and recommended nation-wide mandatory reporting as well. At present, mandatory reporting systems exist in twenty states in the USA. Other countries have also indicated an interest in establishing mandatory systems of this type following the report of the Institute of Medicine and its associated publicity. The report describes the objectives of mandatory reporting as follows: 'Such systems ensure a response to specific reports of serious injury, hold organizations and providers accountable for maintaining safety, respond to the public's right to know, and provide incentives to health care organizations to

---

[35] The issue of the right to silence has become a controversial one in criminal law, where pressure has grown in some jurisdictions to allow adverse inferences to be taken from the accused's silence.

implement internal safety systems that reduce the likelihood of such events occurring.'[36]

In themselves these objectives seem laudable. In so far as reporting is confined to factual information, there can be little objection to such an initiative. There is great value in knowing accurate rates of death and injury in healthcare. However, a recommendation for the public disclosure of information about serious adverse events should at the least differentiate between ascertainable facts and subjective opinion. Requiring individuals or organisations to set aside their legal rights to avoid self-incrimination is only likely to result in the suppression of useful information. This point has been made by Brennan in the *New England Journal of Medicine*.[37]

In the United Kingdom, government concern over the cost, in both economic and political terms, of adverse incidents in the National Health Service has led to the approving of a national system for the mandatory reporting of failures and errors in healthcare. The inspiration for this was the system which exists for the logging of 'near misses' in aviation, which allows for lessons to be learned and avoidance strategies to be developed. Once this system is introduced, procedures for reporting will be standardised and there will be agreed definitions of adverse events which will enable incidents to be classified. It is significant that the Department of Health report which made these recommendations, *An Organisation with a Memory*,[38] stressed that a reporting culture should be encouraged which moves away from blame and sets out to develop an appreciation of the underlying causes of these incidents. The report also recommends that the Department of Health should consider the possibility of introducing clear targets for the National Health Service in terms of a reduction in the number of incidents. These targets included a 25 per cent reduction, by the year 2005, of the number of litigation-triggering instances of negligent harm in obstetrics and gynaecology and, by the same year, a reduction of 40 per cent in the number of injuries caused by negligence in the administration of drugs.

Even in respect of factual information, a requirement for mandatory reporting raises difficult issues. The right of an accused person to remain silent is an important principle in most common-law jurisdictions. Is it

---

[36] Kohn, *To Err is Human*, 8.
[37] Brennan, ' The Institute of Medicine Report on Medical Errors'.
[38] Department of Health, *An Organisation with a Memory* (London, HMSO, 2000).

justified to make an exception of healthcare? Obviously, it is to be hoped that the honest doctor will be completely open and frank in his or her disclosure to any authority concerning an injured patient, but equally there will be those whose approach is understandably more oriented to self-preservation. Does this mean that the requirement for mandatory reporting is placing the honest doctor under unreasonable pressure to set aside personal considerations? The answer to this question depends a great deal on the extent to which blame pervades the response of society to those who honestly disclose errors and mistakes of the type which we have seen will be made by all practitioners at some stage of their careers.

Professional self-regulation and medical errors

Reporting of errors and the creation of a responsive system of safety procedures certainly help to minimise the incidence of iatrogenic harm. Yet once the system identifies doctors whose ability to perform competently is in question, there must be an adequate way of protecting the public from such practitioners. Here the medical profession has been criticised on the grounds that the system of medical self-regulation adopted in many countries has failed to provide patients with an efficient method of monitoring performance and of weeding out those practitioners who are a danger to the public. Typical criticisms of such systems were that they did not prevent a closing of professional ranks, that they were cumbersome and tardy in their response, and that their thresholds for intervention were too high. In the United Kingdom, criticism of this sort which had been levelled against the regulatory body of British medicine, the General Medical Council, became politically irresistible after the conviction of Dr Harold Shipman for the murder of fifteen of his patients.[39] This incident, which followed shortly after the Bristol case, significantly affected public trust in the medical profession's ability to regulate itself. In fact, it may be extremely difficult to identify the homicidal practitioner and these cases will inevitably occur from time to time, no matter what procedures exist for monitoring practitioners' patterns of drug use or for investigating the association of an individual doctor or nurse with a higher than average mortality rate. It is clear that medical self-regulation has been far from perfect, but what may not be

---

[39] B. O'Neill, 'Doctor as murderer' (2000) 320 *British Medical Journal* 329–30.

quite so obvious is the considerable degree to which the profession has in fact been successful in ensuring high standards of medical care for the public. The postgraduate college-based systems for the selection, training and examination of specialist doctors (including, more recently, those who specialise in general practice) have become increasingly rigorous over time – so much so that established doctors are at times accused of setting standards too high in order to protect themselves from competition. An account of how surgeons in a North American teaching hospital recognise and deal with surgical mistakes, and particularly with trainees who make them, has been provided by Charles Bosk,[40] a sociologist who spent eighteen months working with and observing a surgical service. He made the interesting observation that the hesitation and mildness which may often surround such controls relate in part to the uncertainties which frequently exist in pinpointing the cause of a therapeutic misadventure. Partly for this reason, perceived deficiencies in a trainee doctor's honesty and integrity tend to be seen by senior colleagues as more important, and tend to be dealt with more harshly, than issues of technical competence. Bosk made the further observation that, unfortunately, trainee doctors found wanting in one institution may often find employment in another, perhaps less prestigious, hospital.

Even when it has been accepted that professional self-regulation at all levels has been associated with some spectacular failures, it has yet to be shown that alternatives which depend more on external agencies and the involvement of lay people in the processes of professional regulation will be any more effective in identifying dangerous doctors. It is interesting that, in an era which stresses the importance of evidence-based medicine, changes in approach to the regulation or management of healthcare are made with little if any serious attempt to conduct a proper evaluation of their impact. There is good reason to retain those aspects of self-regulation which have merit, and to ensure that doctors continue to have a substantial role in committees dealing with ethics, discipline and regulation. There is certainly value in much greater involvement of non-medical people in such activities, to represent the perspective of the public (or particular segments of the public). In addition, certain non-medical people, such as lawyers, have a training or background that may be of

---

[40] C. L. Bosk, *Forgive and Remember: Managing Medical Failure* (University of Chicago Press, 1979).

great value in managing the process of dealing with adverse events. Nevertheless, doctors are better placed than lay people to understand and identify unacceptable behaviour in the context of the complexities of medical treatment, and there is a risk that an excessive reduction in their involvement in the process of regulating medicine might produce a result which is less satisfactory with respect to the needs of the public. The professional regulation of medicine is not a simple matter; it is important that the need for a well-informed and balanced appraisal of adverse events in healthcare is recognised, and that new measures aimed at improving the situation should build on the strengths of the past and not simply replace one imperfect system with another, possibly an even less effective one. Yet the public may not be sensitive to these difficulties. There may be increasing demands for external controls in healthcare, associated with an expectation that incidents of the Shipman and Bristol sort can be prevented by a rapid, Draconian system of suspension from practice at the first suggestion of incompetence, or the first occasion on which harm has occurred to a patient.

The General Medical Council was not particularly well placed to defend itself in the face of criticism that it had failed to protect the public. It is only since 1995 that the Council has been able to take action in respect of incompetent doctors; prior to that the Council responded only to the professional misconduct of doctors. In 1995 Parliament passed the Medical (Professional Performance) Act, which came into force in late 1997. This legislation gives the Council the power to respond, through disciplinary proceedings, to those doctors whose performance of their duties is seriously deficient. There was some debate as to what this level should be, but in the event proposals to allow for sanctions for 'unacceptable performance' or for merely 'deficient' performance were rejected in favour of the higher level of deficiency. This did not satisfy the demands of organisations which had been campaigning for a more severe response. In a contribution to the *British Medical Journal*, for example, the chief executive of Action for Victims of Medical Accidents wrote:

> Patients who are on the receiving end of poor performance are more concerned with the accountability of those who were responsible than with the definition of seriously deficient performance. If a patient has suffered injury as a result of treatment by a doctor, or as a result of a failure to treat, then surely he or she must have been at risk. If the patient was at risk then there must be a danger that others will be at risk in the future. The problem

is that the new procedures are aimed solely at a pattern of behaviour. How many ureters must a surgeon divide before a pattern is established? How many babies must suffer asphyxia? What patients want to know is whom doctors will be held accountable to after the first occasion that they cause such a serious injury.[41]

This comment demonstrates the nature of the blaming response which we have sought to appraise in this book. In this view, the making of a single error appears to raise a presumption of incompetence; in fact, as we have argued, the making of a certain number of errors is a statistically inevitable feature of any career in medicine. The insistence that a pattern of error should be demonstrated before harsh action is taken at least distinguishes between the normally competent doctor who makes an error and the doctor who clearly falls below a reasonably attainable level of competence. It is very important to understand that the truly malign doctor, such as Harold Shipman, is another matter again. Such a person may be highly competent, may be well liked by many of his or her patients. A truly criminal doctor may be very skilled at concealing harm deliberately caused to patients and may not be readily identified by either approach. Such individuals are in fact uncommon, and, deplorable though the failure to identify them may be, the issue of genuinely criminal behaviour on the part of a healthcare professional must be seen as separate from that of competence.

The use of professional discipline to prevent harm to patients will provide some security against the incompetent doctor, but, by its very nature, it will only deal with the more egregious cases.[42] This has been recognised in the United Kingdom, where the General Medical Council has acknowledged that the price of continued professional self-regulation is the installation of additional institutions with a view to ensuring that levels of competence are maintained and the incidence of medical injury contained. As a result of this realisation, the Council voted for a system of revalidation which will require all doctors – at junior and senior levels – to submit every five years to a process of assessment as to competence. This means that the previous system, which allowed for a doctor to

---

[41] A. Simanowitz, 'Performance procedures for seriously deficient professional performance are flawed' (1996) 313 *British Medical Journal* 562.

[42] This comment applies in Britain, but is not necessarily the case elsewhere; as we have discussed above, in New Zealand the threshold for disciplinary findings at the lowest level is quite low, perhaps in part because of the absence of the option to sue a doctor.

continue to practise indefinitely once he or she had been registered, will be abandoned in favour of a system which places the onus on the practitioner to demonstrate that skills have been preserved and that new knowledge and practices have been assimilated. The United Kingdom comes relatively late to this system, as do Australia and New Zealand;[43] recertification has long been an established feature of speciality practice in the United States, where a certificate in a speciality has to be renewed every seven to ten years.[44] Such approaches have much to recommend them, but there is a risk that they may in the end do little more than create new burdens for the competent and conscientious doctor, and still fail to identify and address the shortcomings of those who are a problem. Greater insistence on continued professional education, along with pro-grammes of clinical governance designed to raise clinical standards, is one of a number of measures that may be expected to have an impact on reducing the incidence of patient injury, particularly when operated in conjunction with effective reporting systems and audit arrangements. The picture that this suggests is one of more highly regulated medical practice with less room, perhaps, for what used to be described as 'clinical freedom'. Yet the consequences should be positive, and the important matter is that this entire approach represents a preventive rather than punitive response to medical error. It is also important, however, that the system of healthcare is considered as a whole, and the many other systemic factors (some of which have been discussed in previous chapters) which predispose to error or promote violations are also addressed.

On the face of it, there will be a considerable financial cost to increased regulation, and to such measures as increasing the levels of supervision provided to junior doctors, limiting the hours worked by any doctor (junior or senior), and introducing initiatives to address the numerous latent errors in the system (poor ampoule labelling, for example). However, this increased cost in the provision of treatment is likely to be more than offset by the savings in respect to the current costs of iatrogenic harm – in both financial and human terms.

---

[43] D. Newble, N. Paget and B. McLaren, 'Revalidation in Australia and New Zealand: approach of Royal Australasian College of Physicians' (1999) 319 *British Medical Journal* 1185–8.

[44] J. J. Norcini, 'Recertification in the United States' (1999) 319 *British Medical Journal* 1183–5.

Conclusions

There is a range of possible reforms with the potential to improve the situation for the injured patient and to reduce unproductive conflict between patient and doctor. A good system should address the following objectives:

1 Patients who have been injured during healthcare should have timely access to adequate support, rehabilitation and compensation without the burden of having to prove negligence.
2 The improvement of safety within the healthcare system must be a priority.
3 There must be effective systems for the early identification and control of those doctors (and other health professionals) who are grossly negligent, incompetent or impaired.
4 At the same time there should be a more sophisticated understanding of the nature of error, and a less punitive approach to those conscientious and competent doctors who, in the course of a medical career, will inevitably make a mistake at some time.
5 The adversarial response to accidents needs to be replaced with a climate in which trust between doctors and patients is re-established, the role of blame is reduced and the focus is placed on co-operation.

How are these objectives to be achieved? It is unlikely that a single model will be universally acceptable. A great deal will depend on the economic, political and social environment of the society concerned. Thus Scandinavian countries, with their long tradition of social welfare, might be expected to favour communitarian approaches, while the USA, with its attachment to notions of individual responsibility, is more likely to prefer a greater role for the tort system. In each case, adjustments to improve whatever system is already in place will probably be more acceptable and successful than attempts at far-reaching and radical reform. The experience of the USA, where tort law reform has been a politically contentious issue, demonstrates the difficulties associated with substantial changes in direction.

There is a strong case for the development of no-fault systems of compensating injured patients, backed up by mediation, and appropriate means of ensuring the accountability of health professionals, including improved approaches to professional regulation. If these work well, there will be little need for patients to resort to litigation, as is the case in Finland. Whatever system is adopted, the value of reporting should be borne in mind, and preserved. One advantage of no-fault systems of compensation is that mandatory reporting of errors and mistakes may more readily be achieved. However, prohibition of the right to sue in respect of personal injury, medical or otherwise, is probably undesirable: tort has its advantages. In particular, it provides an established and useful resort when other approaches prove unsatisfactory. It would be reasonable to require that alternatives be used first, and that settlements and sanctions arising from these alternatives be taken into account in the civil process. Yet, after the less adversarial possibilities have been exhausted, for an individual who feels the alternatives have not worked well, the opportunity to bring a civil action is an important right. For a community that believes other methods are failing in a general sense, tort provides a mechanism for asserting dissatisfaction. A substantial increase in the rate of litigation would signal widespread dissatisfaction with, for example, a no-fault system that was not working well. Sound alternatives to tort should be capable of preventing the excesses which have characterised civil litigation in the past.

A better understanding of the causes of medical accidents, the factors which underlie error or promote violation, and the theoretical basis of safety in complex systems is essential if reforms in the way we regulate medicine are to be effective in achieving their primary objective: improved patient safety and a more acceptable response to the needs of the injured patient.

CONCLUSION

This study started with a chapter of accidents. How those accidents are viewed – and how we regard untoward occurrences in human affairs – has been the subject of our enquiry. It is our view that many of our current responses to such events are not only morally and scientifically unsophisticated, but may also be unhelpful in promoting better and safer practices. If we want to reduce the damage caused by accidents, then we should ensure that the legal response is fashioned with an awareness of the insights which psychology and accident theory can now afford. At present the law in many cases adopts a blunt approach which fails to take these insights into account. This is in the interests of neither the patient nor the doctor.

We have not been concerned with intentionally produced harm, which may quite uncontroversially merit blame. It is worth noting, though, that even in situations where blame is entirely appropriate, a strongly punitive response may not necessarily be the most effective method of dealing with the problem. There will, of course, be situations where a good case can be advanced for a strongly deterrent approach. An example of this is where punitive measures are used to deter the deliberate flouting of safety or environmental regulations by corporate actors. In these cases liability may be imposed on the corporation itself, which may be heavily fined, or there may be prosecution of individual managers or directors. It may be appropriate for both the corporation and individuals within it to be held liable. A striking feature of corporate criminal liability is the fact that it recognises that responsibility for an offence may be institutional as well as individual.[1] In this respect it provides a model for our own critique of the

---

[1] B. Fisse and J. Braithwaite, 'The allocation of responsibility for corporate crime: individualism, collectivism and accountability' (1988) 11 *Sydney Law Review* 468–513.

allocation of blame. We have argued that singling out an individual actor – sometimes one who occupies a relatively junior position within a highly complex organisation – may obscure the real nature of responsibility for an incident. Contemporary legal theorists have stressed the need to escape an individual focus and to recognise the sociological facts and economic realities of corporate wrongdoing.[2] The aim of this approach is to identify what lies behind an individual act. The fact that an employee has breached the criminal law in the context of his or her employment does not necessarily mean that he or she has acted in the pursuit of some personal objective or gain. It may well be appropriate for the individual to bear liability in such a case, but to punish such a person as if he or she had been acting in isolation is to miss the point of offences committed in a corporate context. These offences are often committed in pursuit of corporate gains, sometimes in response to considerable corporate pressure. The real offender may be in the boardroom or may even be the corporation itself. There are, of course, difficulties in conceiving of the corporation as a moral actor but there is a strong consensus in jurisprudence that the corporation is capable of being envisioned in this way.

The social efficacy of blame and related sanctions in particular cases of deliberate wrongdoing may be a matter of dispute, but we accept their necessity – in principle – from a moral point of view. Distasteful as punishment may be – and it is, after all, the infliction of pain – we cannot escape the social, and possibly moral, need to punish people for wrongdoing, occasionally in a severe fashion. The communicative nature of punishment is important. Punishment indicates to all concerned that an act is unacceptable to society, and it affirms the value of the person who has been wronged. These are needs that are deeply ingrained in human society and it is difficult to imagine a world in which the concept of punishment was absent; indeed, such a world would bear very little resemblance to our own. At the same time, we should bear in mind that punishment is in many respects a primitive device and that in some circumstances the forgiveness of wrongdoing is not only the morally correct response but also the most constructive one. Increased interest in

---

[2] C. Wells, *Corporations and Criminal Responsibility* (New York, Oxford University Press, 1993). There is a substantial philosophical literature on the issue of the moral responsibility of the corporation; the classic exposition of the problem, from the point of view of moral philosophy, is that of P. French, *Collective and Corporate Responsibility* (New York, Columbia University Press, 1984).

forgiveness among contemporary moral philosophers and social theorists has drawn our attention to the role which forgiveness plays in the promotion of social healing, most notably in the wake of political and social turmoil.[3] But even at an individual level, the encouragement of forgiveness breaks the cycle of retribution and bitterness and, from a utilitarian point of view, may have the advantage of diminishing social conflict. A society in which blame is overemphasised may become paralysed. This is not only because such a society will inevitably be backward-looking, but also because fear of blame inhibits the uncluttered exercise of judgement in relations between persons.[4] If we are constantly concerned about whether our actions will be the subject of complaint, and that such complaint is likely to lead to legal action or disciplinary proceedings, a relationship of suspicious formality between persons is inevitable. Life in a blame-obsessed system will be very different from life in a supportive and appropriately forgiving system.

Blaming behaviour in relation to deliberate wrongdoing may be morally acceptable, and indeed necessary, subject to a proper recognition of the function of forgiveness, apology and other social institutions of an emollient nature. Its role in the context of non-deliberate actions is another matter altogether, even when those actions have caused harm. It is at the heart of our argument that undue emphasis on blame in relation to such incidents is unjustified and counter-productive. What is required is a clear-eyed, properly informed examination of the grounds for blame, and a firm fixing of these grounds to criteria which are both morally defensible and pragmatically productive.

We have argued that many errors are not the product of failures or shortcomings of a culpable nature. Indeed, we suggested in chapter 2 that certain types of error are inextricably linked to those human strengths (such as distractibility and creativity) which differentiate us from machines and which have contributed to our success as a species. Our

---

[3] There is a burgeoning literature on forgiveness. A work which looks at the topic from a variety of points of view (including the psychological and political) is R. D. Enright and J. North (eds.), *Exploring Forgiveness* (Madison, University of Wisconsin Press, 1998). In the philosophical literature, a useful treatment is the debate between Murphy and Hampton in: J. G. Murphy and J. Hampton, *Forgiveness and Mercy* (New York, Cambridge University Press, 1988). See also R. C. Roberts, 'Forgivingness' (1995) 32 *American Philosophical Quarterly* 289–306.

[4] This theme is developed further in D. W. Shuman and A. McCall Smith, *Justice and the Prosecution of Old Crimes* (Washington D.C., American Psychological Association, 2000).

analysis reveals that to attribute blame for an error is to misunderstand the very nature of what is happening when an error is made. Slips or lapses, for example, will be made by the most conscientious of people, and do not of themselves demonstrate any culpable failing sufficient to justify the attribution of blame. The same is generally true of rule-based and deliberative errors. Errors are not the product of choice.

Why should such errors not be culpable? If one believes that moral culpability depends on the making of a free choice, then any human action which is not the result of such a choice cannot involve blame. In chapter 3 we have argued that errors, under the tight definition which we have provided, are examples of precisely this. This is by no means a novel position in moral philosophy; indeed, the place occupied by freedom in theories of moral responsibility finds its roots in Aristotle and has been central to theories of responsibility since then. It is on the basis of the absence of a free choice of course of action that those who act under coercion are exculpated; similarly, those who act in ignorance are not usually held to be culpable, on the grounds that their actions do not represent an informed choice of the resulting harm.

Culpability may attach to the consequence of an error in circumstances where substandard antecedent conduct has been deliberate, and has contributed to the generation of the error or to its outcome. In these cases, the making of a prior choice by the actor may lead to responsibility for subsequent situations where choice is absent. These choices, which may involve breaking a rule or failing to take proper account of a general principle, are not errors, they are violations. In chapter 4 we made the point that not all violations will be equally culpable; nevertheless, at least some responsibility will always attach to a violation, precisely because violations involve choice. In so far as negligence is constituted by a violation, it will be culpable. If, however, it is constituted by no more than an error, then moral culpability will be absent. In practice, the making of an error will often be construed as negligence. We have argued that, in the case of errors, the only failure is a failure defined in terms of the normative standard of what should have been done. There is a tendency to confuse the reasonable person with the error-free person. In other words, the test has shifted from what *could reasonably* have been expected to have been done to what *ought* to have been done. Even though the courts have repeatedly said that the reasonable person test is anchored in realistic expectations of people, the reasonable person test has progressively failed to take account of the inherent human limitations of actual reasonable people. We have illustrated, in chapter 5, how the precise formulation of the test may change the focus from an action, such as a drug administration error, which may appear unreasonable in itself, to the person. The answer to the question 'Could other people in this position reasonably have made the same error?' will in many cases be in the affirmative, supported by data from incident reporting and other studies which show a widespread occurrence of the same problem.

To help clarify this, we introduced, in chapter 5, a classification of blame in five levels. Level two blame is appropriate for error, in which no moral culpability is involved. In level three, there has been a prior awareness on the part of the actor that the substandard aspect of his or her behaviour fell short of what could be expected. In other words, choice was possible. While nobody can avoid errors on the basis of simply choosing not to make them, people can choose not to commit violations. In level three the actions have genuinely failed the reasonable person test, even allowing for the human limitations of the reasonable people. At level three there is still no intent to cause harm or conscious disregard for the safety of others. We have discussed at length the range of circumstances in which violations may occur.

There is an inescapable tension in the law of torts between the principle of compensation for loss caused by another and the principle that only those who deserve to pay compensation should be required to do so. This contradiction is not one which tort scholars or the courts have resolved satisfactorily. It remains the case that negligence liability in the common-law systems is founded on fault, and this notion of fault is not one which is entirely amoral in nature. The transfer of loss from the person who has suffered it to the person who has caused it depends on the latter having fallen below a standard which it is thought he or she reasonably ought to have met. This is unobjectionable, even if it means that those who were by no means *subjectively* negligent will be held liable. Thus a person may be held liable even if he is doing his best if this best fell short of the reasonable person's expected performance. We would simply add that the reasonable person's expected level of performance must take account of the fact that the reasonable person is a human being, with the normal limitations of even the most conscientious human being. It is this point that has often been overlooked.

If the standard ceases to represent the level that can in reality be expected of the reasonable person, then it could be argued that the moral underpinning of negligence liability has been lost. This possibility is discussed in chapters 6 and 7. The courts have never deliberately sought to produce such a result. They have frequently stressed that the reasonable person test means what it says. Unfortunately, there have been times when a divergence has developed between the standard that the courts clearly intend and that which has in practice been demanded. The reasons for this include the nature of expert evidence, an understandable desire to ensure compensation for loss and, above all, insufficient appreciation of the nature of human cognition and performance.

There are other reasons, apart from those of legal theory, why the standard of care should reflect a reasonably and realistically attainable level. If the standard becomes too high, those who are potentially liable – especially those engaged in high-risk activities such as medicine – will feel that they are the victims of unduly harsh assessment. It could be pointed out to them that civil liability entails no moral opprobrium, and that it is merely a matter of loss redistribution which has the same moral implications as insurance. But this is naïve. The impact of civil liability on defendants *is* serious. A doctor, for example, who is sued for negligence is likely to feel that his professional capability is publicly questioned. Litigation is an intensely stressful experience, from the point of view both of the plaintiff and of the defendant, and to be the object of an action for damages which one feels is not justified is a highly disruptive and distressing experience. It might be argued that this is to place excessive weight on the sensitivities of professional persons, who must accept the consequences of the harm they have caused. Yet this objection ignores the point that there are two sets of interests at stake here: the interests of the plaintiff and the interests of the defendant. A correct balance of these two sets of interests should ensure that tort liability is restricted to those cases where there is a real failure to behave as a reasonably competent practitioner would have behaved. We have suggested that the inappropriate raising of the standard of care threatens this balance. Similar considerations apply to disciplinary measures.

How do we respond to the position of the victim of a personal injury which has been the result of an act which falls into our second level of blame, that is, below the level at which we feel the reasonable person test should apply? Clearly, at this level an injury has been caused by a level of performance that falls short of best practice. One cannot but sympathise with the victim who argues that the accident should not have happened. Such patients are entitled to a timely and satisfactory explanation of events, and usually an apology. Mediation has much to offer. If a way could be found for compensation to be paid without any finding of negligence with all that that entails in terms of blame and moral censure, this would be highly desirable. It is this desire which has fuelled a long-standing debate in tort law as to alternatives to the current system. This debate is by no means over. We have examined some possible solutions in chapter 8.

A consequence of encouraging litigation for loss is to persuade the public that all loss encountered in a medical context is the result of the failure of somebody in the system to provide the level of care to which the patient is entitled. The effect of this on the doctor–patient relationship is distorting and will not be to the benefit of the patient in the long run. It is also unjustified to impose on those engaged in medical treatment an undue degree of additional stress and anxiety in the conduct of their profession. Equally, it would be wrong to impose such stress and anxiety on any other person performing a demanding function in society. There are numerous examples outside medicine of this process: social workers, for instance, face a much higher level of stress in the discharge of their duties knowing of the heightened possibilities of complaint and proceedings for wrong decisions in high-risk activities such as child custody and child safety matters. The same can be said of many other occupations. Although, in this book, we have focused on doctors, it is not the occupation of the individual which is relevant, it is the general issue of culpability in particular circumstances. There is no reason why this pressure should be felt by any reasonably competent person who is conscientious in the discharge of his or her responsibilities. Expectations must be realistic. It is essential that standards are attainable. This implies recognition of the nature of ordinary human error and human limitations in the performance of complex tasks.

The criminal punishment of negligence is a matter of particular concern. Criminal punishment carries substantial moral overtones. The doctrine of strict liability allows for criminal conviction in the absence of moral blameworthiness only in very limited circumstances. Conviction of any substantial criminal offence requires that the accused person should have acted with a morally blameworthy state of mind. Recklessness and deliberate wrongdoing, levels four and five of our classification of blame, *are* morally blameworthy, but any conduct falling short of that should not be the subject of criminal liability. Common-law systems have traditionally only made negligence the subject of criminal sanction when the level of negligence has been high – a standard traditionally described as *gross negligence*. In fact, negligence at that level is likely to be indistinguishable from recklessness, in that some degree of deliberate risk-taking or knowing disregard for the safety of others is involved. Occasionally, however, a criminal prosecution may occur in cases in which this standard is not reached, and some legal systems outside the common-law tradition actually allow criminal prosecution on the basis of ordinary negligence. This is objectionable because it involves the criminal punishment of persons whose moral culpability may be very low or non-existent. In particular, it is inappropriate to convict such persons of a homicide offence.

Blame is a powerful weapon. When used appropriately, and according to morally defensible criteria, it has an indispensable role in human affairs. Its inappropriate use, however, distorts tolerant and constructive relations between people. Some of life's misfortunes are accidents for which nobody is morally responsible. Others are wrongs for which responsibility is diffuse. Yet others are instances of culpable conduct, and constitute grounds for compensation and, at times, for punishment. Distinguishing between these various categories requires careful, morally sensitive and scientifically informed analysis. The law sometimes undertakes this, and attributes liability – civil and criminal – appropriately. In many other cases, however, crude legal notions of negligence fail to achieve a distinction between unavoidable and inevitable mishaps (which are frequently true accidents) and culpable or faulty behaviour. Injustice is the result.

There are too many medical accidents. An important barrier to progress in reducing the incidence of medical injuries and in finding better ways of handling these injuries when they occur is an undue emphasis on blame. Blame promotes an adversarial response, which in turn feeds upon blame. A sophisticated and constructive approach to the attribution of blame is required. In this book we have attempted to provide a reminder of just how important is the link between moral fault, blame and justice.

INDEX